KAREN DOHERTY &
GEORGIA COLERIDGE

BANTAM PRESS

LONDON • TORONTO • SYDNEY • AUCKLAND • JOHANNESBURG

TRANSWORLD PUBLISHERS
61–63 Uxbridge Road, London W5 5SA
A Random House Group Company
www.rbooks.co.uk

First published in Great Britain
in 2008 by Bantam Press
an imprint of Transworld Publishers



This book is a work of non-fiction. In cases, names of people or the detail of events have been changed to protect the privacy of others. The authors have stated to the publishers that, except in such minor respects not affecting the substantial accuracy of the work, the contents of this book are true.

A CIP catalogue record for this book is available from the British Library.

ISBN 9780593059159



Addresses for Random House Group Ltd companies outside the UK
can be found at: www.randomhouse.co.uk
The Random House Group Ltd Reg. No. 954009

The Random House Group Limited supports The Forest Stewardship Council (FSC), the leading international forest-certification organization. All our titles that are printed on Greenpeace-approved FSC-certified paper carry the FSC logo. Our paper procurement policy can be found at www.rbooks.co.uk/environment

Design by Julia Lloyd
Typeset in 10/13 pt Optima by Falcon Oast Graphic Art Ltd

Printed in the UK by CPI William Clowes Beccles NR34 7TL

2 4 6 8 10 9 7 5 3 1

With love

To my husband, Peter, and our children, Natasha, Anya, Cian and Alexandra.

K. D.

To my husband, Nicholas, and our children, Alexander, Freddie, Sophie and Tommy.

G. C.

# Contents

# Introduction

We aren't perfect parents, and our children aren't perfect children.

We met when they were at nursery school, and we became friends when they started getting into all sorts of trouble together. One day there was a call from the headmistress. One of our daughters had stuck paper towels in all the sinks in the bathroom, turned on the taps and flooded her office downstairs.

Then there was the time our boys were caught throwing sand at other children at school (they told us it was flying fairy dust from *Peter Pan*). And the time two of our children squeezed through a gap in the garden fence and were found by a horrified neighbour at the bus stop.

We'd love to tell you we've dealt with all such situations calmly, with the deft hands of real pros. We'd love to tell you we never shout, never get wound up by noise and mess, and never get stressed out when our children fight. And we'd love to tell you we always get our children to the right place at the right time with the right kit. But none of it would be true.

We do lose our cool, we often have regrets, and there's definitely room for improvement. But we do have one thing going for us: we have experience – loads of it. With four children each, there is no shortage of incident and drama in either household.

Like all parents, we love our children passionately and we want our home lives to run as happily and smoothly as possible. We knew that somewhere out there, there must be a better way forward, with less nagging, shouting and stress all round. When life at home was a battlefield, we wanted information from the front line. How did other parents solve the problems we were facing every day?

So we started searching for good ideas. We bought parenting books and attended workshops, lectures and parenting classes. The experts had great advice, but many of the best ideas came from friends and neighbours who were willing to share their secrets.

We found the stories and ideas we gathered were so fabulous, so life-changing, that we couldn't stop. We began asking questions everywhere – at the school gates, at dinner parties, at the sand pit, in the queue at Tesco's.

How do you stay calm? How do you get homework done? How do you handle bullying? How do you get the television turned off? How do you stop your children fighting? What do you do when they won't listen to you? How do you get them to go to bed? How do you persuade them to eat vegetables? How do you cope?

So many parents had wonderful advice and solutions. Some were obvious – why hadn't we tried that one before? Others were unusual, even ingenious.

We were surprised to find how much the answers varied depending on people's personalities and parenting styles. Sometimes the contrast was striking. When their children argued, some parents listened and tried get to the root of the problem, while others told them, in no uncertain terms, to stop fighting. We called the first type **Tuned-In Parents** because they are so good at recognizing feelings, and the second type **Commando Parents** because they have natural authority. Five other successful parent types emerged over time. We've called them **Pause Parents**, **Cheerleader Parents**, **Physical Parents**, **Sorted Parents** and **Laid-Back Parents**, and each has their own unique approach.

In Chapters One and Two we'll introduce all of them and reveal their secrets. You might identify with some of them immediately.

Their ideas will resonate with you and you may find you are already using some of them. Others may need to be adapted, tailor-made to you, your child and your circumstances. Trust your judgement. It's your family and you are the expert.

Then we'll show you how to solve the most common parenting issues, with chapters on getting cooperation, socializing, food, school, bedtime and difficult behaviour. Armed with the seven secrets, you'll feel confident tackling even the most complicated problems. These solutions *really work*.

As Karen has three girls and a boy, and Georgia has three boys and a girl, we have alternated between 'he' and 'she' from chapter to chapter. We've focused on post-toddlers to pre-teens, but we know that very few children, or families, come in neat little packages. Some nine-year-olds convincingly act like thirteen-year-olds. And some of you may have a newborn, a ten-year-old and a teenager. So there are books on siblings and teenagers in the pipeline. We welcome your ideas and stories, so please send them to us at KarenandGeorgia.com and we will include them if we can.

KAREN DOHERTY AND GEORGIA COLERIDGE
London 2008

# 1

# The Seven Parent Types

## What Type of Parent Are You?

Here are the seven parent types, seven different approaches to being a good parent. You will almost certainly identify with one or more of them, and you may even spot your friends here. What type of parent are you?

## The Pause Parent 

The secret of **Pause Parents** is that they don't overreact in a crisis. If their child is arguing, whinging or shouting, they realize it doesn't help to get wound up and sucked into the drama. They know they can reduce the emotional temperature much faster if they keep their cool and give themselves time to think things through. Even if a situation seems overwhelming, they don't panic if they can't immediately see how to solve it. They know that once everyone has simmered down, everything will become clear. Then they can pick up the pieces, solve the problem, and maybe even stop the same scene playing itself out again in the future.

We're not talking about emergencies – **Pause Parents** don't sit back if their child runs into the road, and if she scrapes her knee they'll give her a hug. When it is obvious what to do, they do it.

Being a **Pause Parent** is more about knowing that if you stay calm you will be able to regain control. Some **Pause Parents** feel panicky, like a rabbit in the headlights, because they can't think what to do or say. But it doesn't matter. You are actually doing a lot more good than you think. By staying quiet there's no chance of blurting out something horrible you'll regret later or inadvertently making matters worse.

If you aren't a natural **Pause Parent**, it can be hard not to react to provocation. But if you manage to take a deep breath and stay quiet, the results can be dramatic.

> *My daughter and I used to get into terrible rows. We would scream at each other, and say the most awful things.*
>
> *I knew we couldn't go on fighting like that – something had to change. So the next time she started shouting at me it took all I had, but I stayed quiet. I waited until she calmed down before talking it through with her.*
>
> *It was so much better. What a relief.*

## The Cheerleader Parent

**Cheerleader Parents** know that it's more effective and a lot more fun to motivate children with praise rather than criticism. They know that if they make a point of commenting on the good things their child does, bad behaviour tends to shrivel up from lack of attention. These parents notice when their child does something right and tell her so.

It's not that they don't care if their child misbehaves; they stay positive because they know it gets results. Even when things are going wrong, a drip-feed of kind comments can turn things around and make everyone in the family feel a lot better.

Being a **Cheerleader Parent** works because children crave our attention. This can be hard to believe, especially on those days when they don't seem to listen to a single thing we say. It's even harder to believe when they yell at us to go away and barricade themselves in their bedrooms. But deep down they are desperate for our attention, and they will do whatever it takes to get it. Even being shouted at by an exasperated parent is more satisfying for a child than getting no attention at all.

*I used to have trouble getting my son to wear his seatbelt. He kept taking it off to see how far he could push me until I lost my temper.*

*On one occasion, driving through the pouring rain, I got out of the car and smacked him hard. He howled for the rest of the journey and I felt awful. But I didn't know what else to do. I didn't want him to die if I crashed the car, but I was so angry I couldn't drive properly.*

*I felt so guilty for hitting him, the next time we got in the car I vowed to be nicer. So after he put his seatbelt on and we started driving down the road, I started saying kind things to him. 'Thank you for putting your seatbelt on,' and, a little later, 'I see you are still wearing your seatbelt. I really appreciate that.'*

*To my surprise, it was that easy. He kept his belt on. I couldn't believe it.*

**Cheerleader Parents** are great at turning situations like this around. They know that if they can fill up the attention-seeking hole with positive comments, their child may not try to wind them up. It's so simple, and it really works.

## The Tuned-In Parent

**Tuned-In Parents** know that the way their child feels affects the way she behaves, and that feelings are often the root cause of bad behaviour. Strong feelings can be confusing, stressful and so inconvenient. **Tuned-In Parents** are brilliant at helping their child process difficult feelings so she can cope with them.

When their child is behaving badly or being defiant, **Tuned-In Parents** assume there's a good reason for it, even if they don't know exactly what it is. So before telling her off, they listen. They know that by acknowledging her feelings she will be able to unburden herself, and better behaviour will follow.

This holds true no matter what the feeling is. Whether it's jealousy – 'That's *my* toy', resentment – 'Stop ordering me around', fear – 'I can't do this', sadness – 'No one likes me', or anger – 'I hate you.'

Telling her to stop fussing and behave will get you nowhere.

Pretending her feelings aren't there won't help her either. Instead, listen and try to understand.

*'My son came home from school in a foul mood. When I told him to cheer up, he threw down his school bag and told me to shut up. I didn't like his tone, but I knew there had to be a reason for it.*

*Instead of shouting at him, I said, 'This isn't like you. I can see you are upset. I bet something happened today at school.'*

*Suddenly it all poured out. Two boys had picked on him at lunch and told him they were going to beat him up. He was so upset he had a lump in his throat and couldn't eat. Then, because he was hungry, he felt ill all afternoon.*

*If I had punished him straight away, I might never have found out. But by being sympathetic I got an apology. Even more important, I could help him.'*

When your child knows you understand her, it can make her feel secure and more connected to you.

## The Physical Parent

**Physical Parents** know that if their child has enough exercise, good food and sleep, life is more pleasant. They realize that there don't always have to be deep psychological reasons for bad behaviour; sometimes children get ratty because they are exhausted, cooped up for too long in front of the television or juddering with sugar.

**Physical Parents** don't see the need for too much mind-bending behaviour analysis. If their child is grumpy they are likely to take her out to the park to work off some energy. If their child is tearful they give her a cuddle. They know that when their child feels healthy and well, there tend to be fewer irrational outbursts, fewer arguments, and less drama of every kind.

Fifty years ago it was easier to be a **Physical Parent**. There weren't so many cars on the road and parents were happier to let their children run around outside. There were no computers, Game Boys or PlayStations, so children were less tempted to sit around at home being couch potatoes. There was also less processed food, no television advertisements for sugary cereals and no Gary Lineker persuading children to eat crisps. They say children on post-war food rations in the 1950s had a healthier diet than lots of children today.

But just because it is more difficult to be a **Physical Parent** now doesn't mean it's impossible. All sorts of problems that can plague your family may have an incredibly simple physical solution. Basics like a good night's sleep, a walk, a snack or a hug are easy to overlook, but **Physical Parents** instinctively know that they can work miracles.

## The Sorted Parent

Family life is complicated, and **Sorted Parents** know that when they stay one step ahead of their children, everything is much easier. They are forward planners who think things through in advance to avoid hassle later.

Getting themselves and their children organized removes a whole layer of stress. These parents make a place for trainers, school bags and reading folders, so in the morning they don't have to run around looking for them. If their children fight over the window seat in the car, **Sorted Parents** decide who sits where before they set off on the next journey. They are also good at telling their children in advance what to expect and how to behave on aeroplanes, at restaurants and at other people's houses, instead of hissing last-minute instructions out of the corner of their mouths.

For those of us who aren't naturally sorted, life can be chaotic. When everything spirals out of control, there never seems to be enough time to get organized because you are constantly coping with the latest disaster: searching for lost shoes, scrabbling to find that vital piece of homework, or racing against the clock to get everyone to school on time. If you are stressed, your children are probably stressed too, and acting up.

Being a **Sorted Parent** is about seizing the upper hand and refusing to be a victim of fluctuating circumstances. It is about thinking ahead and setting things up so they go your way.

## The Commando Parent 

**Commando Parents** are good at being in charge and everyone knows where they stand with them. We don't mean the bossy ones who are always on their children's backs, constantly barking orders like 'Get dressed!', 'Tidy your room!', 'Do your homework!' and 'Go to bed!'

The best **Commando Parents** take control and get things done simply and easily without shouting and nagging. Some **Commandos** are easy to spot; they make their views clear and you know there's no point in messing them around. Others are more subtle though just as effective. They rarely even need to raise their voice – all it takes is a polite suggestion and everyone leaps into action. It's an amazing skill that most of us have to learn.

If you aren't a natural **Commando Parent**, you might feel you have to plead and wheedle to get anything done, or ask a hundred times and then lose your temper. Surely life would be a thousand times easier if your children did what you asked without a fuss. It is possible, and **Commando Parents** know how to make it happen. They stay in charge without turning into a dictator or a drill sergeant.

## The Laid-Back Parent

**Laid-Back Parents** let their children do a lot for themselves. They trust their children's judgement and encourage them to develop their independence. Being a **Laid-Back Parent** can be incredibly satisfying. By having faith in your child and giving her a free rein, her confidence will grow, and so will your pride in her accomplishments.

**Laid-Back Parents** know that children love being able to do things for themselves. All the best children's books, from *The Cat in the Hat* to *The Secret Garden, Swallows and Amazons* and *Harry Potter* are about children who have to work things out on their own because their parents aren't around. In real life, of course, children don't thrive on outright neglect, but step back just a little bit and you may be amazed by how competent your child can be without you hovering over her.

It can also be extremely liberating for you when your child starts doing things for herself. If she makes her own bed, this is one less thing you have to do for her. If you chat through a problem she's having at school so she can handle it on her own, she will feel more confident than if you go over her head and fix it for her.

**Laid-Back Parents** don't feel that they have to prove they are super-parents. They are happy to admit that they don't know all the answers and they don't feel embarrassed about asking for help when they need it. They don't feel they have to be in charge of every aspect of their child's life and they know that it's often better when they aren't.

Other parents might find it hard to let go, either because they prefer being in control or because they want to shield their child from the harsh realities of life by cosseting her. Of course it is our job to comfort and nurture our children, but it is also our job to help them learn to cope with the big wide world. **Laid-Back Parents** don't worry that their child will become too independent. Instead, they feel happy that they are helping her to stretch her wings.

# 2

# The Seven Secrets

## How to Make Them Work for You

So often we know there must be a better way. If only we could stay calm, be sympathetic, be assertive, get organized, or whatever. But if it doesn't come naturally, you might wonder how other parents do all these wonderful things.

It isn't as hard as you might think. We will take you step by step through each of the seven secrets. You might be surprised to find how much you are doing right already.

# The Secret of Pause Parents

**Pause Parents** stay quiet in a crisis.

## Zip your lip

It is a myth that good parents always know the right thing to say or do. Lots don't, and it's not a disaster if you haven't got a clue. Some parents discover by accident that doing nothing is often better than getting involved.

*My two girls rushed into the room one day, shouting and complaining about each other. I was so taken aback that I sat there with my mouth open. The awful thing was that I just couldn't think of the right thing to say. The story was so complicated, and the complaints so tangled, I was beginning to panic inside that I was a useless mother. Because*

*I didn't know what to do, I just kept looking dumbly at them.*

*Suddenly they stopped, looked at each other, and left. Maybe they'd let off steam, or maybe they just got bored because I wasn't saying anything. I don't know. Anyway, it worked.* '

If you can stop whatever you're doing and give your child your full attention without saying a word, you may not need to do anything else.

## Wait until later

It is another common misconception that parents need to solve every problem instantly. If an argument blows up or someone is feeling upset, it is incredibly tempting to jump in immediately and try to sort it out. If you are the kind of person who hates children bickering, you will do anything to get them to stop. If you feel miserable when your child is unhappy, you would move heaven and earth to cheer him up.

But sometimes it simply isn't appropriate to launch yourself into the fray. When everyone is already in a state, they won't appreciate your advice. You won't be able to help and sometimes you can actually end up making a bad situation worse. Get the timing wrong and your child may well become even ruder, more hysterical and more obstinate.

**Pause Parents** realize that life can be much easier and more pleasant if they hold off. Difficult situations are easier to handle after everyone has calmed down.

' *Every time my son treated his sister badly, I always reacted instantly. I'd tell him off, order him to apologize, and then threaten all sorts of punishments when he refused. Each time the situation escalated; my son would get more and more furious, my daughter would be in tears and I'd be tearing my hair out.*

*Now, with great self-control (which goes against all my instincts) I say we'll discuss everything later, when there's no shouting. Usually, if I let him calm down on his own, he will come straight back and apologize. The amazing thing is that when he explains himself rationally, I can see his point of view. When he's angry, I'm angry, and neither of us can think straight. Waiting until later really helps.* ❞

Sometimes you may have to wait a while for your child to deal with his feelings.

❝ *We had a huge argument about turning off the television. I was so angry I threatened to throw it out of the window. The children burst into tears and started yelling at me. We all had to go off to different rooms to calm down. They kept throwing me dirty looks all afternoon. But that night at bedtime, I had a really good chat about it with each of them and they agreed to watch less television.* ❞

Even if something seems really important, it can be a complete waste of time trying to deal with it immediately and you can end up feeling like you are beating your head against a brick wall. But pick your moment, and it will be much easier.

It might be tempting to ignore problems completely and never go back to them. Who wants to dredge up old issues when everyone has moved on? But **Pause Parents** know that waiting until later does not mean avoiding your responsibilities. Even if a situation feels out of control, if you don't do anything about it immediately you are actually being proactive; you are giving yourself the time to think. So when you go back and address the problem later, you'll know how to handle it and it won't be as hard as you think.

**Pause Parents** also know that they don't need to have the answer for everything and that it's fine to have conflicting feelings, and they explain this to their child.

❝ *My son asked for a PlayStation for his birthday, but I couldn't say yes straight away. I said I'd have to think about it. On one hand I wanted to buy it for him; most of his friends had them, and I didn't want him to feel left out. On the other hand, I felt the games would be violent and I worried that he already watched too much television. I thought it over for a few days. In the end I bought it, but not before setting limits on his screen time and the type of games he could play.* ❞

If you have mixed feelings about something it doesn't mean you are indecisive. It simply means that life can be complicated. There is no point in being rushed, bullied or embarrassed into making a hasty decision. Pondering out loud can also open the door for further discussion.

‘*My daughter was invited to a birthday-party sleepover. I told her I was in two minds about it. I said I was sympathetic and didn't want her to be the only girl in her gang to miss it. But I was hesitant because we were visiting her grandparents the next day. The last time she went to a sleepover the whole weekend was a write-off. She was shattered because she had stayed up until three o'clock in the morning and gorged herself on sweets.*

*Perhaps because I was open about my reasons, she didn't take it too hard when I didn't let her spend the night. Instead she went for the dinner and movie, and I collected her at nine thirty for bed.*’

## Calm down fast

Even **Pause Parents** can't stay relaxed all the time (is there a parent out there who can?). But when they feel they are losing their cool, they know how to calm down so they don't make a bad situation worse. They might try taking a deep breath, counting slowly to ten or leaving the room. Just use whatever works for you. Here are some other simple ideas:

- *'I drink a glass of water.'*
- *'I go out for a quick run. If I can't get out of the house, I close my eyes and imagine it instead.'*
- *'I lock myself in the bathroom and call a friend on my mobile.'*
- *'I run up and down the stairs or hit a pillow.'*

We've even heard of one mother who vents her frustrations by jumping up and down on a packet of biscuits until it's nothing but crumbs.

## Keep things in perspective

When your child has a problem, it can be hard not to overreact. But **Pause Parents** try to keep everything in perspective.

If your child is picky and won't eat his vegetables, you might start to worry. But think back – did you like vegetables at his age? If he is taking a vital exam or playing an important match, of course you want him to do well. But there is no point getting neurotic; it's not a matter of life or death and he doesn't need to cope with your stress as well as his own.

The hardest time to keep things in perspective is when you are already under pressure. If your boss is coming for dinner and you find mud tracked through the house, you may feel like throttling the child who did it. But thinking through the worst-case scenario (your boss sees mud on the carpet) can help keep the calamity in perspective. If your child was seriously ill or had been in some sort of accident, none of this kind of thing would matter.

## Expect to get wound up

**Pause Parents** know it's inevitable that children and situations will wind them up. They can anticipate when something might get under their skin and prepare themselves for it. That way, when a situation becomes stressful, they don't get completely taken by surprise or overreact.

If you can guess beforehand that something is going to irritate you, it helps to give your child a bit of warning:

- *'This car journey is going to be very long, and I am already feeling anxious about it. I need you to keep the noise down while I'm driving so I can concentrate.'*

If you are already stressed out (whether it's because you're running late, have too much to do, or are simply exhausted), your child can seem a hundred times more annoying. But if you are aware of how you feel, you can explain it to him. That way you are less likely to snap and he might even behave.

# The Secret of Cheerleader Parents

**Cheerleader Parents** focus on their child's good points.

## Notice the good, ignore the bad 

**Cheerleader Parents** give their children lots of praise and encouragement for the good things they do, and try not to be critical. Though we'd all like to think we're kind parents, it's easy to take it for granted when our children are being good. When we're busy, it's such a relief when they go away and play quietly. When they're occupied, we can get on with the thousands of things we have to do before they come and disturb us again.

So if you were a child looking for attention, how would you get it? By sitting quietly in your room, colouring a picture in total silence? Or by winding up your brothers and sisters, whining that you are bored or refusing to do what you are told?

When a child behaves badly he suddenly comes back into focus, looming large in your field of vision. When he behaves really badly, it's hard to think of anything else. Your whole life seems to be dominated by worrying about how you can get him to stop fighting, arguing back, having tantrums or whatever it is you can't stand. Sometimes the bad behaviour takes up so much space in your head that it seems as though your whole family life is a disaster. There's no room left to see anything good, particularly about the child who is causing the most problems.

*'I was worried sick about my oldest son and angry with him all the time. He was bullying his little brother and sister, and it was affecting the entire family.*

*In desperation I enrolled for parent classes. The homework the very first week was to ignore all his bad behaviour and notice every good thing he did, however small. I went away feeling cynical. I honestly thought he wasn't doing anything right and I'd come back with nothing to report.*

*It was a revelation. I discovered that my son, the black sheep of the family, had been doing so many good things right under my nose, and I had been blind to them all. On the first day, when it was time for breakfast I called everyone and he was the first to come thumping down the stairs. OK, it was a little loud so early in the morning. But was he always the first down? I didn't know.*

*Then on the way to school I saw him glance back to make sure his little brother was safe crossing the road. Did he do this every time? I had no idea. I was usually still seething after the arguments getting out the door.*

*He did all sorts of bad things too, but suddenly they didn't bother me half as much, and I let most of them go.* ’

This mother's only task was to make a simple mental shift, and the effect was dramatic. By noticing the good things her son did, she felt the atmosphere in her family start to turn around.

**Cheerleader Parents** know that if you concentrate on the good instead of the bad you can feel totally different, more positive and more hopeful. Suddenly your family's troubles don't seem so overwhelming and out of control.

But there is another benefit. The atmosphere won't just feel better; it can genuinely improve as your child's behaviour starts to change.

## Be specific

Starting to notice the good things your child does is half the battle. He will pick up the fact that your attitude is generally more positive, rather than hostile or nit-picky, and he will probably start behaving better. But it's even more effective if you can tell him out loud exactly what he is doing right, and the more specific you can be, the better.

Be careful not to go over the top and gush out generalized praise. It can be tempting to tell your child he is 'Super! Wonderful! Marvellous! Brilliant! Amazing!' It's better than no praise at all, but he may have no idea what he has actually done well.

‘ *My daughter came home from school and showed me the gold star she'd been given by her teacher. I asked her what it was for and she looked at me blankly. 'I don't know,' she said.* ’

Sometimes general praise can backfire because your child feels it isn't justified and suspects that you are being insincere.

> *My son showed me a picture he did at school. I told him it was brilliant, and that he was a great artist.*
>
> *'No I'm not,' he snapped. 'Stop saying such stupid things. This picture is rubbish.' Then he ripped it up. I was so surprised. I was just trying to build his confidence.*

Some parents worry that if they give their child too much praise he will become big-headed, self-absorbed and attention-seeking. Others worry that it will make him falsely confident, and horribly unprepared for the harsh realities of life. But if you stick to being specific, this doesn't seem to happen. Just describe what you see and be truthful.

- *'You worked hard at that maths problem'*

is better than:

- *'You are a maths genius.'*
- *'You've been running and kicking that football all afternoon. Great ball control'*

is better than:

- *'You are brilliant at sport.'*

If you praise his small achievements, he is more likely to believe what you say. This will give him the incentive and confidence to carry on. But if you gush, he may feel he can't possibly live up to your inflated image of him. Though he may get big-headed, it's more likely he'll be embarrassed and reject what you say.

> *The next time he brought home a picture I was very careful not to go overboard. Instead I just tried to point out the things I noticed. 'I like the way you coloured the front door red . . . You've drawn lots of trees.' He was so pleased he launched into a detailed description of what he had done.*

You can also show your appreciation by asking your child to show you what he's done. And even if you don't like the picture, you can always find something nice to say.

> *You worked hard on this picture. No wonder you carried it home so carefully without creasing it.*

## Praise on the spot

We know it sounds contradictory, but the best way to change behaviour you don't like is to catch your child when he does something right, rather than criticizing him when he does something wrong.

Take untidiness, for example. If you keep criticizing him for it, he'll internalize the message:

- *'I'm not good at being tidy, so there's no point in even trying.'*

But there's no point in lying to him, either. If you tell him he is a tidy person when he isn't, he simply won't believe you. In fact, he'll probably laugh in your face. So here's the clever bit. Try catching him when he *is* tidy – that one time he puts a T-shirt on the chair instead of on the floor – and tell him how pleased you are. Be specific, but neutral (no gushing). Even if it's the first time in a year he's done it, a **Cheerleader Parent** seizes the moment and comments on it, describing what they see, being specific and being truthful. Though it may not be much, you have to start somewhere.

- *'I can see you hung up your wet towel.'*
- *'Thank you for putting that in the bin.'*
- *'You've started to tidy up your desk. It looks nice.'*

Then your child knows what he has done well, knows you've noticed and knows you are pleased. Over time he can take in more messages that he is a tidy person.

Just commenting on good behaviour is enough, but you can also try giving the behaviour a name. Again, don't go overboard or you'll start to get irritating.

- *'You put the ketchup away on the right shelf. That was very organized.'*
- *'You wiped up the milk you spilt. Thank you for being so conscientious.'*

If he begins to see himself as an organized, conscientious person and has the evidence to back it up, he is more likely to live up to this positive image. The idea is for him to want to be tidy from the inside, rather than being tidy because you nag him.

If you have a child who feels manipulated or embarrassed by compliments, he may be rude to you when you praise him on the spot. Generally this happens more with older children, but even some younger children feel awkward if the spotlight of your attention is too bright. Don't take it personally. Even if he shrugs off your approval, remember that deep down he needs it, so find a subtle way to show him that you appreciate his efforts. Try a quiet thumbs-up, a quick nod or smile, or leave a brief note for him in his bedroom.

If you aren't a natural **Cheerleader Parent**, catching your child when he does something right can be very difficult at first. It's so much easier to spot his mistakes. For example, if he shows you a page of sums, where does your eye go? Straight to the one that's wrong, of course. It just leaps off the page and you can't help pointing it out. Because we love our children we feel it is our duty to show them where they are going wrong and help them on to the right path. How amazing that they aren't grateful for all our good advice.

Even if you don't praise him the moment he does something right, showing your appreciation weeks or months later is better than not mentioning it at all.

*It didn't occur to me how well behaved my children were at Hallowe'en until a friend started complaining about hers. Her children always fought over sweets – who had more, who got what. She said it was a nightmare.*

*My children came home, dumped all their sweets out on the kitchen table and had a great time swapping and trading them. They even gave some to their little sister who had the least. Though Hallowe'en was long past, I told them how much I'd enjoyed it and how nice it was that they'd shared.*

## Be positive

One of the reasons **Cheerleader Parents** are so successful at promoting a happy atmosphere is that they make the unpleasant stuff palatable. Even when they need to criticize or remind, they manage to get their point across in a positive way.

Instead of:

- *'You still haven't finished tidying your room. I've told you a million times to pick up your dirty underwear'*

they might say:

- *'You've done really well. I see you've already picked some things off the floor. I can see 95 per cent of the carpet.'*

With a bit of luck their child will think:

- *'Yes, I have done well, and what else is there? Oh yes, my pants.'*

The added bonus is that by letting him figure out the missing piece, you have yet another opportunity to praise him.

- *'Thank you for picking up your pants and finishing your room off.'*

The difference may sound quite trivial, but if you encourage your child he is much more likely to try harder next time, whereas if he gets discouraged he might not bother trying at all.

**Cheerleader Parents** know that saying things in a positive way can swing round potentially difficult situations. For example:

- *'Well done looking both ways before crossing the road'* (if you're not sure he's fully concentrating).
- *'Well done holding on to the dog's lead so tightly'* (if the dog is about to run off).

- *'Well done for not hitting your sister'* (when you can see he's about to!).

## Be open-minded

It can be a very fine line between praising your child and putting pressure on him. The thing to remember is to be open-minded. Children are always changing. **Cheerleader Parents** are wonderful at understanding this and appreciating all the little phases and stages along the way.

Part of being open-minded is realizing that your own expectations can cloud your vision, like a coloured filter or distorting lens, so you can't see your child clearly for who he is. If you were quite academic or sporty, you might be hugely disappointed if he isn't, and this can prevent you from noticing his other talents. But stay open-minded and concentrate on specifics, and you will see what he's doing well. Maybe he is more interested in art or drama than maths, or more into books than rugby.

Each child's needs and capabilities are different; different from your own at that age, different from his siblings' and different from other children's in his class. If you accept this, it's easier to notice the wonderful things your child has to offer.

The other part of being open-minded is not generalizing about your child. Labelling him 'the good one', 'the naughty one', 'the helpful one', 'the difficult one', 'the musical one' or 'the mathematical one' can put him into a rigid box that's difficult to live up to or get out of.

One of the biggest problems with labelling your child is that he might believe you. If you tell him he is lazy he may think of himself that way, making it harder for him to change. True, he may go through idle phases or be less active or helpful than his siblings. But if you don't call him lazy or 'the lazy one', he may not consider laziness to be a defining part of his character, which will make it easier for him to change as he grows up.

Even when you think you are complimenting your child, labels can be a bad idea.

*'My parents used to tell everyone I was the good one, and at home I was an angel. I never talked back. I never put a foot wrong. But with my friends it was another story. I did all sorts of stupid stuff. Even when I needed their help, I could never confide in my parents. I never wanted to ruin their image of me, so I've spent a lot of time hiding things from them and not letting them know what is really going on.'*

At some point, possibly much further down the line, your child is going to have to reconcile your label with the person he really is.

*'When my daughter was younger she did beautiful drawings and I felt she showed great promise. I wanted her to feel good about herself and develop her talent, so I used to tell her she was the artist in the family.*

*One day when she was eleven I asked her how 'my artist' was doing. She screamed at me at the top of her voice, 'Why do you keep calling me that? I am so sick of it. I am* not *your artist. I* hate *art.'*

*Now she won't do any art, which is disappointing. But when I was little I wanted to be a Merry-Go-Round driver. It seems ludicrous to think what my life would be like if my parents were still holding on to that one.'*

If your child loves football, encourage him, by all means. But be open-minded and notice his other interests and talents as well.

Not labelling one child also leaves possibilities open for siblings. There's room for more than one football star in the family. Even if your second child doesn't seem as interested, don't give the title away to his older brother or he may feel he can't compete and give up without trying.

# The Secret of Tuned-In Parents

**Tuned-In Parents** understand the feelings behind their child's behaviour.

## Listen to their feelings

When their child feels strongly about something, **Tuned-In Parents** try hard to listen and understand. If your child is angry or unhappy, he can let go of his feelings more easily once you've listened to him. So when he says something like 'I hate homework' and flings down his pencil, try not to contradict him or talk him round. Instead, just confirm that you've heard. Try:

- *'You really can't stand doing homework'*

or:

- *'You wish you didn't have to do this.'*

This might sound counter-intuitive, but you are not saying that he doesn't have to do his homework. You are only acknowledging that he wishes he didn't have to do it, and showing him you understand how he feels.

This little trick is amazing and often works wonders. It can save you a lot of pointless arguments when the outcome is obvious. Your child doesn't expect to be let off the hook, he simply wants you to understand him. Once you show that you do, he'll often drop the topic altogether and start cooperating.

*'My daughter used to complain every night about putting on her pyjamas. It was a real battle persuading her to get changed. One evening I tried something different. When she started moaning, I said, 'You don't want to put on your pyjamas. You wish you could stay in your clothes all night.'*

*She looked at me, bewildered. She'd been waiting for me to nag her, but it didn't happen. She said wearily, 'Yeah, I don't like getting changed. But I don't want to wear my school clothes in bed.' Then she got undressed. I wish I'd known it could be so simple.'*

Many parents find it very hard to tune in properly when their child is upset. It's our natural instinct to comfort our children and tell them things aren't as bad as they think. So if your child says:

- *'I don't have any friends. No one likes me'*

you might be tempted to reply:

- *'Don't say that. It's not true. You have lots of friends.'*

You are contradicting him to try and stop his suffering. But if you deny his feelings, he's likely to become more vehement to prove his point:

- *'It is true. I told you! No one likes me.'*

Accepting your child's feelings straight away is actually much kinder and more productive. When it works you can feel like a superparent, because your child feels you understand him and the two of you connect. Once he feels understood, he may also be able to think through his problem for himself.

> *My daughter poured out a long story about how no one liked her at school. I was desperate to give her advice, but instead I made sympathetic noises and tried to show that I understood. 'So your best friends have been ignoring you? That must really hurt your feelings. No wonder you're so unhappy.'*
>
> *After twenty awful minutes of tears, she began to cheer up. 'I know,' she said, 'I can be friends with some other people instead.' And she made a list of three girls she wanted to invite over to play. She worked it out all on her own.*

Listening will help your child cope with his feelings so they turn into more of a spring shower than a thunderstorm. When you acknowledge his feelings, they may blow over surprisingly quickly – don't be surprised if he blows up with even more intense emotion.

- *'Yes! I told you. I hate Jack! I wish he was dead!'*

If things seem to be deteriorating, your natural impulse might be to call a halt before he says or does anything worse. But if you can stand it, try to sit tight and let him blow off steam. Things may have been building up for a while and you are lifting the lid on an emotional pressure cooker. Though it might feel awful at first, just keep listening, or confirm what you hear:

- *'You are* furious *with him.'*
- *'It makes you* crazy *when he does that. You really hate it.'*

Don't start criticizing the person he is ranting about, especially if it's a sibling. Your feelings aren't the issue, and making judgements won't help. Your job is to give him a safe space to talk about his feelings. If they have been building up for a while he may need to vent more than once, but eventually he will calm down. Afterwards he will feel happier and more rational and be able, at last, to move on.

Some parents worry that they won't be able to say the right thing. But try anyway. It isn't a problem if your guess is wrong, because your child will quickly set you straight.

- *'You are angry because he borrowed your Lego.'*
- *'No. I hate him because he smashed up my Lego car to make a spaceship.'*

An added bonus of listening to feelings is that you can try to give him new words to describe them.

If he says:

- *'I hate Jack,'*

you can say:

- *'You are really irritated because he smashed up your car,'*

or:

- *'You're annoyed because he keeps pestering you,'*

or whatever.

By showing him how to pinpoint his feelings, he can learn to understand them better, and they may not feel so overwhelming next time. By identifying the problem, you are also helping to normalize it, which can take away a lot of his angst.

> *My daughter used to have huge meltdowns whenever she couldn't get her hair smoothly into a ponytail. Finally I told her she was having a 'bad hair day' and that we all had them.*
>
> *It hasn't been a problem since. If she gets frustrated, she laughs and says she's having a bad hair day, and that's the end of it.*

Don't hesitate to use sophisticated words for different shades of emotion. If they describe how he feels, he'll understand what you mean.

- *'I bet you were discouraged when he said you were a hopeless goalkeeper.'*
- *'You must have been pretty envious when she was boasting about her holiday.'*
- *'It can be disheartening when your teacher doesn't notice your hard work.'*

**Tuned-In Parents** know that although some children will come and tell you what's wrong, others are like unexploded bombs, lips sealed with all sorts of frustration or anger boiling up inside. If he isn't talking, guess what you think your child is feeling. You can start off by being quite general:

- *'You look like you've had a bad day.'*
- *'I can see you 're not very happy about something.'*
- *'Something's bothering you.'*

If you suspect you know what the answer is, you can always be more specific:

- *'I guess you're upset because Joe yelled at you for borrowing his iPod.'*

It seems to work best if you stick to statements rather than asking questions. Even simple questions like 'Why are you upset?' can put too much pressure on a child. He may be confused about how he feels, and questions will only muddle him further. Or he may feel got at and not want to answer. Somehow a statement – 'You look upset' – is less intrusive.

If he really doesn't want to tell you what's going on, don't keep pushing him unless, of course, it's an emergency or someone's hurt and you urgently need to know what happened. In most cases, when you're dealing with difficult or painful feelings, if your child doesn't want to talk, it's not worth badgering him. If you've expressed your interest and sympathy, he'll feel comforted and continue sorting things out on his own. The chances are he will come back to talk to you later, when he is feeling less raw, and will pour out the whole story.

Though tuning in to your child is usually helpful, some parents can take it too far. They understand and sympathize so deeply with their child that they can't see where he's gone wrong. They make excuses for him when he's upset, even if it's his own fault, and find it hard to say no when he wants something. Sadly, some parents over-identify with one child, completely tuning in and understanding him, to the detriment of their other children.

> *‘When I was younger my little sister used to whinge and cry all the time. My mother couldn't bear to see her upset, and took her side on everything. I hated both of them for it.’*

## Accept difficult feelings

Being empathetic can be very difficult for a lot of parents. When your child misbehaves it's all too easy to point out where he's gone wrong and set punishments, without finding out why it happened.

- *'There is no excuse for hitting your brother.'*
- *'You shouldn't ever be rude to your teacher.'*
- *'Don't you ever speak to me like that.'*

Of course he needs to know how to behave, but instead of criticizing or punishing, **Tuned-In Parents** begin with the assumption that whatever their child has done, he must have done it for a reason. If his reaction was excessive, he must have felt so strongly about something that he couldn't think of another way to express himself.

> *The headmaster telephoned to say my son had punched another boy in the face. I was so shocked I wanted to ground him for a year. But when I picked him up, I could tell from his face he was really upset. So instead of shouting at him, I listened.*
>
> *It turned out this other boy had been picking on him and teasing him all term. The final straw was when he grabbed my son's book bag. All his papers spilled out and lots of them blew away. He shouldn't have punched the other boy, but I could see why he lost it.*

Letting your child say things you don't want to hear can be extremely hard.

> *I always thought I was a relaxed and sympathetic parent. But when my son said he hated his sister, I wasn't sympathetic at all and told him never to speak like that again.*
>
> *But then I remembered that I used to hate my little brother sometimes, too. He annoyed me so much. And guess what? My mother would never let me say so either, and it made me hate both of them even more. If I wanted my own children to get on, maybe I was going to have to let them hate each other sometimes.*
>
> *So later, at bedtime, I said, 'You were very angry with your sister today.' I felt really scared, like I was standing on the edge of an abyss. It was horrible. He listed all the things he disliked about her, all the ways she bugged him, even some of the things he'd like to do to her. It was almost more than I could take, but I kept quiet, and eventually he stopped. After that he was about a hundred times nicer to her.*

Using some of the tools of **Tuned-In Parents** can be very frightening at first for those who get overwhelmed by their child's emotions. But by doing so you can avoid all sorts of head-to-head clashes, and end up having a much better relationship with him.

By tuning in to your child and understanding him better, you may find ways to solve problems that work for both of you.

> *My son kept nagging me to let our dog sleep in his bed. I wanted her to stay downstairs because she can be filthy, but he said he was scared of night noises. So we compromised and let her sleep in a basket in his room.*

Even if you decide not to compromise, your child is far more likely to accept your decision if you listen to him first.

## Respect their feelings

Because **Tuned-In Parents** understand how their child feels, they try hard not to talk rudely to him or about him, especially in front of other people. They know how humiliating it can be, and how angry or sad it can make him feel. So they don't make comments like 'My son's a demon' or 'He can be so incredibly selfish' when he can overhear.

However tough children may appear, inside they are usually more vulnerable than we are. Though they might pretend not to care what we say about them, they tend to believe us.

Ideally we would all be so tuned in that we'd never say anything unpleasant about our children, because we'd know there's always a reason behind bad behaviour. However, in practice we all need to let off steam sometimes, or at least talk through some of their more irritating habits. But you can respect your child's feelings by waiting until he is out of earshot, asleep or, better still, out of the house.

## Imagine it could happen

This is another miracle-worker, particularly for younger children, and it's capable of defusing all kinds of arguments and tantrums. Instead of arguing their point when their child won't back down, **Tuned-In Parents** might take their child's wishes to the extreme by imagining what would happen if they were fulfilled. Their child still doesn't end up getting what he wants, but he stops being unreasonable because he feels understood.

*I was collecting my daughter from a friend's house, but she made a huge fuss and refused to leave. I tried everything – pleading, threatening, even pretending to leave without her. I thought I was just going to have to pick her up, kicking and screaming, to get her out of there.*

*But her friend's mother solved the problem. She said, 'You wish you didn't have to go home. I bet you wish you could stay here overnight. Wouldn't it be great if you could stay here until Christmas!'*

*My daughter stopped struggling immediately and started to smile at this outrageous suggestion. 'I'd like to stay here for a hundred nights, and eat sausages and chips for dinner,' she answered. Then she put on her shoes and socks quite happily and we left.*

In a lot of ways, this is not dissimilar to listening to feelings and accepting them. But imagining that something could happen takes the process one step further. By taking your child's wishes to the wildest extreme, you can often end the episode on a positive note.

*My kids were desperate to have an ice-cream in the park. I told them they couldn't because we were on our way home to have dinner. They started begging and pleading and I thought it was going to end in an argument. Instead I said, 'Wouldn't it be great if we could have a huge ice-cream sundae with ten monster big scoops each!' My daughter added, 'Smothered in chocolate sauce.' Then my son said, 'With hundreds and thousands and chocolate chips.' We all agreed, 'Yes – wouldn't that be great,' and carried on home. I couldn't quite believe it worked, but it did.*

Don't worry that your children will misunderstand and insist on having giant ice-creams – somehow they can always tell that it's just a wonderful fantasy. The important thing is that you have acknowledged their intense desire to buy, have or do something.

## Reconnect

Even sensitive **Tuned-In Parents** blow it sometimes. They get into arguments with their children, lose their temper and say things they don't mean.

They might feel horrible about it all day, but they know it isn't a disaster. One fall-out doesn't mean they've damaged their child or lost him for ever. There's always the chance to go back, say sorry and smooth things over. They know that it's good for their child – and good for them – to reconnect, say goodbye to the guilt and start again. But however desperate they are to make things better, like **Pause Parents** they know how important it is to wait for the right moment. Your apology won't work if you are still angry, and if your child is still angry, he won't listen anyway.

If **Tuned-In Parents** regret shouting or saying something hurtful they will say so, but they won't grovel or change their mind about something important. For example, if the trouble started because their child flatly refused to feed the dog, they won't excuse him from looking after it in future. But they might say sorry if they over-reacted by yelling or threatening to give the dog away.

Some parents feel that apologizing isn't appropriate when their child has been defiant. But **Tuned-In Parents** know that it is vital to reconnect with their child, and they aren't too proud to make the first move.

On a good day you will get an apology in return. But what do you do if your child just grunts and rolls his eyes? **Tuned-In Parents** might assume that he's still angry or upset and be compassionate about it. But apologizing needn't be a one-way street. Parents have feelings too.

*My son and I got into an argument. I felt bad afterwards and apologized, but he just looked at me sarcastically and raised his eyebrows. This irritated me all over again. So I took a deep breath and explained how apologies work.*

*I said, 'If someone says "sorry" to you, they need something back. Here's how to do it. Look at them and say, "I'm sorry too," as though you really mean it.'*

*'But what if I haven't done anything wrong?' he mumbled.*

*'Then you can say, "Thank you. That means a lot to me," or, "It was kind of you to say that." Then the whole thing is done and dusted.'*

*'OK, Mum, sorry,' he said.*

*I went to bed feeling much happier than I'd been all day.* ❞

## The Secret of Physical Parents 

**Physical Parents** know that when their child feels well he will usually behave well.

### Get them moving

**Physical Parents** know that children are a bit like dogs: they need lots of exercise. If you are trapped inside on a rainy day it's a miracle if everyone stays in a good temper. But get everyone outside and somehow all that aggravation evaporates. **Physical Parents** intuitively know that exercise makes children feel good, and scientific studies back them up. A little exercise can raise a child's endorphin levels, boost his immune system and even make his brain work more efficiently.

The hard bit is persuading your child to get his backside off the sofa. If you are lucky, you have a naturally physical child who loves being active. If you are not so lucky, you will have to be clever about it, because if you are heavy-handed or over-competitive, you can turn him off exercise totally. Here are some suggestions from successful **Physical Parents** we know:

- ***Walk to school*** *Build that extra ten to twenty minutes into your routine – it's worth it. Think laterally to make this work – if you live a long way off, drive part of the way. Bring heavy things to school once a week in the car and leave them there.*
- ***Get your child to do some chores*** *It's much better for kids to rake leaves, mow the lawn, hang out the laundry or do the washing-up rather than sitting hunched in front of the computer or the TV all day. It won't kill them and they might*

*even enjoy themselves. Some parents give pocket money in return.*

- ***Sign your child up for a club or class*** *Even if he hates sport at school, you should be able to find something he'll enjoy. Try trampolining, yoga, judo or modern dance. The local sports centre is a good place to start.*
- ***Organize fun family outings at weekends and in the holidays*** *Take your child swimming or skating, go on bicycle rides, organize long walks, rent paddle boats. If you are into it, he'll get into it.*
- ***Get a dog*** *This makes walking much more fun, and has to be done every day.*

If you live in a city you can still be a **Physical Parent**, but you may have to be creative about it. One mother, who brought up four strapping boys in a house in Fulham with no garden, told us how she did it.

> *The thing that kept me sane was getting them outside every single day, whatever the weather. It wasn't always easy because I couldn't open the door and shoo them out. To cut out the moaning, I did everything I could think of to make our expeditions fun. We had footballs and a frisbee, we played tag, we had snail races in the rain, we played hide and seek, we'd go out on bicycles with the baby in a seat behind me. It was an effort, but I was determined. I would have strangled the lot of them by now if we'd stayed cooped up inside.*

## Feed them well

**Physical Parents** know that the food their children eat can affect the way they behave. Not everyone is the same, but the most common triggers of bad behaviour are sugar, caffeine (which is in chocolate and cola drinks as well as coffee), preservatives, food colourings, flavourings and flavour enhancers like monosodium glutamate. If a child is sensitive to any of these they can make him become highly emotional, cry or scream, buzz around the house like a hyperactive bluebottle, suffer severe mood swings, or collapse in an exhausted heap. If your child shows any of these symptoms, it is worth considering whether he has a food sensitivity or intolerance. Many schools have banned vending machines that sell sweets and fizzy drinks because students' behaviour gets worse straight after lunch. With doctors in the UK handing out 250,000 prescriptions for Ritalin-type drugs every year, parents need to be aware that hyperactivity can sometimes be prevented simply by sorting out their child's diet.

*My son was diagnosed with Attention Deficit Disorder. His school suggested I move him somewhere that could deal with his behavioural problems and the doctor said the best thing for him was Ritalin. It was horrendous, but I was determined to sort him out without drugs. It took a long time, but with a lot of testing and exclusion diets we worked out that he was very sensitive to tartrazine (a food-colouring in orange squash) and gluten (the sticky component of wheat). He also got moody if he ate more than a little sugar. We cut these out of his diet and it was like a miracle. The hyperactivity completely disappeared, and I feel like I've got my son back. He doesn't like being out of control, so now he's pretty careful about what he eats.*

*My son always looked white and felt permanently exhausted. Eventually we worked out that he was intolerant to wheat, dairy products and Brazil nuts. All things that I thought were good for him! At one point, he was so pale and withdrawn the school suggested I take him to a child psychologist. I am glad we never had to get into all that.*

**Physical Parents** also know the benefits of drinking lots of water. Even after just a few hours without it, children can become lethargic and irritable. Some **Physical Parents** don't bother with juice drinks, which tend to be full of flavourings, colouring and sugar or artificial sweeteners. Instead they favour good old water, and you'll find a glass of it for each child on the table at every meal.

## Get them to bed

**Physical Parents** realize that the most disagreeable children are often the most exhausted ones. When a child is tired, he can be absolute hell to live with: first thing in the morning he is demanding and unreasonable, when he gets home from school he antagonizes his siblings, and by bedtime he is so obstreperous you are ready to throttle him. So they make sure their children go to bed at a reasonable hour and get plenty of sleep.

*I woke our youngest up for school on Monday morning and she was so nasty everyone in the house was angry with her. But I knew she was tired, and told everyone to try to be understanding. We'd had friends over at the weekend and she'd had a couple of very late nights. It was all too much for her.*

*That afternoon when she came home from school she fell asleep until dinner.*

## Be affectionate

**Physical Parents** know that a hug and a cuddle can solve a thousand problems, so they give them out readily whenever there's the chance. They know that there is no better way to comfort and reassure their child or let him know that he is loved. If he can't or won't talk about his feelings, **Physical Parents** aren't fazed. They might sit him on their knee, hold his hand or put an arm around his shoulder. Often they find that does the trick.

**Physical Parents** don't just kiss and hug their children when they are babies and toddlers; they know that children need affection at every age. But as they get older, there are fewer opportunities to be affectionate, so you may have to start getting clever about it.

*As my daughters get older, the chances for me to give them a cuddle are fewer and further between. They stay late at school with clubs, they go to friends' houses. They're busy and I'm busy. I find putting them to bed is the only time left. So when I read each of them a story I hop into their beds. And when we turn out the light I just lie there for five minutes. They hold my hand or I put my arm around them. It's a lovely cosy time.*

*My son is trying to be macho. He hardly ever lets me kiss him any more, especially not in front of other people. Sometimes I know he needs a cuddle but he would die rather than ask for one. Instead we play this game we've invented which involves a lot of wrestling as we try to push each other off my bed. It sounds really silly but it is a lot of fun and it allows him to get some physical contact without being sissy about it.*

## Just be there

There is no doubt that exercise, healthy eating and cuddles can work miracles, but they aren't the only answers. Sometimes **Physical Parents** need to remember that listening to feelings can be just as important. Although **Physical Parents** don't always find it easy to talk about feelings, just being there gives their children the chance to open up and talk if they want to. Sometimes children don't want a long discussion about what's on their mind. All they want is for their mother or father to be around. You don't have to do or say anything – just watch television together, or read while your child does his homework.

**Physical Parents** know that their children may need them to be around at any time, and this includes night time. Lots of parents let their kids hop into their bed or sleep in the same room if they need reassurance in the middle of the night.

*My son comes into my room if he has had a nightmare. I don't bother to go through it with him. I just let him go to sleep beside me. It's so nice that this is all it takes to comfort him.*

*When my daughter comes home from school, she doesn't always want to talk. If I question her she'll clam up. So instead, I carry on doing whatever I'm doing – peeling potatoes, washing up, whatever. When there is no possibility of my making embarrassing eye contact, she'll tell me what's on her mind.*

# The Secret of Sorted Parents

**Sorted Parents** are forward thinkers and stay one step ahead of their child.

## Bite the bullet

When we have problems, many of us cross our fingers and hope the difficulties will magically disappear if we ignore them. We are too overstretched and over-committed to squeeze in another thing. **Sorted Parents** are as busy as the rest of us, but somehow they manage to give problems their undivided attention and make the effort to solve them.

For example, if **Sorted Parents** want their child to eat healthier food, they might organize regular supermarket deliveries, rather than scrabbling in the cupboard at teatime for bread and jam. When important exams are coming up, they might make a timetable to help their child revise. If bedtime is becoming a long-drawn-out nightmare, they might spend a week or two concentrating on establishing a new routine.

All of these problems can be a pain to resolve, and you might not feel that you have the mental energy to tackle them. But **Sorted Parents** know that if you take the time to untangle your most pressing problems, in the end you will have more time to deal with everything else.

It's hard to get organized if something seems too daunting or difficult. You might feel ambivalent about finding a solution, or simply out of your depth. Either way, it's much easier to put off making a decision or even thinking about it. **Sorted Parents** realize that it's better to bite the bullet and dive right in, because this will save them hassle later on.

*It used to be so difficult getting my children out of the house in the morning that I couldn't even bear to think about it. I hoped that if I ignored it, the problem would somehow go away on its own. So of course it got worse. The solution would have been to get everything ready the night before. But I never wanted to ruin my evening. The more disorganized we got, the more reluctant I was to come downstairs in the morning and face the chaos. But now I've faced up to it, it's really not so bad. I get all the kit and packed lunches together at bedtime.* ’

## Sort your systems

One of the greatest strengths of **Sorted Parents** is that they look ahead, see what's coming and get organized.

‘ *When I bought my son's school uniform there were dozens of bits and pieces. I realized they would get lost all over the house. So I made a place for everything right by the door – his coat, scarf, gym bag, shoes, lunch box, reading folder, you name it. I figured if he put it all there at night, we'd have a decent chance of finding everything in the morning before school.* ’

**Sorted Parents** also have the uncanny ability to notice that birthdays and Christmas happen at the same time every year. So while the rest of us struggle along and are perpetually taken by surprise, they're never caught off guard.

‘ *I'm the kind of parent who sits up on Christmas Eve frantically wrapping up presents. The same flipping thing happens every year and I hate it. Every year I run out of time, and every year I get stressed out and exhausted. My excuse is that I have four children and no time to get organized.*

*Then I read that the fund manager Nicola Horlick buys presents every year for seventy children. Seventy children! I can barely manage four. Apparently she has a list of all their names, ages and addresses, and every September she spends a few hours ordering all their presents from mail-order catalogues.* ’

**Sorted Parents** also notice when a problem keeps on rearing its ugly head, and they set up a system to take care of it.

‘ *Every night my children used to scatter their dirty clothes all over their bedrooms. I was forever nagging them to use the laundry basket in the bathroom, but it didn't work. So I decided we needed a new system. Now there is a laundry basket in each bedroom and the problem is solved.'*

When something goes wrong over and over again, it's worth considering whether there is a system you could use to stop it happening. It feels wonderful once you get a few successfully up and running, and you will save yourself an enormous amount of time and hassle. If you do decide to introduce a new system, there is one thing you can do to make your life easier: give some advance warning and explain to everyone what's going to happen.

## Give advance warning

**Sorted Parents** know that if they want their child to behave in a certain way, it is best to talk things through beforehand. This is much more effective than giving a stream of last-minute instructions or expecting him to work things out for himself. They might try to give their child a mental picture of what the situation will be like, and then tell him how and why they expect him to behave.

*'When we had guests for Sunday lunch I was so embarrassed. My children slouched around and barely said a polite word. Next time, my husband explained to them before the guests arrived exactly how he wanted them to behave. It worked. On the day they were so much more polite; they even seemed to be semi-present. What a difference.'*

## Set up rules

If you have a contentious issue with your child, like getting the TV turned off at a reasonable hour, it's tempting just to dive in and switch the damn thing off when you've had enough and want everyone to go to bed. You may win the battle, but the chances are there will be a huge argument and you'll have to go through the same thing all over again next time.

**Sorted Parents** would set up a simple, consistent rule instead, giving plenty of warning so everyone has time to get used to it.

Here's how they might do it:

- ***Tell your child in advance*** *using as neutral a voice as you can manage. 'I don't like arguing when it's time to turn off the TV. So starting next Monday, we are only going to watch TV after dinner until eight o'clock. I know it's going to take a little time to get used to this idea, so I'm telling you now.' Then remind him a couple of times over the next few evenings what is going to happen.*
- ***Let him moan*** *In fact, expect it. You can listen sympathetically and help him to think laterally round his objections. For example, if he is going to miss his favourite programme, you can show him how to tape it and let him watch it the next day.*
- ***Enforce the plan*** *This part shouldn't be as hard as you might think. The idea is that by the time the new rules actually start, your child will be used to the idea and won't kick up a fuss. Instead of complaining because you're swooping in with no warning to spoil his fun, he knows what to expect. It's just another family rule – the way we do things around here.*

If you aren't naturally sorted, setting up rules ahead of time can seem like a big hassle, but in the long run it can make your life a lot easier. If you allow plenty of time for your child to get used to the idea of the new regime, you shouldn't have to argue your case over and over again. You'll probably get through first time.

As well as being easier, giving advance warning takes the heat off you and means you don't sound like a tyrant every time you insist something has to be done. The TV doesn't get turned off because you are a mean, horrible, unsympathetic parent. It gets turned off because everyone knows that homework comes first. That's just the way it is and there is no point in arguing about it.

Some parents find the idea of setting up lots of rules oppressive. There is certainly a danger of being too sorted and going overboard. If you're not careful you could end up with thousands of rules and regulations, and you're likely to have a rebellion on your hands if you legislate over every aspect of your children's lives. So focus on the things you are sick of arguing about or that are really important to you.

The scary thing about very **Sorted Parents** is that they seem to be able to anticipate a lot of problems. But the rest of us don't have to aim that high. Often it's more of a case of working backwards, trying to figure out what has gone wrong and then working out how to sort it before it happens the *next* time round.

## Train them up

If you train your child up by spending a few minutes a day for a frustrating week teaching him how to do things – like making his bed or loading the dishwasher – you will save time in the long run when he can do these things for himself. At first this can be slow and tedious. It's usually far easier and quicker to do everything yourself, or even to pay someone else to do it. However, the danger is that you'll end up with a pack of pre-teens who've never made their own bed, or a bunch of twenty-year-olds still living at home who don't know how to use the washing machine. And why haven't you had time to teach them? Because you've been so busy struggling along coping with all the chores.

Training your child up also has another benefit – knowing how to do things can work wonders for his self-esteem.

> *My son is dyspraxic, so he is a bit clumsy and finds some ordinary tasks more difficult than other children do. Long after he should have been doing up his own shoelaces I was tying them for him so we wouldn't be late for school. Then I realized that unless he practised, he would never learn. For two weeks I got the whole family down for breakfast twenty minutes earlier so he had as much time as he needed. I sat with him and encouraged him every step of the way. After a fortnight he was up to speed, and being able to do it himself really boosted his confidence.*

If you take the time, you can teach even very young children to help out. Two-year-olds love helping to make beds and empty the dishwasher. And on a good day, you might even get your older child to help you cook or fold laundry.

Some **Sorted Parents** are so efficient that they do everything themselves because it is quicker, but in the long run it's better to teach children to do things themselves.

> *I was surprised to find that my very organized neighbour was still brushing her children's teeth and dressing them – including putting on her girls' tights – and her oldest was ten. She said it was quicker. But when she found that mine got ready on their own, she had hers trained up within a week.*

# The Secret of Commando Parents

**Commando Parents** have natural authority and get things done without shouting or nagging.

## Give orders that don't sound like orders

Like good teachers, good **Commando Parents** have an amazing ability to get their child to cooperate willingly. Instead of ordering him to do something, 'Because I say so,' they manage to make him buy into the whole process so he actually wants to do the right thing. If a child thinks that something is a good idea, or his own idea, he is far more likely to get on with it.

- Parent: *'There's a damp towel on the floor.'*

With luck, the child thinks: *'Oh yes, I know what to do about that. It goes on the towel rail.'*

If the penny drops and your child thinks of the towel rail on his own, he is more likely to follow the idea through and pick the wet towel up. It's the difference between being forced to do something and feeling motivated.

After he has come up with the right answer all by himself, you can then praise him not only for doing the right thing, but for doing it without even being asked. This is a win-win situation, because he will feel proud of himself and, with luck, be keen to get it right again next time.

**Commando Parents** often use orders that don't sound like orders, because they get results without putting their child's back up. If you start barking out commands, your child is sure to resist and you are more likely to end up with an argument on your hands.

Here is a whole selection of orders that don't sound like orders. They are lifesavers when you need cooperation. They are a non-aggressive way to get your child to do something, and should be made in a calm, neutral voice. You'll find they are great alternatives to nagging, which drives your children as crazy as it drives you.

- ***Give options*** Ask your child which option he would prefer. This lets him know what has to be done, but allows him to keep his dignity by choosing the outcome.

So instead of:

*'how many times do I have to tell you to put on your clothes?'*

try:

*'Would you like to wear the blue trousers or the green trousers today?'*

Child thinks, *'The green trousers'* and puts them on, bypassing the whole argument about whether or not it's time to get dressed.

- ***Say it in a word*** Instead of going into a long, boring explanation which he's heard a thousand times before, try using just one word.

So instead of:

*'You have to put your pyjamas on because it is time for bed. If you don't hurry up and get changed now, then . . . blah, blah, blah,'* (child switches off)

try simply saying:

*'Pyjamas,'* in a clear, direct tone.

With luck your child thinks: *'Oh yes, pyjamas. I need to get my pyjamas on,'* and does it.

- ***Describe what you see*** **Commando Parents** know that if they describe what they see in a pleasant voice, their child will often figure out what he needs to do, and then do it without fussing.

So instead of:

*'Clean up that juice you spilt'*

try:

*'There's some juice on the floor.'*

Pointing out what you see is a lot nicer than telling him what he has done wrong. If the penny still doesn't drop, you can always add more information.

*'We need a cloth. I can see one in the sink.'*

Child thinks, *'Oh yes, juice on the floor. I can fix that.'*

- ***Ask what comes next*** Ask your child what comes next, rather than telling him what to do. This is particularly useful for regular events in a child's life.

So instead of:

*'Hurry up. You still need to get your coat on'*

try:

*'You've put on your hat and gloves. What comes next?'*

Child thinks, *'Oh, I know. I need my coat.'*

- ***Give a quick reminder*** Rather than saying something negative, which might make your child feel ashamed or uncooperative, a kind reminder is less threatening.

So instead of:

*'You've forgotten your school bag – again'*

try:

*'There's something you need to remember.'*

Child thinks, *'Oh yes, my school bag. Got it.'*

Then you can say:

*'Well done remembering your school bag.'*

If he begins to see himself as someone who remembers things, rather than someone who forgets them, you may not even need to remind him in the future.

You could also try:

*'I'm sure your teeth are brushed, or are just about to be.'*

- ***Whisper*** If you say something very quietly, it sounds more like a suggestion than an order, and your child is more likely to be receptive. It's a great way to give him instructions that might be embarrassing or humiliating if spoken out loud.

For example:
*'Your trouser zip is undone.'*
Or, at the table:
*'Elbows.'*

Whispering can be surprisingly effective when your child is being so noisy that you feel as if your head is about to split open. Though you might be tempted to yell at him to keep it down, it will work better to draw him in close to you and whisper in his ear.

- ***Give thanks in advance*** Thanking him in advance for doing something is like a very friendly reminder.

*'Thanks for shutting the door'* (as he goes out of the room).

*'Thank-you for putting the ice-cream back in the freezer'* (as he spoons it into a bowl).

*'Thanks for putting your clothes in the laundry bin'* (as he's getting undressed).

- ***Write a note*** **Commando Parents** understand a mysterious phenomenon – if something is written down, children usually take it seriously.

So instead of giving instructions out loud, try putting:
A note on the bedroom wall:
*'Morning jobs: Make bed. Fold pyjamas. Get dressed.'*
(This can be done as pictures if your child is too young to read.)
A sticky label on your computer:
*'Reminder: No one can touch this laptop except me. Signed, Mum.'*
A Post-it on the hamster cage:
*'Please feed me on Mondays and Fridays.'*

- *Refer to the rules.* **Commando Parents** get things done without arguments by referring to simple, consistent rules.

  Good rules make life easier, because they let everyone know where they stand and how things are done – like hanging up your coat on the same peg every day at school.

You probably have all sorts of rules already, like:

*'We clean our teeth at bedtime'.*

*'We don't hit people'.*

*'No mobile phones at the table.'*

All you need is a short reminder. Try:

*'Teeth!'*

*'We don't hit.'*

*'You know the rule.'*

If you find this doesn't work and your children argue back, you might need to borrow a trick from **Sorted Parents**. Set up the rule more explicitly by giving plenty of advance warning about what you expect and why the rule is important (see pp. 50–52).

## Give information

**Commando Parents** realize that if their child understands why something is important he is much more likely to do the right thing. So instead of:

*'Move your mug off that table, now!'*

try:

*'If you leave a wet mug on a wooden table, it will leave a ring.'*

Child thinks, *'Oh – quick! I need to move that mug,'* and will probably remember not to do it again.

When giving information, you are teaching your child about the implications of his actions. Giving information works very well if you have a good relationship with your child, or if he is naturally cooperative and helpful. What you are saying is really no big deal. It's a straightforward, no-nonsense way of communicating.

But if your relationship with your child is stickier or he's angry or upset, giving information won't work on its own. You may need to tune in first and understand how he is feeling before he will listen.

## Express your feelings

**Commando Parents** know that children simply don't care about the same things that we do. You may hate it when your child runs around the house shouting like a maniac, but he probably thinks it's fun. So try explaining how you feel and why:

- *'When you shout and jump around like that it makes my head hurt. I'd be grateful if you could please tone it down.'*

If you can state your own feelings clearly, you might be amazed at your child's reaction. He may seem thoughtless, but underneath it all he does care. The more clearly you can understand your own feelings and explain them, the more effective you will be.

*My son likes to walk to his friend's house a couple of streets away. I'm all for it, as long as he rings me when he gets there so I know he has arrived safely. He used to forget to call, so I'd watch the clock and worry, and then phone up to check. I'd get so cross with him, but he just didn't seem to understand.*

*Then one day I said to him, 'It really worries me when you don't ring. I start thinking you might have been hit by a car, or something terrible may have happened to you, and I can't relax until I know you're safe.' I could see it was like a light bulb switching on in his head. He looked right at me and said he was really sorry and that he wouldn't forget again. And he hasn't.*

Explaining how you feel can get you out of a tight spot, especially when other people are watching.

*My daughter started showing off like crazy at my mother-in-law's house. 'Hello stupid poo-poo Mummy. Hello Mrs Wee-wee.' With her grandmother standing there I couldn't ignore it, but I didn't want to tell her off, either. My mother-in-law was looking at me as if I was totally useless and her granddaughter was totally out of control.*

*So I took a deep breath and told my daughter the truth. 'You know,' I said, 'I feel embarrassed listening to you talk like that. I don't like hearing it and I feel uncomfortable that Grandma is hearing it too.' It was amazing. She stopped immediately.* ❞

Talking like this isn't about embarrassing your child into behaving well, just expressing how you feel in a quiet, straightforward way.

Sometimes, expressing your feelings means standing up for what is important to you.

❝ *Whenever I told my daughter what to do, she whinged and argued. So I told her straight, 'You mean a lot to me, and I want to bring you up properly. It is my responsibility to make sure that you clean your teeth, do your homework and say "please" and "thank you". That is my job – to make sure those things happen. When you are older you will be able to look after yourself.' By being very clear and direct, she got the message and the backchat almost completely stopped.* ❞

It is not always easy to explain everything so calmly. Uncooperative children can send the most saintly parents over the edge. Even trained-up **Commando Parents** lose their temper, especially after they've tried every other humane technique. The truth is, as long as you usually express yourself appropriately and don't make a regular habit of blowing your top, showing your true feelings is no bad thing. If it's obvious you are *furious*, your child will probably stop doing whatever it is that set you off.

❝ *I try very hard not to shout at my children, but this morning I'm glad I did. My younger two woke up at half past six, and immediately started arguing. That woke up my older daughter. When she got up, they all started bickering and picking on each other. I shouted at them and stamped my foot, and told them how upset I was to be woken up by such a racket. They were all shocked by my outburst, and looked at me dumbfounded. Then they really surprised me – they all apologized and went off to play.* ❞

The key is to describe how angry you feel, rather than blast your child with criticism. 'I feel . . .' is much kinder and more effective than 'You always . . .'

> *If I say, 'I'm not happy with this mess,' my children will often start cleaning it up. It sounds much better than 'You always make such a mess. You are so selfish,' which only leads to resentment, arguments and absolutely no cooperation. It saves me having to get really angry with them.*

## Stand your ground

**Commando Parents** have enough natural authority to give their children clear, direct orders, and expect them to work:

- *'Please put on your seatbelt.'*
- *'Hold my hand, we're crossing the road.'*
- *'We've got to leave, and I mean now.'*

But sometimes this isn't enough. Some tasks – like homework, cleaning out the fish bowl or taking out the rubbish – are so unappealing that **Commando Parents** know they have to go further to make sure the message gets through. For a start, they know that shouting orders up the stairs and hoping for the best won't do the trick. You need to make eye contact. You also need time to stand there and make sure your child carries out your instructions. If you are just about to rush out of the door, this isn't the time to try this technique. But if you have got the time, here's how to do it:

- ***Make eye contact*** *This is the most important part and can be really hard, especially if you are trying to get your child to turn off the computer. If he is gazing with glazed eyes at the screen, start by chatting about the game. When he turns to look at you,*
- ***Tell him succinctly what you want*** *'I need your help to take out the rubbish. The bin men are coming in the morning.' Then, whatever you do,*
- ***Don't say anything else and* don't leave!** *Stay there, in his*

*space, looking right at him, watching him until he gets up. If that doesn't do the trick, try asking him to repeat what you've said (trying to keep the mood light). If he gets it right or makes any move in the right direction,*

- ***Praise him** For getting the right answer or thank him for getting started on it.*

This sounds so basic you probably can't help but wonder if it really works. We can assure you it does, but it's not for the faint-hearted. You really have to stand there, holding your ground and keeping your temper.

*‘My daughter loves playing in the garden, and sometimes she doesn't pay the slightest bit of attention to me when I call her in for dinner. She tries to ignore me because she'd rather stay outside. Shouting at her doesn't work. I've found instead that I need to go right up to her, look directly at her and tell her it's time to come in. Sometimes she is still reluctant, but when I'm standing right there waiting, she usually cooperates.’*

## Use rewards and consequences

- *Rewards*

**Commando Parents** might start gently with orders that don't sound like orders, expressing their feelings or giving information, and when they need to, they stand their ground. But they know that sometimes children need an extra incentive to do the right thing.

To get cooperation, **Commandos** might offer a reward. But this doesn't mean bribing children with sweets or toys; they actually have something more tempting at their disposal. You may not believe it, but the best incentive for your child to behave well is the chance to spend time with you. It's worth far more than a bag of sweets, or a toy he'll tire of in ten minutes.

A wrestling match with Dad is far more fun than a plastic Mr Incredible. A game of tag with you in the garden is more exciting than a new racing car. An extra story at bedtime, or extra time lying with you while he falls asleep, will make him feel happier and more secure than an extra hour on his own watching television. Tell your child you like spending time with him when he behaves well, and try to spend more time with him when he does.

Try:

*'If you help me tidy up, I will have more time to help you with your project'*

instead of:

*'If you help me tidy up, I'll buy you a treat on Saturday.'*

- *Consequences*

**Commando Parents** aren't shy about getting tough and using consequences when necessary. This is the tool they keep in their back pockets at all times to get things done. This is no more Mr Nice Guy. They tell their child what he needs to do and what will happen if he doesn't. For example, if they've asked him on numerous occasions to chew with his mouth closed because the sight and sound puts everyone else off their food, a **Commando Parent** might say:

*'We don't want to see the food in your mouth or listen to slurping noises. If you can't chew with your mouth closed you will have to eat your dinner alone after the rest of us have finished.'*

Consequences work best when they relate to the problem, so your child learns the real effects of his actions. If he eats like a pig, other people won't want to eat with him, so he will have to eat on his own. If he refuses to clean his teeth, then he can't have any sweets or puddings.

This is different from punishments which aren't directly related to the crime. If he won't get ready for bed, you can cancel his weekend playdate. But when the time comes, he'll probably resent you for it. If, on the other hand, you point out that there will be no time for a bedtime story if he doesn't get into his pyjamas, he'll learn the immediate consequences of his behaviour.

Consequences can also work well for older children. Try:

*'If you leave your clothes on the floor, you will have to collect them and wash them yourself'*

instead of:

*'If you leave your clothes on the floor, I'm cancelling your pocket money.'*

Be extremely careful what you say when you lay down the law, because you've got to be able to follow through every time. The minute you start threatening consequences you can't enforce (or don't really want to), your child will twig that you don't mean what you say, and you'll have lost the upper hand. So if you threaten that he'll have to stay behind if he doesn't hurry up and get ready, be prepared to leave him at home with someone if he doesn't.

It's worth remembering that consequences don't work by themselves. If they did, all the prisons in this country would be empty. Your child has to want to do the right thing from the inside, not just because you say so. Make sure you listen to his feelings and take time to explain why some things are forbidden.

# The Secret of Laid-Back Parents

**Laid-Back Parents** encourage their child to do things for himself.

## Allow them to do more 

**Laid-Back Parents** are confident that even young children can do a lot of things for themselves. We aren't talking about potentially dangerous things here, like allowing toddlers to cross the road on their own. We're talking about little things like letting them comb their own hair and choose their own clothes. **Laid-Back Parents** don't care if their child's hair is messy or his clothes don't match for a while until he gets the hang of things. As long as he is happy with his appearance, they are proud of him and consider his efforts a success.

*One morning my daughter announced she wanted to choose her own clothes for nursery school. She picked a purple flowery dress, green striped tights and red wellies. I thought for a second about being embarrassed, but let it go. How could I possibly make her change? She looked so cute! And she was so proud. Her teacher remarked how well she had done to choose her own clothes (it was quite obvious she had), and that really boosted her confidence.* ’

Letting your child make mistakes without being critical can be difficult at first. Start by letting him do tiny things for himself, and over time he can move on to bigger things.

‘ *My son, who is ten, cooks breakfast for all of us on Sunday morning. We've had a few rubbery eggs along the way, but now he can do bacon, fried eggs, sausages, toast and coffee. He loves doing it, and I'm happy he won't be living on Pot Noodles when he eventually leaves home.* ’

You know that being a **Laid-Back Parent** is working when your child feels good about being able to do things for himself. Of course it's possible to be too laid back, by not doing enough for your child or noticing when he needs help. For example, if he is struggling to keep up at school because he is disorganized and isn't getting his homework done, you may need to step in.

## Ask for solutions

**Laid-Back Parents** know their children are full of good ideas. So when their child has a problem, they will often ask, 'What do you think you should do?' This isn't being lazy, it's encouraging him to think for himself and develop his own judgement. When he comes up with answers himself, something amazing is happening on a neurological level and new connections are being made in his brain. This is much more effective than telling him what to do. You may get some pretty creative answers, or at least a place to start talking about the problem. If he looks well and truly flummoxed and mumbles, 'I don't know,' give him a moment to think about it, and then ask him to guess. If he knows you aren't going to laugh or criticize, you're likely to be pleasantly surprised at what he can come up with.

‘ *My daughter got very upset because she felt she had too much homework. She asked me what she should do. I gently asked her,*

*'What do you think?' Even though she was in a real stew, the answer tumbled out. 'Well,' she said, 'my geography isn't due until Friday, so I can leave it until Thursday night. Maths is due tomorrow, so I'll do that now. Then I'll start writing my story. I could finish it off tomorrow morning if I get to school early.' She worked the whole thing out on her own.* ❜

Encouraging your child to make decisions and solve problems for himself can be a huge confidence booster, especially if he is the quiet, hesitant type who wouldn't normally volunteer suggestions on his own. You can ask him for all sorts of ideas: how to get the kitchen tidied up before you go to the park, what to do when he is being bothered by his sister, even what you should give him as a punishment (go easy on this last one as sometimes children are harder on themselves than you'd ever be). When he does come up with a good solution to a problem, remember to praise him and say something nice about it.

Asking your child questions can also be a very good way to help him learn.

❛ *When my daughter asks me how to spell something, I try to get her to work it out for herself. I might say, 'What do you think it starts with? What's the next letter? What's the next sound?' She's usually able to work it out.* ❜

You don't have to be extreme about this. If it drives your child nuts when you don't just tell him the answer, it won't hurt to help him out. Better still, you could show him how to use a dictionary. But not always answering questions can be a good way of stretching your child and encouraging him to explore new things.

❛ *My son asked me when the new James Bond film was coming out. I asked him if he could work it out on the internet. He not only found the movie, he came up with a really cool site which we use now to check out cinema listings. I'm glad I left it up to him.* ❜

## Ask the family for ideas

Lots of issues affect the whole family, like turning the television off without backchat, getting organized to go on holiday or solving children's arguments. **Laid-Back Parents** might sit everyone down together and ask them all for good ideas. This way everybody feels as if they are part of the process and takes an interest in making it work. They may not realize they are doing it, but many **Laid-Back Parents** run their families like companies, with regular informal board meetings to make sure everyone is on track and pulling together. Try writing down every suggestion, no matter how silly. That way everyone feels their contribution is important and will keep coming up with new ideas. Even children as young as two or three have opinions, and older children are much more cooperative if you get them involved. After you've all come up with ideas, read them out and you can each choose the one(s) you'd like to try.

*'Whenever one of my kids invited a friend over, the others would drive them crazy, following them around the house. So we all sat down one day to work out what we could do about it. I wrote down everyone's ideas on a sheet of paper. Then my girls took the list, typed it out in bright colours and taped it to the kitchen door. All the children are so proud of that list. They agreed that anyone who's being irritating has to spend five minutes out of the room on their own. Now if a friend comes over and anyone starts bugging them, that's what happens.'*

If your children are normally quite volatile or if they are particularly wound up about something, you don't have to sit them all down together to discuss it; you can always ask each one separately for their ideas. Pick a time when they are calm – bedtime is often good – and ask them for ways to solve the problem. Being consulted and listened to will take a lot of the heat out of their indignation. As before, write down every single idea, no matter how silly. Then you can all decide together which ones to try. If you have an ongoing problem, agree to try out one solution for a fixed period of time, like a couple of days, and see if it is working. If it isn't, try another one.

## Be a role model

**Laid-Back Parents** realize that when they are a good role model their child instinctively absorbs what he needs to know. This is far more subtle and effective than telling him how to behave. They wouldn't expect their child to hold a knife and fork properly if they didn't do so themselves. They wouldn't expect him always to wear his seatbelt if they didn't always wear theirs. **Laid-Back Parents** realize their child is constantly learning from them. Your child listens to everything you say, from how you talk to the cashier in the supermarket to how you interact with his teacher.

Being a good role model is just as important when it comes to not doing things. If swear words don't slip out of your mouth, there is much less chance they will start slipping out of your child's. Studies show that if you don't smoke, your child is much less likely to be a smoker.

We can never be perfect all the time, but there is no doubt that children are influenced by our behaviour. The good news is that you are probably already doing many more good things than you realize – being kind to animals, being polite to the postman, recycling your rubbish, tidying your house occasionally. Your child logs it all without you ever having to say anything at all.

## Get help

Many **Laid-Back Parents** don't have a problem admitting when they need help. They know it doesn't mean they are useless failures who can't cope on their own. They are open-minded enough to know that they don't have to.

> *'I tried to teach my son to tie his laces and it was a disaster. He kept getting frustrated and crying. So I asked his teacher to help and she worked her magic and taught him in a day.'*

**Laid-Back Parents** aren't embarrassed to ask for advice when they need it.

*When my daughter was being bullied at school I didn't want anyone to know about it. But she was so miserable and I couldn't help her. Eventually I confided in a friend, who encouraged me to call a bullying helpline. I talked to a counsellor and so did my daughter, and now she is through the worst.*

Nor are they embarrassed if they have to ask their partner to back them up.

*My boys left toys and rubbish all over the garden. I asked them six times to clear up the mess but they ignored me. So I asked my husband to help me out. He came downstairs, got heavy, and they tidied everything away.*

*Then my son tried to annoy me by accusing me of being weak and unable to control them (he was being a monster that day). But I told him that at least I was smart enough to know when to ask for help.*

*I felt so confident saying it that he actually dropped the subject.*

If they feel overwhelmed, **Laid-Back Parents** might find someone nearby who can help for a couple of hours in the evening with homework, cleaning up the kitchen or getting school stuff organized for the morning. Nursery-school teachers are often interested in doing a little evening work. If you can't afford to pay for help, try making plans with a good friend to help with each other's children.

*I often look after my neighbour's kids if she needs help, and she takes mine when I need a break. I can't do it all on my own and neither can she.*

3

# Getting Cooperation

## When Your Child Won't Do What You Say

In any family there are always things that have to be done. But left to themselves, there's no chance most children would do any of them. If your children already tidy up, clean their teeth and do their homework willingly and without being reminded, there's not much we can tell you about motivating them.

For most of us, however, it can end up a daily battle of wills. If children aren't in the mood they can drag their feet, argue, or go mysteriously deaf in both ears. We shouldn't be surprised. Is there a child on the planet who would rather take out the rubbish than loll on the sofa in front of the television?

Even if your children are reasonably helpful and cooperative, you still might wish you didn't have to remind them to do things so often.

> *I don't expect my children to be perfect and jump up and do everything the minute I ask. But I'd love it if they just did some things without waiting for me to nag them.*

When you have to ask five or six times, then lose your temper and shout like a maniac before you get a flicker of cooperation, even an ordinary day can become exhausting. It's no fun repeating instructions over and over again while your child pretends to ignore you.

## Reasons Why You Might Nag Your Child

- ***Things have to get done*** Your child's bedroom is a health hazard, and so are her teeth.
- ***You need help*** and she won't stop MSNing her friends.
- ***It's a re-run of the same old situation*** How many times do you have to tell her to do the same things? Clear the table. Put the dirty dishes in the dishwasher. It's like being trapped in the film *Groundhog Day*.
- ***You are already stressed*** This is one of the worst. You're pressed for time and she's footling around, ignoring what you say and holding everyone up.
- ***You feel everyone should contribute*** Why should you have to do everything when there are other able-bodied people in the house who are capable of helping?
- ***She needs to learn*** It's your job to teach her good habits and how to do things so she can look after herself one day.

Sometimes you might feel you're nagging for a good reason. You're hoping she'll finally get the point and stop wasting time arguing about things she has to do anyway. If she'd just get on with it, you wouldn't need to keep reminding her. So even if you regret the atmosphere in the house, you'll do whatever it takes – cajoling, bargaining, bribing or threatening – to get her moving.

But if she hates being nagged, she'll probably resent your behaviour. She might reluctantly obey, but you'll get a whole lot of attitude and very little effort. Plus there's the danger that, over time, you'll have to turn up the volume and frequency of your requests because she'll start tuning you out altogether. In the end she'll hate doing the things we all have to do every day, and she might hate you, too.

If you don't like confrontation, you might be tempted to let things slide instead. It's sometimes easier to give in and do everything yourself, or give up and leave her bedroom to fester. You might wait until your partner gets home so he can be the disciplinarian, or, if you can afford it, hire someone else so you don't have to deal with these issues at all. Most of all, you may not want to create a bad atmosphere or compromise your relationship with your child, so if you come up against any resistance you won't press the point.

### Reasons Why You Might Not Insist On Cooperation

- *It's too difficult* You'd honestly like some help, but it's too much trouble to get your child to lend a hand. You'd rather avoid a confrontation.
- *Lack of time* You're busy and it's easier and quicker to do things yourself, or not do them at all.
- *You want the job done properly* If you do things yourself, you know they'll be done the way you want them.
- *You don't mind* It gives you satisfaction to know you're doing everything you can to look after your family.
- *You're soft-hearted* She's still your baby and she has enough responsibility with school. You want her to enjoy her childhood.
- *Past experience* There was a bad atmosphere in your house when you were a child and you don't want to re-create the same thing.
- *Inertia* You'll get round to it, one day. Maybe.

Your hope might be that if you don't put too much pressure on your child there will be a good atmosphere in the house and a strong bond between you. Eventually she'll appreciate all your generosity and kindness, and start making a contribution.

But the danger is that she gets to wriggle out of the most basic jobs, like clearing the table, but has plenty of time to sit around texting her friends all day. She may have no idea how to make her bed or organize her things, and expects to have everything done for her. Another problem may be that by trying to avoid any hassle, you take on far too much. Even if you want to be kind, if you become exhausted, run down and feel taken for granted, then you're likely to get angry with her anyway.

Most of us swing between these two extremes. Sometimes we nag our children to cooperate, and sometimes we figure it's easier just to do everything ourselves. Either way, if we get over-tired and frustrated, we can say things we don't mean, threaten punishments we don't intend to enforce and then feel racked with guilt.

Most of us are aiming for broadly the same things: for everyone to cooperate willingly and pull together as a family. Actually, most of us would be delighted with something far less ambitious, like occasionally being able to ask for help and get it without a fuss. We're going to show you effective ways to get cooperation and help you feel better about standing your ground when you have to. Even if your child is already quite helpful and you only want to do some fine-tuning, these ideas will help.

## What to Do When Your Child Refuses to Do What You Ask

There are some things that absolutely need to be done, like cleaning teeth and wearing a seatbelt – there's no room for negotiation. But what do you do when your child refuses?

*'One of my biggest bug-bears on holiday is getting my children to put on sunscreen. They make such a big deal about it that I can't make them. Then they get burned and I feel guilty.'*

*'When my daughter came home from school with nits, I tried to deal with them before they multiplied or the rest of us caught them. But she kept running away from me and wouldn't let me do it properly. And then we all had them for months.'*

*My son leaves old apple cores and used ice-lolly sticks and tissues all around the house. I've asked him countless times to put them in the bin, but he won't do it.*

So what can you do?

## *Try being a PAUSE PARENT* 

**Wait until later** As with so many family problems, the best place to start is by pausing. If you're used to nagging to get things done, this isn't going to feel natural. If she is actually disobeying you, pausing is going to be the last thing on your mind.

But try it, because nagging and shouting can make her resentful and leave you feeling horrible.

*This morning my daughter wouldn't get ready for school. I must have asked her a dozen times to get on with it. In the end I lost my temper and we had a huge row. By some miracle we got to school on time, but I felt guilty all day, like I was the worst mother in the world.*

Being slow might be your child's passive-aggressive way of winding you up. She'll get an even bigger reaction if she's rude, so be prepared. The next time you feel yourself getting sucked in, make a heroic effort to pause. This will give you a little time and space to think through your next step.

You might also need to pause if you do too much around the house and want things to change.

*I don't have the patience to wait for my children to get round to their chores. Instead I launch in and do them myself, complaining all the time. They don't enjoy the grumbling, but they've got me where they want me. I'm the one who tidies the bedrooms, sorts the washing and loads the dishwasher.*

If you are running out of time it can be tempting to step in, find your child's shoes and pack her homework folder. But if you can, stand back and work out how you can try to get her to do it. We'll give you plenty of ideas.

***Zip your lip*** If your child isn't doing what you've asked, try your hardest to keep quiet. Even if other people are watching and you're breaking out in a sweat, staying silent is still the best first option. You're not giving up on the problem, just preventing yourself from making it worse.

***Expect to be wound up*** Your child may be winding you up on purpose. Younger children think it's great fun to run round the house, dodging furniture, with you in hot pursuit waving pyjamas or a toothbrush. Older children get a sense of power by refusing to budge and watching you get frazzled. It's easier to pause if you expect this, and your child may stop trying to annoy you if she doesn't get a reaction.

It's also worth remembering that when you ask your child to stop doing something, she will often do it one last time. Like when you ask her to stop making an irritating noise. You can bet she'll make it once more, and look at you to see what you do. If you expect it, you won't get wound up and can just let it go. She usually won't do it again.

It sounds obvious, but when you're stressed about other things, an uncooperative child seems a hundred times more annoying.

> *'I was trying to pack for our summer holiday. I had lists coming out of my ears – passports, tickets, telephone numbers, baby kit – on and on it went. When I asked my daughter to fetch some shampoo, she gave me a sulky look and went back to her Tamagotchi. I lost my temper and hurled it into the bin. The Tamagotchi died and she burst into tears. Total disaster.'*

When we're busy we're completely focused on something other than our children. They know it and can resent it. So when we most need their help, they may go out of their way to wind us up. You'll be better off if you expect this to happen.

## *Try being a TUNED-IN PARENT* 

On the surface it can seem as if your child is defying you simply because she wants her own way: she doesn't want to help tidy the kitchen, she doesn't want to put the sweets away, or she doesn't want to get ready for bed. And this could be the case. But if you tune in you might find there is more going on than you think.

Children are often more cooperative once they feel understood, so listening to her feelings may be enough to get her moving. But even if it isn't, at least you'll have a clearer understanding of why she's stalling.

*Listen to their feelings* Instead of reasoning with her, try:

- *'It looks like you don't want to . . .'*

(Substitute whichever one of the umpteen million things she is refusing to do.)

It might sound unlikely, but this little phrase can often do the trick. If there's a reason or feeling behind her disobedience, you are allowing it to come out into the open. Though you might not feel you can spare time to chat, this is often a very quick and efficient way to get her to help.

### Reasons Why Your Child Might Not Do What She's Told

- ***She may want attention*** If your child wants your attention, she may defy you to get it. Being chased around the house or nagged is better than getting no attention at all.

  With a younger child, try stopping what you are doing, getting down to her level and saying it straight: *'It looks to me like you want my attention.'* Often five minutes of chatting and a hug is enough to make her feel like co-operating.

  Older children may not admit they want attention, but

the basic premise is the same. Stop what you are doing and focus on your child. Then she might do what you've asked.

- ***She may feel nervous or unconfident*** She may be digging her heels in because she feels frightened or unsure of herself.

*My son refused to come to the park, and he complained, grumbled and clung to my arm the whole way. Eventually he confessed he was scared of meeting a big dog. Last time an Alsatian had bounded up to him and growled in his face.*

By tuning in you can work out whether your child is being defiant or needs your help. If she doesn't know how to do something, she might stonewall you when you ask her to get on with it.

*I nagged my daughter to tidy her bedroom until I was blue in the face. Finally she broke down and confessed that she didn't know where to start. There wasn't room to cram anything else in her cupboard and she couldn't work out what to throw away.*

- ***She may need to calm down*** If she has something else on her mind, she won't feel like cooperating. If you can wait until she calms down or take the time to listen to her feelings, she'll be far more likely to be helpful.

*My son had promised to clean out the fish tank after school, but he refused to come out of his bedroom. I asked him nicely three times and then roared that I was going to give all the fish away. He flung himself on to his bed and buried his head under the duvet.*

*That evening he told me that he'd had a terrible day at school. He got caught writing on the desk with Tippex, was sent to the headmaster and given a detention. The tank got cleaned the next morning.*

- ***She may have her reasons*** She may seem defiant, but if you take the time to listen, you'll understand her better.

*My daughter pushed her plate of roast chicken away and said, 'Yuk, I'm not eating this.' Eventually it came out that she had watched a programme about battery farms, and felt that eating them was cruel. Once I understood, I let it go.* ❞

- ***She may be sick of you nagging*** It's not easy to admit, but your child might not be cooperating because she doesn't want to listen. She may be closing her ears because your tone of voice and the stressful atmosphere in the house are too much for her. If you tune in and try to be sympathetic, you might find it easier to get through to her.

*Accept difficult feelings* Lots of parents hate confrontation, so if their child refuses to help, they back off. They might not want to make her unhappy by forcing her to do something against her will, or perhaps they simply can't face an argument.

Trying to make sure your child has a happy childhood is a wonderful aim, but if she has to pick up her dirty clothes or sweep the kitchen floor, it won't ruin her life. Nor is it a disaster if she gets angry about it. In fact, quite the opposite: she needs to learn how to handle herself when she doesn't want to do something. There are going to be plenty of times in the future when she will have to do things she doesn't want to do.

Listening to her whinging or shouting because she doesn't want to do what you ask can be hard. Even looking at a long face is more than some parents can bear. But instead of pleading or trying to reason with her, the best and easiest thing is to say something like:

- *'I see. You hate cleaning your room and you wish I would do it for you for ever.'*

You aren't letting her off the hook. If she keeps protesting, listen, try to be sympathetic, but stand your ground. Once she feels you understand, she may even go and tidy up.

Sometimes, accepting difficult feelings is the only thing you can do. It worked for these parents who found themselves in hot water:

*One day when our son was little, he wanted to help make tea. So I let him put teabags in the pot and milk in a jug. But when the kettle boiled he grabbed the handle to pour the water. I grabbed it too, gibbering, 'No, let go, let go. You can't pour the water. It is too dangerous. It could burn you. Let go now!' He kept trying to pull it from me shouting, 'I'm going to pour it. I want to pour it.' It was a tug of war and getting more dangerous by the second.*

*Thank heavens my husband was there. 'You want to pour that water for Mummy. You got the teabags ready. Now you feel big enough to pour the kettle too.' My son nodded and his hands relaxed on the handle. Crisis over.*

***Reconnect*** However good our intentions, we all say and do things we regret.

*My daughter's room is a disgusting tip. However much I nag her, she won't tidy it. This morning I totally lost it, yelled at her and confiscated all her CDs. The room is still a disaster, but she won't even talk to me, let alone clean it up. What do I do now?*

If you get frustrated and blow your top, you will probably feel horrible afterwards and worry that your child will never speak to you again. But you haven't lost her for ever. Wait until you've both cooled down and then go back and say sorry. You don't have to apologize for asking for help, or let her off her chores. Your apology is only for overreacting. If you're big enough to admit where you went wrong and to say how much you regret it, you may not get an immediate apology in return, but at least you'll be speaking to each other again. You're also teaching her how to say sorry.

## *Try being a CHEERLEADER PARENT*

***Notice the good, ignore the bad*** **Cheerleader Parents** know that if their child is being openly defiant or ignoring them, nagging or shouting can make it worse. If she enjoys the attention she gets from messing around, she will carry on doing it. But if you send a couple of nice comments her way, she might try and get your attention for doing something good instead. She will certainly be more receptive.

So before you lose your temper or give up and give in, it's always worth looking round for something, *anything*, that's going right. If you're lucky, mentioning it will be enough to break the deadlock and turn the situation around.

For example, if it's time for school but your child is still dancing round the living room in her underwear, try:

- *'Well done. You've got your pants on already.'*

What if she's completely starkers? Try:

- *'Well, done. You've taken your pyjamas off.'*

There is almost always something positive you can say if you look hard enough. Try it next time you start to feel stressed.

- *'We're starting to run a bit late, but I see you've nearly finished your breakfast.'*

This technique works for parents because once you can see a ray of light, the situation suddenly seems less overwhelming and stressful. And it works for children because once they get some positive attention, they'll usually stop blocking you out and listen.

## Strategies to Motivate Your Child

Pausing, tuning in and noticing the one thing that is going right can get you out of a deadlock fast. They are helpful techniques at the very moment when your child is dragging her heels or flatly refusing to do what you say.

But how can you motivate her in the longer term? Instead of just persuading her to put her dirty laundry into the basket today, it would be wonderful if she did it every day, without you ever having to mention it again. It may sound too good to be true, but it is possible. Here's how the different parent types can help.

## *Try being a CHEERLEADER PARENT* 

**Cheerleader Parents** are very good at getting their children to want to do the right thing. Their secret is to bombard them with praise and attention. They know that when a child feels good about doing something, she's more likely to do it willingly.

*Notice the good, ignore the bad* Focusing on the good bits and downplaying the rest can help in a tricky situation, but it is also brilliant for changing long-term habits. You can make your child more cooperative by highlighting the behaviour you want to encourage.

*Praise on the spot and be specific* Don't feel you have to wait until your child does something major for you to praise her – you could be waiting for ever. Think small and keep your eyes open. Even if it is the first time in a year she's fed the cat, seize the moment and make a nice comment about it.

- *'You fed the cat. That was thoughtful.'*

Once you start looking, you'll probably be surprised at all the good things she's already doing. Don't gush, but tell her specifically what she's done right or what you liked about it.

- *'Thank-you for putting away your plate.'*
- *'You've made your bed and pulled open the curtains.'*
- *'Thanks for helping me make the salad.'*

These small comments add up. It obviously isn't going to work if you tell your TV-addict couch-potato that she's 'always so helpful and energetic'. If your praise isn't sincere, she'll feel she's being manipulated. But if you pick up on small, specific things, she'll know they are true. Once she begins to see herself as a competent, helpful person, she is more likely to live up to this positive image.

*‘My son never helped much around the house, but one day we put together a flat-pack bookcase. He was great – deciphering the instructions, sorting the screws and slotting wood together. I gave him loads*

*of compliments, and now he can't wait to do another one. Since then he's been so much more helpful. Yesterday we unloaded the shopping from the car, and then he helped me bring some boxes up from the basement.* ❞

**Be positive** Sometimes, of course, you can't wait around for your child to do the right thing. The job has to be done immediately. If you do have to remind her, try to keep the message positive. Instead of:

- *'You still haven't packed your football boots. You're driving me crazy'*

try:

- *'You need to remember something for your match today.'*

Instead of:

- *'Why haven't you finished clearing up the living room? You promised, but it's still a pigsty'*

try:

- *'Thanks for starting to put away the cards. What comes next?'*

**Be open-minded** We know how hard it is not to criticize when your child is being unhelpful. But calling her lazy or uncooperative is like stamping the title on her forehead in indelible ink. She might be going through an unhelpful phase that can last from minutes to months. But it's a lot easier for her to grow out of it if you don't entrench the problem by banging on about it.

Playing children off against each other can also make the problem worse. Phrases like 'He's the helpful one, but she never lifts a finger' get siblings stuck in roles which are hard to get out of. This kind of label can also make them hate each other, as well as you. Of course it's fine to praise the one who is being helpful or to try to kick-start the other, as long as you don't compare them.

## *Try being a SORTED PARENT*

If you keep pausing and tuning in when your child won't do what you say, and praising her when she does, you'll find she starts to be a lot more cooperative and you have to nag a lot less. But if some of your instructions or requests are still being ignored, try tackling it like a **Sorted Parent**.

> *'Every day, as soon as we park, my children jump out of the car and I'm left to struggle with the school bags, trainers and discarded snack wrappers. I can't praise them for unloading the car, because they never do it. So I lose my temper and yell. But that doesn't work either. So what am I supposed to do?'*

***Give advance warning*** If you want to change habits long term, don't wait for the problem to happen yet again, and then react. Instead, talk to your child about it well in advance. This way you can tell her exactly what you expect from her. Setting things up beforehand gives you a much better chance of being obeyed than rapping out orders on the spot.

Here's how a **Sorted Parent** would retrain their child to unload the car:

- *Find a quiet time to chat about it.*
- *Tell her how things are going to change.*
- *Listen to her moan, but don't change the plan.*
- *On the day itself, remind her again. 'In five minutes I'll be parking the car. What do you need to do?'*

When it comes to the crunch, you'll probably find that there's no resistance left. But if she still keeps 'forgetting', even after all this preparation, you may need to get tougher. See the **Commando** section (pp. 92–7) for more advice.

As well as changing long-term habits, being sorted helps a lot with day-to-day instructions. Instead of ordering your child to do something at the very moment you need it doing, try giving a tiny bit of warning by saying:

- *'This afternoon we are all going to . . .'*
- *'Straight after lunch I need you to . . .'*
- *'In ten minutes, when we get home . . .'*

**Set up rules** Your child might not do what she's told because she knows there's a very good chance that whinging or arguing will get you to change your mind. These are the kind of trouble spots we mean:

- *'But it's a really good film. Can't I watch to the end?'*
- *'Just one more story, plee-ease?'*
- *'You never told me I had to clean up the bathroom when I'm finished.'*
- *'But it's his turn to . . .'*

But children of **Sorted Parents** tend to cooperate without fussing because there is a set of simple, consistent rules and very few grey areas. They know what time the TV is going to be turned off, how long story time will last and in what state they're meant to leave the bathroom.

No one can be consistent all the time, but if you have a lot of nebulous areas and your children exploit them, you might consider setting up rules so there's no ambiguity. This may sound boring, but it's a lot less boring than wasting time negotiating over and over again.

Your rules should be very clear.

- *'You are only allowed one hour of screen time a day. That includes the TV, the computer and your Game Boy.'*

Keep the rules simple, because you're the one who has to enforce them. If your child is still finding ways to argue, you may need to be even more specific.

- *'I'm sick of this fussing and I can't keep track of every sliver of time you spend in front of screens. From now on, the only computer, television or Game Boy time in this house is from six until seven. That includes watching someone else play. If you miss a night, then that is tough. You can't make it up later.'*

It may take time, but eventually the rule will become a fact of life. This will take the pressure off you and give you more authority. You can just say, 'You know the rule,' and they'll know there's no point in arguing.

*Bite the bullet* **Sorted Parents** are very clear and don't give instructions until they've thought them through. Nor do they bark half-hearted threats they have no intention of enforcing. If you tend to muddle through, making things up as you go along, your child will know you don't really mean what you say.

- *'It's your turn to lay the table.' (I think – it's hard to keep track around here.)*
- *'It's bedtime.' (But I'm tired. Maybe you could watch just a bit more TV?)*
- *'Tidy your room.' (But can I really face the hassle of making sure you do it?)*
- *'If you want clean kit, you need to put it in the washing machine.' (Maybe I'm asking too much and I should be doing that.)*

If your child thinks you might let up or change your mind, she's far more likely to whinge and be uncooperative. But if you are clear about what you are asking and what you expect, there's much less chance she'll mess you around.

Biting the bullet may not come naturally to you, but it may not be as hard as you think. If you have to be tough, you'll feel better if you think through why it's important.

> *'I don't like forcing my children to tidy up and get ready for bed. But 'Just another ten minutes, just another ten minutes' can drag on for ages. And when they get to bed too late, they're tired for school in the morning. Once I got that straight in my mind it was much easier for me to insist.'*

*Sort your systems* If your child is still reluctant, try setting up systems to make things easier for her, and take the time to explain them.

Why is it that two-year-olds can tidy up at nursery school but you can't get your child to put anything away? Part of the reason is because at nursery school everything belongs in a particular place and the children know exactly where that is.

If your child's bedroom is a tip, she might not know where to start. Tackle it together and find a home for everything. Then she won't find the day-to-day upkeep so daunting.

*'My son would never clean his bedroom, and we had so many arguments about it. One weekend we blitzed it together. We chucked out all the broken toys, gave outgrown clothes to the charity shop, reunited scattered games and put them in clear plastic boxes, put hooks up on the door for clothes and more on the ceiling for model aeroplanes. Then we bought a bookcase, a CD tower and put up a high shelf for cuddly toys he never played with but didn't want to give away.*

*Now it's no longer a festering heap, it's much easier for him to keep it under control.'*

Children are far more likely to clean up a mess if they know where to find the dustpan and brush, or to pick up their dirty clothes if there is a convenient laundry basket.

If your children constantly argue about whose turn it is to take out the rubbish, set up a system. Hanging a chart in the kitchen can put an end to the bickering.

*'My children won't help if they suspect that someone else is getting away with less work. 'But I did it last time, it's* his *turn . . .' I can't stand the whinging, so when it gets bad, we do a job rota for a few weeks until they settle down.'*

Rotas don't suit everyone because someone – namely, you – has to oversee them. But if you take a tip from **Laid-Back Parents** and get your children to help set them up, they may not be so hard to monitor.

***Train them up*** Children often don't do chores willingly or well because they don't know how. They don't realize that plates have to be scraped before they go in the dishwasher, and they won't know how to stack them properly if you've never shown them how.

At the moment when something needs to be done, it's often quicker and easier to do it yourself. But if you are constantly rushing from one job to the next and never get the chance to delegate or explain, you'll always be short of time.

**Sorted Parents** know that it's worth training their children to be capable around the house. Yes, it can be time-consuming to teach your child how to make her bed, fold her clothes or separate the rubbish for recycling. You might have to show her many times how to do it. You may think you haven't got time for all this. But in the long run, she'll be able to do these things on her own – she'll be more independent, and you'll save time.

Seriously **Sorted Parents** start this training when their children are very young, because little children love to help out and are much easier to motivate than sulky pre-teens. But it is never too late to start.

Getting organized can make your life easier. But you can take things one step further. If you find you have to supervise everything – arbitrating on turns, putting stars on charts, reminding when it's time for music practice, you may want to try stepping back and becoming more of a **Laid-Back Parent**.

## *Try being a LAID-BACK PARENT*

**Laid-Back Parents** are good at encouraging their children to do things for themselves. From an earlier age than most, their children can get dressed in the morning, prepare a meal or do their own laundry. Children who never learn these things aren't well prepared for the future.

*'My father was an only child and the apple of his mother's eye. She did everything for him; she waited on him hand and foot. He is a great guy, but he's still completely incompetent. Even now, in his seventies, he can't change a light bulb. It's a miracle he survived!'*

*'I sometimes wonder, as I pick up another soggy pile of clothes off the*

*bathroom floor and flush the loo for the ninety-third time, who is going to want to share a flat with my son, let alone marry him one day?*

**Laid-Back Parents** have also worked out that if they do all the chores themselves, there's often no time left to spend with their family.

*After a busy week at work, I spent all weekend running round after my children. I cooked them fantastic food, washed and sorted all their clothes for school, deep-cleaned their rooms. Did they do anything to help me? Not one thing. And the result was that we barely spent any time together at all.*

But apart from running off to Ibiza and leaving your child alone for a fortnight, how are you supposed to encourage her to do things for herself?

***Allow them to do more*** If you are not a naturally **Laid-Back Parent**, the first step is subtle. It's accepting the possibility that your child can take on more responsibility and that you can step back a bit. Don't worry, this doesn't mean leaving her to fend for herself. If you get sorted first and let her know what's going to happen, she'll be fine.

*My daughter often telephoned from the school office. 'Mum, I've forgotten my recorder (trainers/charity money/textbook). And I really need it. Will you bring it for me?' And I'd feel sorry for her and drive over.*

*Finally I warned her that after half-term, there'd be no more courier service. We talked through her timetable and made a list of what she needed on what day. Since then she's become much more organized and responsible.*

If you're used to rescuing her every time she messes up, it can be a hard habit to break. But until she knows that something really is her job, she won't make it happen. If you nag her to unpack her smelly sports kit, but always do it yourself in time for the next games lesson, she has no incentive to put it in the laundry basket herself. So warn her in advance that you are not going to do it.

You aren't being mean if you follow this one through. Ultimately, doing things for herself can help her feel more confident, and neither of you will miss the nagging.

***Ask for solutions*** **Laid-Back Parents** know that asking their children for ideas is a very good way to encourage cooperation. If your child comes up with an answer, she is more likely to follow it through. It makes life so much easier: no conflict, no buts, no argument and no time-wasting.

> *After years of nagging my son to get out of bed in the morning, I asked him what we should do about it. He said he'd like a clock radio. Now he gets up and dressed before I do.*

***Ask the family for ideas*** If there is an issue that affects everyone – from how to get the toys tidied to how to take care of the cats – ask your children for solutions. If everyone feels part of the process, they're more likely to make it work. Even boring jobs like the weekly supermarket trip can be transformed.

> *My sons hated going to the supermarket until one of them suggested we make it a race. Now, before we go, we split the shopping list. I take one trolley, they take another, and we see who can get their list done faster. Sometimes I bump into them rushing around. It is such a change. They even help me pack the bags.*

***Be a role model*** It sounds obvious, but if you want your child to help you, don't grumble and complain about the job.

> *My mother cleaned the house on Sunday mornings. She hated it, and she was horrible to be around. Did we help her? Not at all. We did anything we could to stay away from her.*

It doesn't matter what the job is – washing the car, weeding the garden or cleaning out a cupboard – if you are a resentful, ranting old battleaxe, your children won't want to come anywhere near

## Setting Up a Family Meeting

If you want your children to take on more responsibility, try discussing it with them round the kitchen table. It's a good way to ask them for help.

**How to start:**

***Express your feelings***

- *'I have been doing too much of the housework lately and I'm tired.'*

Substitute whatever problem you want to discuss.

***Ask your children to solve the problem***

- *'Does anyone have any suggestions?'*

***Choose a solution***

- *'Good idea. From now on, on Saturday mornings let's all work together to clean the bathrooms and fold the washing. Then you can each tidy your bedroom.'*

***Listen if anyone starts complaining, but don't change your mind***

- *'I agree. Spending the morning doing chores isn't as fun as playing.'*

***After the meeting, follow through***

Give your children praise and attention for any effort they make:

- *'You did a nice job on the basin. Now let's go and fold the laundry.'*

***Set up consequences if you have to***

- *'If your bedroom doesn't get cleaned this morning, then we'll stay at home and wait for you to do it instead of going to the park.'*

you. But if you're pleasant or at least neutral about it, they're more likely to stick around and help.

> *I'm a caterer, working from home, and I love my job. I think my children have picked up on this. We sit happily together, peeling potatoes and carrots. Even my four-year-old can do saucepans of them.*
>
> *But I loathe gardening, and when I expect some help, they're nowhere to be seen.*

## *Try being a PHYSICAL PARENT*

There is definitely a link between how your child feels physically and how cooperative she'll be. Anything can tip the balance: a cold coming on, too little exercise, too much sugar, too many E-numbers, not enough water or proper food, or food sensitivities.

> *If I eat a big bowl of pasta I feel so tired afterwards I can't get up off the sofa. If my daughter eats too many sweets or too much junk food, the same kind of thing happens. She just mopes around.*

Overcoming inertia can also be part of it. Once your child is sitting in front of the TV, she isn't going to feel like getting back up to do anything. So catch her early or ban TV until the jobs are done.

## *Try being a COMMANDO PARENT*

The final words on getting your child to cooperate come from **Commando Parents**. Lots of the ideas we've suggested work over time, and if you can be patient you'll get there. But what do you do when something has to be done *right now*? When there's no time to wait around, there's no time to listen to your child's feelings and you can't compromise?

This is where **Commando Parents** have the edge. These are parents with natural authority. We're not talking about shouters; we mean the kind of people who are naturally tough but rarely, if ever, need to raise their voices. A suggestion or a look is all it takes and their children leap into action. It can be fascinating – and baffling – to watch, until you figure out how they do it.

When it comes to the crunch, **Commando Parents** are confident and stand their ground. They don't become intimidated and they don't give up until their child gets moving.

*Give orders that don't sound like orders* **Commando Parents** don't always go straight in with the heavy artillery. They might start by giving strong hints, and letting their child work out for herself what needs to be done.

For example, if you say:

- *'Your shoes are in the garden and it's starting to rain'*

with luck, she thinks:

- *'Oh, that's right. My shoes. I'd better go and get them.'*

We're not saying you can't be explicit. 'Get your shoes from the garden' is fine. But she is more likely to want to rescue them if she isn't feeling bossed around.

## Orders That Don't Sound Like Orders

Here's a quick recap of orders that don't sound like orders. We've explained them in much more detail in Chapter Two. Notice there are no direct commands. The hope is that your child won't get defensive and disobey you, and her next step should be clear to her from what you say, whisper or write down.

***Give options*** *'Do you want to wash or dry?'*
***Say it in a word*** *'Hairbrush!'*
***Describe what you see*** *'There's a banana skin on the floor.'*
***Ask what comes next*** *'You've finished your tea. What's next?'*
***Give a quick reminder*** *'There's something else you need for gym.'*
***Whisper*** *'Say "thank-you".'*
***Give thanks in advance*** *'Thanks for putting on your seatbelt.'*
***Write a note*** *'This door should be left locked at night.'*

***Give information*** Remind your child every so often that you're asking for her help for the benefit of the entire family.

- *'When we tidy the house together, we're doing something for the good of all of us.'*

- *'I like it when we work together. The time goes quickly and then we have time to spend together doing other things.'*

It's important for children to understand why you want them to make a contribution. Over time, these are extremely powerful messages.

In some cultures, it is much easier to get children to cooperate because faffing around isn't an option. Everyone has to help simply to get food on to the table.

> *I grew up in Mexico. There was no ambiguity; everyone in the family had to work. When I was six I was washing clothes and looking after younger brothers and sisters. We helped out with pride, knowing we were making a contribution.*
>
> *Now I live in America, I find it much harder to get my children to help. My family aren't around and none of my children's friends are expected to do a thing.*

You can't create a supportive culture from scratch, but you can remind your children that when everyone works together, the whole family is happier.

***Give rewards and consequences*** You will be even more effective if you can back up your rules or requests with rewards and consequences, especially if they are directly related to whether or not your child does what she is told.

**Reward**

- *'If you help me tidy up, I will have more time to help you with your project'*

is better than:

- *'If you help me tidy up, I'll buy you a treat on Saturday.'*

Even though she may not admit it, the best rewards for being cooperative aren't sweets and toys, but your good opinion of her and your undivided attention. So when your child helps around the house, tell her how happy you are and spend some of the time you've saved talking to her or doing something she enjoys.

**Consequence**

- *'If you don't get ready now, there'll be no time in the park'*

is better than:

- *'If you don't get ready now, there'll be no TV for a week.'*

Some consequences are easy to work out.

- *'If you don't put your shoes away when you get home, you will continue having a tough time finding them in the morning.'*
- *'If you don't turn off the television, you will lose screen time tomorrow.'*

But what do you do when it isn't so obvious?

- *'If you don't put your plate in the dishwasher, then . . .'* Then what?

Your child doesn't care if her dirty plate sits on the table all night. But she might care if you aren't so inclined to help her next time she wants something. Children need to learn that their actions (or lack of them) affect others. If they sit around and don't help out when we ask, it can make us feel uncooperative as well.

*My son said, 'You can't make me do it,' and I said, 'You're right. I can't. But bear this in mind: next time you want something from me I might still be annoyed, and then I won't feel like helping you.' He thought for a moment and then reluctantly got to his feet and cleared his plate.*

This also works if your child pretends not to hear you.

*My son wouldn't get ready for bed. I asked him six times, but he put his fingers in his ears. 'Blah, blah, blah,' he chanted.*

*But later he understood how I felt. After ten minutes he came back to show me his latest drawing. He started explaining all the blasters and rockets, but I said, 'I'm sorry, but I don't want to listen to you right now. You didn't want to listen to me and now I'm irritated and I don't want to listen to you. So you are going to have to wait until I've calmed down.'* ❜

***Express your feelings*** One of the main reasons why children don't cooperate is that they simply don't see the point. Why clear up the sitting room? The mess doesn't bother them. Who cares about the crumbs and smears of jam on the kitchen table? What's the point of changing their underwear or washing their hair? Why go to bed when they'd rather stay up?

Even though your child doesn't care, explaining exactly why you feel strongly about something can often get her moving.

- *'I know you don't see the point of getting changed, but it means a lot to me that you turn up at our friends' house properly dressed. That means clean trousers, not dirty jeans.'*
- *'I mind a lot about the mess in the hall because I don't like to trip over bags and bikes and I'm embarrassed when visitors arrive. Please go and put the bikes in the garden and hang the bags up on the rack.'*
- *'I don't like listening to you shouting and arguing about this. It gives me a headache. Please make your bed and draw your curtains.'*

Some situations make it hard not to lose your temper. This doesn't have to be a complete disaster. If you can stick to 'I feel . . .' rather than 'You always . . .' it can even be helpful.

- *'Walking into this bathroom makes me so angry. There are wet clothes and towels all over the floor and hair in the bath. I am steaming.'*

***Stand your ground*** Even cooperative children have their off days, and there are so many temptations. If your child is in the middle of a DVD or playing on the PlayStation, this isn't the time to fire out quick instructions over your shoulder. Nor will it work if you shout up the stairs. You need to be right in front of her, eyeball to eyeball, and stand your ground until she gets moving. See p. 60 for more on this, but here is a quick review:

- ***Make eye contact*** *(especially if she is in front of a screen)*
- ***Tell her succinctly what you want***
- ***Don't say anything else and don't leave!***
- ***Praise her*** *(for any small step in the right direction)*

For this to work you need to keep your nerve and give the impression that you can stay there all night if necessary. Go in prepared for a long wait. If you waver, lose your temper or flounce off, you'll lose face and it will be more difficult next time. If you're in a hurry, keep this technique for another day.

For a smaller child, a variation on this is to bend down to her level and say, 'Would you like me to help you?' Again, praise her for anything she does right and tune in if she does any complaining, but don't leave until the job is done.

# Travelling with Children

For some parents, the hardest time to get cooperation is in the car. Just driving down the road can be a nightmare. If children keep taking off their seatbelts, kicking your seat and shrieking, you can't concentrate on the road.

Even the thought of going on holiday – spending hours cooped up in a metal box, whether it's a car, train or aeroplane, with your children – can bring you out in a cold sweat. You know everyone else manages to get from A to B with their family. But how on earth do they do it?

## Getting Cooperation in the Car

When you have children in the car, you need to find a way to make them behave because it's dangerous when they don't. You can't drive properly if you're turning your head every ten seconds to check their seatbelts, or reaching behind you to break up arguments.

## *Try being a SORTED PARENT*

Don't wait until your children are misbehaving. Talk to them in advance and tell them what you expect, i.e., seatbelts on at all times, no arguing or kicking, and no loud noises that can distract the driver. If they fight over the seats, agree beforehand who sits where.

## *Try being a CHEERLEADER PARENT*

Compliment the child who is wearing her seatbelt or sitting quietly.

## *Try being a TUNED-IN PARENT*

Listen to their feelings and try to be understanding when they whinge. Wearing seatbelts can be uncomfortable and car journeys can be long and boring.

## *Try being a COMMANDO PARENT*

If your children are still whooping and hollering in the car or refusing to wear their seatbelts, this is where **Commando Parents** come into their own. They come down hard and don't put up with any nonsense.

> *It's simple – I refuse to start the car until everyone has their seatbelt on, and I stop the car if anyone misbehaves. I won't drive if it isn't safe.*

We know one mother who pulled over to the side of the road and turned off the engine while her children carried on fighting and screaming in the car. No nagging, no pleading, no shouting – she simply sat quietly. Eventually they realized they'd have to be quiet before she carried on. Now if they start misbehaving one of them will say, 'Stop it or Mum won't start the car again.' It may sound harsh, but it's the right thing to do.

*I've had two minor accidents in the last month, bumping into the car in front at traffic lights and backing into a car that pulled up behind as I was about to park. Both of them happened when I was yelling at my children to be quiet and stop fighting. When they're raising hell in the back, I can't keep my mind on the road. I'm afraid we are going to get into a serious accident one day.*

You might think it's impossible to stop the car if you are already running late. But it really is your best option in the long run.

*My son refused to put his belt on and so we sat there for fifteen minutes. Yes, we were all late for school. But it was well worth it. He got the message and never took it off again.*

Another mother we know cancelled a trip to Legoland halfway along the motorway because her children kept taking off their seatbelts. She said she wasn't in the mood to spend the day in hospital.

## Going on Holiday

### *'I find travelling with my children so stressful I need a holiday to get over it.'*

If you are going on holiday, it can seem to take almost as long getting your family out of the house, packed and ready to go, as you spend on the holiday itself. It's not as if any of the preparation is really that difficult. It's trying to do it all while keeping regular everyday life under control that causes the overload. It is amazing that no matter how much you accomplish every day, how fast you move, how late you stay up and how many things you cross off your list, the whole process always expands to fill every second you have. You can find you're busy right up until the very moment you all troop out of the door.

The one crucial thing you need – without which the whole operation is doomed – is for your children to cooperate. But do they?

*When I've got a list a mile long and I'm struggling to get ready to go, my children start fighting and demanding my attention. I wish they would watch TV or go outside, but they're right in my face.*

Travelling itself can be incredibly stressful too.

*Flying with our children wasn't really a problem, until we took a quick trip within Europe – a one-and-a-half-hour flight – and my youngest threw a fit the whole way. It was turbulent and she screamed persistently, at the top of her lungs, because she didn't want to put her seatbelt on. My heart went out to anybody on that flight who was afraid of flying. What with the turbulence and the histrionics, their nerves must have been completely shot.*

## Ways to ease the stress before a journey

### *Try being a SORTED PARENT*

Travelling with children is much easier if you get sorted and do as much as you can well in advance.

*Give advance warning* You can save yourself an enormous amount of grief if you talk to your children and tell them what to expect. The first thing to mention is that you are going to be very busy preparing for the trip, and you really need their help. You need time now to get everything prepared, so you can spend lots of time with them while you're on holiday. If you warn them in advance, they may be remarkably thoughtful and cooperative.

*Sort your systems* You can keep on top of the chaos if you get as organized as possible before the trip. For example, everyone will be much happier if there's a snack bag packed, the Game Boys are charged, you've brought audiotapes or music, and you've got a series of songs you can sing or games you can play along the way.

*When we travel on long-haul flights I always bring a reading and puzzle book for each child, just in case the in-flight entertainment system goes down. We had that happen once, and it was awful.*

You might also warn them that everyone is expected to wear their seatbelts on the plane, and decide in advance who gets the window seat.

### *Try being a COMMANDO PARENT* 

*Express your feelings* Telling your children in a clear, matter-of-fact way how you feel often gets results. It makes what you have to say so much more palatable.

> *'I find travelling with everyone very stressful. I get especially worried when you start running around the airport and I can't see you.'*

### *Try being a LAID-BACK PARENT* 

*Ask for solutions* You get extra points if, instead of organizing everything yourself, you enlist the entire family to help. Ask them for their suggestions on how to make the journey better for everyone.

> *'My children like to pack their own backpacks with things to keep them busy in the car or on the plane.'*

## Ways to ease the stress during a journey

### *Try being a PAUSE PARENT* 

*Expect to be wound up* You're going to stand a much better chance of enjoying yourself on the trip if you are mentally prepared for the onslaught. Instead of thinking of it as your time, think of it as theirs.

> *'When I fly with my children I bring along magazines for me, but I don't expect to read them until we've arrived, or assume that I'll get to see the film. If I go with the assumption that I'll be looking after my children the whole time, jumping up and down fetching drinks and snacks, going back and forth to the loo, reading stories, and wandering up and down the plane with a fretful baby, I'm in a much better frame of mind. I don't get so wound up when they want me to do things for them. If, by chance, they're settled for any length of time, I've got my magazines just in case.'*

## *Try being a PHYSICAL PARENT* 

***Feed them well*** The last thing you want is to be trapped with a hyperactive child who then crashes with the sugar blues. So try not to get sucked into buying chocolate or additive-laden snacks if you are going to be in a confined space for any length of time. Do yourself a favour and pack things like fruit, pretzels, organic crisps and biscuits, natural fruit juice and water.

## *Try being a CHEERLEADER PARENT* 

When they are behaving well, remember to tell your children how lovely it is to travel with them.

## *Try being a TUNED-IN PARENT* 

***Listen to their feelings*** Travelling is hard and no matter how much preparation you do your child may have the occasional meltdown. If you tell her she's got to shut up immediately, you run the risk that she will push you to see just how far she can go. This is one power struggle you don't want to get into at 32,000 feet or halfway up the motorway, because there is a real danger you will lose. Your best chance of rescuing the situation is to listen and try to understand your child's feelings.

- *'I know you're fed up. So am I. This is so boring. I wish we were there already.'*

4

# Making Friends and Handling Bullies

## Helping Your Child to Get on with People

Some people are blessed with impeccably behaved, outgoing children. When you meet them they don't scowl, mumble or stare at their shoes. They look you in the eye, smile and even manage to string a sentence together. Immediately you get the feeling they've got it all going for them and will go far.

These children find it easy to get on with other people. They pick up on social cues and seem to know by osmosis how to behave. It's a real wind-up for parents whose children just don't get it. Some children only need a bit of fine-tuning, like learning to say 'hello' when they meet someone instead of grunting. But others can get seriously out of control.

*'I took my children to my sister-in-law's house and I've never been more ashamed. Her children were so good at lunch, but mine kept interrupting, showing off and burping. They grabbed food and never said thank-you for anything. After lunch she caught them jumping on her furniture and they refused to apologize. Oh – and my daughter picked her nose at the table. It was awful. I can't bear it.'*

Even quiet children can be embarrassing.

*'When my friends come over, my son won't look at them or say hello. Even if they bring their children, he isn't friendly. He just slopes off to another room to watch TV or play on his own. I know he's shy, but to everyone else he just seems rude.'*

There are any number of reasons why children don't do the right thing: bad habits, attention-seeking, insecurity, trying to be cool, and (let's face it) copying us at our worst. Personality can also play a big part in it. At one end of the scale there are shy children who don't have the confidence or skills to make friends. At the other end are the boisterous ones who ride roughshod over other people's feelings and don't pick up the signals when their behaviour is irritating or unacceptable.

There is no one right way to get your child to behave appropriately. Each child and each problem is different and you will tackle things differently depending on which type of parent you are. Your views about appropriate behaviour might be different from those of other parents. You might not be too concerned about table manners or how your child answers the phone, while for others these might be priorities.

In general, we feel that socializing your child is about encouraging behaviour that makes him feel comfortable in any situation and helps others to like him. Manners do come into it; the basics of saying 'please', 'thank-you', 'hello' and 'sorry' will help children through almost anything. Table manners come into it too; your child needs to know how to use a knife and fork and how to behave at the table so he doesn't draw too much attention to himself or put others off their food. But socializing is about far more than etiquette. The underlying goals are courtesy, responsibility and sensitivity to other people's feelings.

It's also about discouraging behaviour that other people find offensive. Your hit list will be personal, but ours includes whinging, bragging, lying, rudeness and any bodily functions, like farting and nose-picking, that are best done in private.

As well as making other people feel at ease, socializing helps a child feel happy in his own skin. By learning how to handle himself, he will find it easier to make friends, cope in new situations, stand up for himself and keep his cool under provocation. A child who gets on well with others is also far less likely to be bullied or to become a bully, though at times even well-adjusted children need help.

# How to Encourage Good Manners

***'My child has such bad manners I'm too ashamed to be seen anywhere with him besides a dark cinema. What can I do?'***

If you want to encourage good manners you need to get to the point where you can give information and know your child will do the right thing. Where you can say in a neutral, matter-of-fact voice, 'We don't eat baked beans with our fingers,' and he immediately picks up a spoon. Or better still, when you don't need to say anything at all because you can trust him to do the right thing.

But what if you aren't there yet? What if your child can't be bothered to behave, or completely ignores your instructions? Trying the approaches of the different parent types will help.

## *Try being a PAUSE PARENT*

When the atmosphere is relaxed and there is no one else around, it isn't usually a problem reminding your child to say 'thank-you' or 'sorry'. Unfortunately, when you need to correct him you're nearly always in front of other people. But criticizing him in public can backfire. If he feels resentful or embarrassed, he'll either ignore you or do something worse to get more attention. Further, you're setting a terrible example – no one can describe nagging, nitpicking or humiliating children in public as good manners.

***Zip your lip*** You will both be far better off if you start by pausing and keeping quiet, but we know how hard this can be. Without a doubt, one of the most difficult times to pause is when your child behaves inappropriately in front of other people and there's maximum chance of embarrassment. The classic example is when he refuses to apologize for something.

*' My son, Jamie, kicked over another boy's sandcastle and then refused to say sorry. The other boy started crying and his mother was furious. Everyone around the sandpit was watching us. I tried everything to*

*make Jamie apologize, but he refused to budge. The other mother was so angry she took her son and left in a huff. It was excruciating.* ’

Depending on how wilful he is, forcing your child to apologize in front of other people can be a disaster. If he won't back down you can end up even more embarrassed.

Not making him apologize immediately might feel as if you're letting him get away with bad behaviour. But we aren't saying you should ignore it. We're saying don't make matters worse. Getting into a power struggle or humiliating him in public isn't the answer.

You'll have a better chance of getting a 'sorry' out of him if you take him aside and talk about it semi-privately.

## *Try being a TUNED-IN PARENT*

***Listen to their feelings*** If he feels worked up, he won't apologize until you've got to the root of the problem. There must have been a reason in his own mind why he didn't do the right thing. When you dig deeper, you'll probably find out what feelings are lurking under there. 'I'm too embarrassed to apologize,' or 'I don't care about his stupid sandcastle. He took my bucket.'

Once you understand what's going on behind the scenes, you'll probably feel more sympathetic and you can help to solve the problem. And once he feels understood, he's more likely to do the right thing and say sorry.

If this doesn't work immediately, all you can do is swallow your pride, apologize on his behalf and leave the scene. You will need to do quite a lot of tuning in, so resolve to discuss it with him later, perhaps at bedtime. If you can finally get to the root of the problem, he'll listen to you and he'll be more likely to behave better next time.

***Accept difficult feelings*** Tuning in is often your best bet when you want your child to have good manners and you suspect there's going to be trouble.

*When my daughter saw her bridesmaid's dress her face fell. She shouted, 'How old does she think I am? I'm not wearing that! It looks like a fairy outfit for a baby. I'm not going to the wedding.'*

*For two days I tried to talk her round, but she refused to listen. 'I won't go and you can't make me.' I panicked. It was too late to bottle out. But I couldn't drag her up the aisle. What if she ruined the wedding?*

*The breakthrough only came when I sympathized. I said, 'I understand why you're upset. You've been looking forward to this wedding for months. And this dress isn't what you expected at all. You are so disappointed.'*

*The more I agreed it was a disaster, the more compliant she became. On the day, she wore the dress and she behaved beautifully. Thank God.*

This sounds like a risky strategy. It's tempting to say, 'You will wear that dress and you will behave.' But if you tune in, you generally don't need to get heavy. Once you've acknowledged your child's strong feelings, he will usually do the right thing.

Tuning in is also a good way to help children understand the difference between good and bad behaviour. When your child moans about one of his friends and says things like:

- *'I hate Simon. He's always saying his house is so big'*

seize the moment. Try:

- *'You're right, it's irritating. It's bad manners for him to boast like that.'*

We aren't suggesting you encourage your child to bad-mouth his friends. Focus on the behaviour, not the person. But if he sees how certain types of behaviour make him feel, he'll be less likely to behave that way himself.

## *Try being a CHEERLEADER PARENT*

One of the best ways to teach good manners is by encouraging your child when he does something right.

***Notice the good, ignore the bad*** It's so simple. All you have to do is make nice comments when he does something polite, and he'll be more inclined to do it again.

- *'Thanks for passing the peas.'*
- *'Well done remembering to flush the loo.'*
- *'That was thoughtful, hanging up Grandpa's coat.'*

If he feels appreciated, he may be less likely to close his ears to: 'You need to say sorry' or 'Please ask me in a nice voice.'

Even if he behaves badly a lot of the time, make a heroic effort not to react. Instead, turn things round and start giving him positive attention when he does something right. In most cases it's even worth praising him if he does something only half right. So instead of:

- *'That's not a proper sorry. That was a snarl. Say you're sorry properly'*

try:

- *'That was big of you to say sorry. I could tell you didn't really want to.'*

***Be specific*** When trying to teach your child good manners, it is very tempting to point out when he's done something wrong. For example:

- *'You didn't even shake Mrs Lake's hand or say one word to her. How do you think that made her feel?'*

But a comment like this will only make him feel resentful and self-conscious. If you want him to be polite, give him some specific praise to build his confidence. Even if he doesn't do exactly what you want, you can always find something good to mention and build on that.

- *'I liked the way you smiled at Mrs Lake when you met her. Perhaps next time you could say a quick hello.'*

**Praise on the spot** This is particularly helpful if you are working on table manners. Though it may be tough, try and ignore the fact that he is rocking in his chair and comment on anything you can find he is doing right.

- *'Eating rice with a fork can be hard. You're doing a good job balancing it like that.'*

If he is eating with his mouth open and making horrible chewing noises, give him attention the moment he stops.

- *'It's so nice when you eat with your mouth closed.'*

This works especially well if you have more than one child. If you find you're always paying attention to whoever's misbehaving, try noticing the one who is sitting quietly doing the right thing.

- *'I like the way you are sitting properly in your chair.'*

Nine times out of ten the sloucher will sit up straight too, and then you can compliment him as well.

**Be open-minded** Even if your child has manners from hell, you'll find it much easier to help him if you don't go on about it, and don't discuss his uncouth behaviour with other people so he can overhear you. If he believes he is rude, a whiner or whatever, it will be ten times harder for him to shake off the label. And if he enjoys the attention he gets from behaving badly, he'll keep doing it.

You may also need to lower your expectations. Children aren't adults, and it's unfair to expect your child to behave like one. It may be unrealistic to expect him to be able to sit quietly for hours on end or to be on his best behaviour every time guests arrive.

## Try being a SORTED PARENT

One of the best ways to encourage good manners is to discuss beforehand what you expect. If you are a very **Sorted Parent**, you will naturally do this long before troubles appear.

***Give advance warning*** This is a particularly good way to tackle long-running battles that keep erupting over and over again.

- *'Lunch is ready. I said LUNCH IS READY. Get in here NOW! Remember to wash your hands. Why? Because they're filthy. Don't tip your chair. I said, don't tip your chair! Sit back down. You've only had two mouthfuls. This is our one chance for a civilized family lunch. What do you mean, you're not hungry? Come back here . . .'*

If you are concerned about table manners, for example, decide what really bothers you and talk to your child before the problem crops up again. By talking it through in advance, he can mentally gear up to the new regime. This generally works much better than dishing out instructions on the spot, especially if you tend to boil over with frustration.

So try something like:

- *'It is very important to your dad and me that you make an effort for Sunday lunch. That means coming to the table when I call you, washing your hands, and sitting through the entire meal. From now on I'll give you a fifteen-minute warning so you can turn off the PlayStation and get ready.'*

***Train them up*** Quite a lot of anti-social behaviour is triggered by uncertainty, when children feel uncomfortable or aren't sure exactly how to behave. If this is the case, try a little practice.

*When anyone came to the house my children used to stare at the ground. So I dreamed up this character called Mrs Peabody, and we all took turns acting her out and practising how to meet her. I showed them how to hold out their hand, look at her and say, 'Hello, Mrs Peabody.'*

*It was so much fun that a few days later they said, 'Can we do the Mrs Peabody thing again?'*

Children also tend to behave badly in situations when they'd rather not be there at all. By being a **Sorted Parent** you can help soften the blow by preparing your child and explaining exactly what to do.

- *'I know you don't like it when Great-Aunt Lucy comes to visit. It's boring and it's hard for you to think of anything to say to her. But when she is our guest we have to make her feel welcome. I want you to smile at her, say hello and chat for a couple of minutes. Why not start by asking her about her cats?'*

## Try being a LAID-BACK PARENT 

One of the best ways to reinforce good habits is to get your child to come up with answers for himself. If he does he will be more likely to follow them through, which means you won't have to nag him.

**Ask for solutions** When you're trying to teach your child the right thing to do, try asking him questions.

- *'When someone says hello to you, what do you think you should say to them?'*
- *'It's hard to remember to take a message when you answer the phone. What would help you?'*

This is also very useful if you ask your child to do something (or stop doing it) and he rolls his eyes and says, 'Why should I?'

Instead of justifying yourself with a lecture on manners, try:

- *'Good question. Why do you think you should?'*

If you keep smiling and looking friendly, he might dredge up an answer. Of course he knows the answer already – you've been through this a hundred times.

He may reply, 'Because you are annoying, and make up stupid rules?' But try your hardest not to react. You could say, 'Good guess. Try again.' If you're lucky he'll come up with something sensible. If not, just leave it.

Asking questions is also brilliant when your child is in trouble. You'll be amazed how often he can think his way out of a problem.

*My son chased a little girl with a stick, and frightened her so much she wouldn't go back into the playground. Understandably the girl's mother was upset about it, and I was furious.*

*But instead of punishing him, I asked him what he thought he should do about it. He suggested he could say sorry to her. He did, and that was the end of it. I actually ended up being quite proud of him.*

## *Try being a COMMANDO PARENT*

There are times when you need to be a **Commando Parent**. There are certain things your child needs to know in life so that he doesn't make an idiot of himself, and you are the one who needs to tell him.

Manners are about making other people feel comfortable. If he can understand this, everything else should follow.

***Give information*** Rather than criticizing or embarrassing him, tell him in a straightforward way how to behave and why. What you say is up to you, but some examples might include:

- *'You need to sit quietly in restaurants because other people don't want to be disturbed.'*
- *'If someone gives you a present and you don't like it, it's important to thank them anyway so you don't hurt their feelings.'*
- *'Chewing with your mouth open is off-putting for the people who have to see and hear it.'*
- *'It's good manners to flush the loo and open the bathroom window, because it's nicer for the next person.'*
- *'It's fine to laugh and joke, but we stay off subjects that put people off their food.'*

You may also need to help him to understand when and where behaviour is appropriate. For example, it might be all right for him to wrestle with his brother at home, but not OK in a public place. It's fine for him to pour his feelings out to you about the annoying boy in his class, but not OK to bad-mouth him at school.

***Give consequences*** When your child does something really awful that you can't ignore, just giving information may not be enough. You may have to threaten consequences, and carry them through if necessary.

> *'My daughter bit another child at a birthday party. I made her say sorry and told her that if it happened again we would have to go home. Ten minutes later another little boy snatched her piece of pizza, and she bit him, too. I could see why she did it and I didn't want to manhandle her out of the door. But I had to. She has to understand that she can't bite people, however cross she is.*
>
> *Two weeks later she bit another little boy at the park, and I took her home immediately. After that she stopped.'*

When you need to follow consequences through, it helps to get sorted first. If you are clear in your own mind what is and isn't acceptable you will have more authority, and if you talk through the consequences with your child, he's more likely to accept them when he misbehaves.

The consequences will depend on the situation. If your child is small enough, you can pick him up and take him out of the room or remove whatever is causing the problem. It is not polite to bang a drum, for example, when adults are trying to talk, so take it away. If he's bigger, you'll have to be more creative and plan your campaign more carefully. (See Chapters Three and Eight for more advice.)

# Difficulty Making Friends

Some children are naturally sociable, but others find it harder to make friends. While nearly all children will have to deal with friendships breaking down (see below), for some they never quite get started.

If your child doesn't have a best friend or isn't part of an obvious group, you might be quite sanguine about it and figure he will get there in the end. But lots of parents worry.

***'My son just seems to float. Is this normal? I don't want him to end up as some sort of loner.'***

In a way, what you feel doesn't really matter. The question is whether or not your child is bothered about it.

> *Lots of children started on a round-robin of play dates as far back as nursery school. But two of my children weren't interested. They didn't even want to go to birthday parties until they were seven and eight.*
>
> *Some of the parents thought we were snubbing them. But my children didn't want to play with other children after school. It wasn't their thing and they weren't ready for it.*

## *Try being a PAUSE PARENT*

***Keep things in perspective*** If your child isn't unhappy or doesn't particularly want to spread his wings, don't panic about it. He may be quite happy drifting at school and hanging out with whoever comes along, rather than making one or two particular friends. If he has siblings, he may be perfectly content to come home and play with them, or do things with you.

It might bother you that other children get together and play after school (while their mothers get together for lovely cups of tea), but give it time. He will make friends and want to have them over to play when he is ready.

It is a problem, however, if your child isn't happy and wishes he had friends. You might even feel worse about it than he does. If you ever felt left out and miserable when you were younger, those old feelings might get churned up and can be quite painful.

There are endless reasons why he may not be making friends. The most common are: difficult circumstances, irritating habits and bad behaviour, confidence issues and shyness. The good news is that there are loads of things you can do to help him, and we're going to talk you through them.

### *Try being a TUNED-IN PARENT* 

Whatever the reason, if your child is unhappy, the first and best thing you can do is to listen. Feeling lonely or awkward can be pretty awful for anyone, and he doesn't have enough experience to know that things will probably get better in time. Let him pour his heart out, without interrupting or giving advice. You can help him to solve his problems soon, but for the moment, just let him talk.

## When Circumstances Make Friendships Difficult

Whatever's going on at home can affect your child's ability to make friends. If you're getting divorced or moving house, he'll feel the strain. He may become rude, bossy or withdrawn around other children, and if they start to exclude him, he'll feel worse. Talk to his teacher and let her know what's going on. Even if you have almost no emotional energy left yourself, make some time to listen to him.

Sometimes children don't make friends simply because of bad luck. It could be that the children he likes don't include him because they all live in the same street or on the other side of town, or because they've known each other since nursery school. If there isn't anything else that makes him unappealing (like irritating behaviour – see below), the simplest and easiest thing is to get out your diary and organize a couple of play dates. He may find it easier making friends one-to-one, when there aren't dozens of other children around. Or talk to his teacher about pairing him up with another child, or including him in a group project.

Sometimes, even if there are thirty other children in the class, things just don't gel. He may be happier in a different class, and you may want to consider moving him.

*My daughter didn't have any friends in her class, and she was very unhappy about it. She would bring a deck of cards to school and play on her own during break times.*

*I told her she should try to stick it out. But in the end she did change forms, and what a difference it made. She never had any problem making friends after that.'*

## Irritating Habits and Bad Behaviour

If your child has a disgusting habit, like burping in public, he might be popular with a few children if it makes them laugh. But it's likely to put the rest of them off. Dealing discreetly with bodily functions is a major part of learning to fit in.

*'There is a boy in my daughter's year who has a very runny nose. My daughter says he sits all through class sucking rivers of snot into his mouth. Everyone thinks he is disgusting and no one ever wants to sit next to him.'*

*'The girl who sits next to my daughter at school is only ten, but she has BO and very greasy hair. I feel sorry for her because no one wants to be her friend. But I also feel sorry for my daughter. She says the smell is really awful.'*

You don't want to give your child a complex about his body or its natural functions. But he needs to realize that there are certain things he can't do if he wants other people to feel comfortable around him.

Some of the most common unpopular habits include: bogey-picking of any sort (but especially eating or flicking); spitting phlegm; picking earwax, scabs or belly-button goo; and making loud or smelly burps or farts. Flashing your bottom or genitals depends so much on circumstances – inevitable in the pool changing room, but not appropriate in the classroom, the play-ground or on the school bus. There are also a number of small things that can irritate other children, including: sniffing, thumb-sucking, head-scratching, chewing and clothes-sucking.

Use the tools for encouraging good manners (pp. 107–15) to make your child aware of what he is doing and change his irritating habits.

Bragging, lying and cheating are other common traits that irritate children. If your child constantly does one of them he is likely to find himself being ostracized. This is especially true if he makes direct comparisons, like:

- *'My trainers are cooler than yours.'*
- *'Well, we have five TVs.'*

Some children can't seem to help being irritating, and if your child is unlucky he might be one of them. He may not quite get how to behave, and if he doesn't conform, the others in his class will notice and find him annoying.

If no one wants to be your child's friend, do lots of tuning in to help him feel understood and try to encourage him to have better manners (see pp. 108–9). If it seems as though he's being bullied, see pp. 141–2 on irritating children who get bullied.

## Shyness and Confidence Issues

### *'My child doesn't have bad manners, he's just shy. It's painful to watch. How can I help him?'*

In previous generations, being shy wasn't such a problem. Children were expected to be seen and not heard. But modern life is busy, complicated and full of people. If your child doesn't have the courage to join in, you might be worried.

> *I was a shy child myself, and I know it limited my opportunities. Now I find it almost unbearable to see my daughter suffer. At school she never gets picked to be anyone's partner, she doesn't put her hand up in class, and she is always hidden in the back corner of the school productions. It's just so sad because she is such a lovely little soul. If only someone else could see it and appreciate her as well.*

There's nothing wrong with being shy. We all sit somewhere on the line between outgoing and bashful, it's just a matter of degree. Even the most extrovert characters feel tongue-tied in certain circumstances. But outgoing, gregarious children don't usually have trouble making friends. It's easier for them to go up to other children and start a conversation, and others are more likely to gravitate towards them.

Shy children, on the other hand, can find talking to people excruciating. If your child feels nervous on the inside, his manner may be misinterpreted as stand-offish or arrogant. If he doesn't speak up in class, he might seem immature or less bright than extrovert children and may be misunderstood by his teachers.

So how can you help him?

## *Try being a PAUSE-PARENT* 

***Expect to get wound up and zip your lip*** Lots of parents find it annoying or embarrassing when their shy child won't perform in public, and worry that his gauche behaviour reflects badly on them. But it doesn't help to draw attention to it or apologize. You'll be in a much better position to help him if you are ready for it and aren't wrong-footed every time he hides behind your legs or refuses to acknowledge people.

## *Try being a TUNED-IN PARENT* 

***Listen to and accept difficult feelings*** Even if you're frustrated or embarrassed because he isn't being friendly, try tuning in. He is likely to feel far more confident about new people and places if you acknowledge his uneasy feelings and let him take things more slowly.

> *'When I was a child I was desperate to do ballet. I begged and begged, and finally my mother took me to a class. When we got there I was struck with a bout of nerves, and I just couldn't join in. My mother forced me to stand with the other girls. I had a total confidence crisis. I bowed my head and tried to have a go, but tears were streaming down my face. Then I ran out the door. My mother was so embarrassed she shouted at me the whole way home. She said she would never take me to another ballet class ever again.'*

This mother's approach is so much more helpful:

*My daughter is a great one for wanting to go to music classes and birthday parties. But when we get there she only wants to sit on my knee and watch. I really don't mind. I know she will join in when she is ready.*

If you suspect your child is worrying or feeling upset, listen and let him know his feelings are important. Everyone feels shy sometimes, so don't be dismissive or try to cheer him up by saying, 'Don't fuss. It's not that bad. You'll be fine.' To him, at that moment, things *are* that bad. So listen to him.

## *Try being a SORTED PARENT*

Being the parent of a shy child can be heartbreaking, especially if you know he would genuinely like to join in. Some shy children are perfectly happy not to participate, and they shouldn't be forced. Others would like to get stuck in, but can't or don't know how to go about it. In either case, you can try being a **Sorted Parent**.

*Train them up* **Sorted Parents** help their children to practise things step by step. First you can help your child with what to say if someone speaks to him, then work up to introducing himself or asking a question. He may feel better trying these things out on home territory.

Role-playing can work well for practising making eye contact, shaking hands or saying thank-you, all of which can be torture for shy children.

*I showed my children how to hold out their hand and say 'hello' when they met someone. While we were practising, my shy daughter asked in a quiet voice, 'How do shy people do it?'*

*I thought about it for a moment. Then I said, 'First they take a deep breath, and then they do the same thing. They hold out their hand and say "hello".' So we practised that, too.*

You might try it first with just two of you, then with other family or close friends, and finally with people he doesn't know so well.

It's a bit like desensitizing him through gentle exposure until it feels natural.

***Give advance warning*** If something is coming up that you know is going to be difficult for your child, keep your instructions simple and specific. Shy children don't find social rituals quite so bad if they know exactly what they are expected to do.

- *'We are visiting Aunt Jane today to collect your birthday present. It will make her very happy if you smile at her and say 'thank-you.'*

## *Try being a LAID-BACK PARENT*

***Be a role model*** Shy children are often ultra-sensitive. If they see what it is like to be on the receiving end of their unintentional rudeness, they will often try to make more of an effort.

> *My children are shy, and they used to ignore family friends who'd come to visit and turn their back if an adult said hello or asked them a question.*
>
> *While we were eating dinner one night, I told them to ask me the same question twice. The first time, I turned my back and didn't answer; the second time I looked at them, smiled and answered.*
>
> *I asked them how it felt. They said the first time was horrible, as if I didn't care. Now they know what it feels like, they are trying to be more friendly.*

Though you don't want to draw attention to your child's shyness, you can demonstrate how people behave in certain situations by being a good role model. Show him how to be polite and friendly by your own behaviour, without putting any pressure on him.

> *I am shy myself, and I have three shy children. I've made an effort to smile at them as much as possible to encourage them to smile at other people. It's important because shy people who don't smile can seem stuck up.*

## *Try being a CHEERLEADER PARENT* 

**Be open-minded** There is nothing to gain by labelling your child, so don't keep calling him shy, or going on and on about the 'problem', because it will make it harder for him to change.

> *My first daughter was very shy. I worried about her a lot, and drew an unbelievable amount of attention to it. I discussed it endlessly with everybody we met, and did everything I could to 'cure' her. The result? She rebelled and didn't speak at all at school for three years!*
>
> *My youngest is shy, too, but this time around I haven't gone there. I've never felt compelled to apologize for her behaviour and if other people comment that she is shy, I simply agree that she is taking her time. If she wants to talk to me about feeling shy, that's fine. But I am very careful to use the word 'shy' to describe her feelings rather than to describe her as a shy person.*

As well as not labelling your child, resist the temptation to compare him with other children:

- *'Watch how Billy does it. See?'*
- *'It's no surprise Emma is so popular. Look at how friendly she is.'*

This kind of comment can put an unbelievable amount of pressure on a child.

Should your shy child surprise you and be polite or friendly in a social situation, this is one time when praising him on the spot might do more harm than good. He will almost certainly feel awkward if you draw attention to him in public. Instead, give him a quick smile and make a mental note to mention it later:

- *'Well done saying "hello" when our guests arrived.'*
- *'It was kind of you to show Robert the puppies.'*

# Difficulties with Friends and Bullies

Perhaps there are people out there who met their best friend on the very first day of school, are life-long bosom buddies and have never had a single argument. But most children go through a complicated and sometimes painful process, making and breaking up with friends, and forming and re-forming new groups.

All children have to deal with social difficulties along the way. The list of possibilities is endless. Your child might be left out when partners are chosen, blamed for something that isn't his fault or talked about behind his back. He may have his feelings hurt, things taken from his desk or school bag, or get dragged into scuffles.

Though some parents feel that anything on this list is bullying, a certain amount can be just normal stuff between friends, and your child may be able to deal with it on his own. But if he feels it is malicious or it carries on for a long time, he may need your help.

> ‘*My daughter knew that two girls in her class sometimes whispered about her behind her back. We talked about it, but she didn't seem too bothered. But then they stepped it up. They started calling her names and turning other girls against her. She got very upset and started crying at bedtime. That's when I knew something had to be done.*’

It might seem strange that we've put difficulties with friends and bullies in the same section, but the line between the two is often blurred. Without underplaying how serious some bullying can be, it's worth remembering that there's a huge grey area. Your child might easily fall out with his friends, even if they are nice children you've had round to play. If they get into a fight, or go off each other, your child's best friend can quickly become his worst enemy. Paradoxically, bullies can turn around and become friends. How other children affect your child emotionally can change considerably from day to day and year to year.

If your child is feeling demoralized, you might find you get sucked right down there with him. Whether it makes you angry or sad, if he is being bullied it can get you right in the guts. Even issues with his friends can upset you.

> *My son says he has two best friends. But when they have to choose partners, he gets left out. He's the gooseberry, tagging along with the others. I remember how awful that feels. In fact, I think I mind much more than he does.*

While some parents worry about minor issues and can't keep things in proportion, others are horrified to find their child has been bullied for months and they knew nothing about it. The spectrum is very wide.

> *My daughter and her best friend told me they were being bullied, and I was so worried about them. But when I called the other girl's mother, I was shocked when she put it down to playground fun and refused to do anything about it. So I went in to see the headmistress myself the next morning and she put an end to it.*

If you suspect that your child is being bullied, don't close your eyes and hope it will go away on its own. Bullying is something you can't ignore. The intention is to hurt or intimidate your child, and it can range from short-lived bouts of exclusion or nasty text messages to months of emotional and physical abuse. The worst cases of taunting, tormenting and violence are heartbreaking. The victim's self-confidence plummets, and he can become severely depressed and refuse to go to school.

If the situation is serious, you may need professional advice. But there are also many things you can do to help. Dealing with bullies and soured friendships require very similar sets of skills, and this section will give you advice that helps with both.

If your child is going through a particularly rough time, the only chink of light may be that he still has the support of his family at home. Of course you would prefer it if he didn't have to go through it at all, but at least he has you there to pick up the pieces. You can let him know you love him, help him deal with any emotional fall-out, and try to help improve the situation.

## When Your Child Is Being Bullied

When children fall out with friends, it can severely affect their confidence. Bullied children can have a particularly hard time. Every remark, every sideways glance from any quarter, can hurt.

*'A boy in my daughter's class was badly bullied, and after that the slightest thing would set him off. One day he burst into tears because a couple of girls said 'nice pants' as they walked past. The edge of the elastic was sticking up above his trousers.*

*My daughter was there and she said they weren't being nasty at all. They felt terrible and kept apologizing, but he couldn't stop crying.'*

It's so unfair, but sensitive children are like bully magnets. Bullies always seem to go for them because they know they will get a reaction. The same dynamic is often true of siblings. In either case, if the victim isn't bothered, it's not worth bothering him.

*'My older boys never pick on their little brother, but they tease their sister mercilessly, and I can see why. If they make fun of her she gets furious. She goes bright red and starts jumping up and down or crying. It's worth needling her because she gets so worked up.*

*But when they tried to wind Danny up by telling him that he looked like a girl, it didn't bother him at all. He laughed, did a little curtsey and went back to his Lego.'*

### Cyber Bullying

Cyber bullying is a new form of bullying which is becoming increasingly common. It means harassing someone electronically, by text or email, or on a website. It can smash a child's confidence because he can never relax or feel safe, even at home. The bully can get to him at any time.

*'At half-term we rented a cottage, miles from anywhere. At ten p.m. my daughter's mobile pinged to show she had a message: 'UR a*

*wannabe. We R all here. U suck.' She cried all night, and spent all week worrying about it.* ❜

**If your child is getting horrible cyber messages, tell him not to reply, no matter how much he's tempted to do so. The bully wants a reaction, and if he gets one he will send more. So no matter what the provocation, don't give him the satisfaction of responding. If it's a persistent problem, save the messages and report them. It is now a criminal offence to harass anyone by text or email, so in theory the bully could be charged. If the teacher (or, if the problem warrants it, a local policeman) explains this to the class, the problem may stop without drawing attention to your child.**

When your child is being bullied, it isn't always clear exactly what you should do to help. You might not want to focus on the problem and make him feel even worse, and you certainly won't want to antagonize the bully further. Anything you can do to build up your child's confidence is good (see pp. 208–20 for more advice). But what else can you do to help?

## *Try being a TUNED-IN PARENT*

Whether it's a minor incident or a serious problem, start by tuning in so you can find out what's been happening. This might be easy if it's a minor problem and your child is coping quite well. He may even enjoy telling you about the latest outrage.

- *'Guess what, Mum. Jonathan's at it again. Today he stole my sandwich.'*

It's much more difficult if he doesn't tell you what's going on. You have to trust your instincts that something's not quite right. He might be unusually quiet or aggressive, or you might notice a couple of bruises. His work might start to suffer. He might be super-hungry when he gets home if someone is pinching his lunch. He might complain of stomach aches and not want to go to school, or you might overhear him crying himself to sleep.

*'All of a sudden, my son's behaviour got very bad. After school he was rude to me, and appalling to his younger brother, bossing him and pushing him around. It finally came out that he was having a terrible time at school and no one would play with him. He could hold it inside all day, but when he got home he took it all out on us.'*

If you suspect something is up, try gently tuning in. It often helps to start with a statement rather than a direct question:

- *'Something happened today at school.'*
- *'I see you've got a bruise on your arm.'*

Don't worry if this doesn't do the trick. We will give you more strategies in this chapter to encourage your child to open up.

***Listen to and accept difficult feelings*** If your child has a problem that's upset him deeply, it can be hard for him to explain, and hard for you to stomach. Your natural instinct may be to try to make him feel better immediately, but resist the urge to give advice or say you will sort everything out.

First take the time to listen to his feelings. He needs to talk before he can accept your help or find answers within himself. He needs to know it's OK to feel upset and angry. Being bullied and falling out with friends can churn up strong emotions. Though you might be desperate to stop his suffering, let him stamp and shout about his tormentors, or cry his eyes out. You could simply stay quiet and listen, but phrases that are helpful include:

- *'It's painful when a friend behaves like that.'*
- *'You must have felt lonely today, when no one would talk to you.'*
- *'I bet you were angry with him for pushing you around.'*

Phrases that aren't helpful include:

- *'Stop crying, sweetheart. It isn't as bad as it seems. Crying won't change anything.'*

- *'It doesn't matter. You don't need them. Why don't you find a new set of friends?'*

Keep tuning in until he feels a bit better. If a close friendship is blowing up in his face or he is being systematically harassed or humiliated, this can take a while. You can't go into school with him and shelter him from the shrapnel, but if you spend time listening to him, he may feel strong enough to manage on his own.

In general, the more you've been able to tune in to him in the past, the more open your child is likely to be when he has a problem. But don't count on it. If the problem is a big one, the dynamics may be very different.

There are plenty of good reasons why he may not want to confide in you or anyone else: he may be too ashamed of what's happened or how he feels about it, he may not want to worry you, or he may be afraid the bully will find out and torment him further.

From his perspective it might come down to, 'If I don't do anything and don't tell anyone, at least my life won't get any worse.' Even if you suspect something is wrong and ask if he is OK, he might fob you off with, 'I'm fine. Stop bugging me.'

One way you might try to encourage him to talk is to reminisce about your own experiences:

- *'When I was at school, there was a boy who gave me Chinese burns. He said if I told anyone, he'd do it harder.'*

It doesn't matter whether your story ends well or badly. The point is to open up the discussion and show him you understand his feelings.

But if you are still having trouble getting him to talk, you may need to work on generating an atmosphere where he feels comfortable discussing his problems. One of the best ways to do this is by being a **Pause Parent** and staying calm yourself.

## *Try being a PAUSE PARENT* 

If you suspect your child is having a problem and you start nagging him to tell you about it, he may clam up completely. It's so tempting to badger him for the details. But pause and wait.

***Wait until later*** He may not want to rehash a hellish day at school the moment he walks through the door. So don't pressurize him. Just tell him that if he wants to talk, you are there to listen. Then leave it. The details may bubble up later after he has had something to eat or time to play, or when he is lying in bed.

> *'My daughter was bullied by some girls at school. Every day I asked her how it was going. I guess I went a bit too far, because one day she snapped and shouted at me, 'What is it with you? Why do you keep going on and on about it? Can't you just leave it and leave me alone?'*

***Calm down fast*** Try and stay calm. The more emotional you become, the less information you may get. Your child might not be able to handle your feelings on top of his own. So whatever he says, try not to react in an extreme way. Instead of:

- *'Oh my God! I can't believe it! That's appalling'*

or:

- *'I've had enough. I'm calling the headmaster immediately,'*

quiet sympathy is more likely to encourage him to talk:

- *'Maybe you could tell me a bit about how it started.'*
- *'Mm, I see.'*

Once you get a whiff that something is going on, of course you'll want to get to the bottom of it straight away. But if you want your child to talk, avoid bombarding him with questions like:

- *'Why didn't you tell the teacher? Why didn't you fight him back? What did you do to make him so angry? Exactly what did you say happened? Why are you so scared of him?'*

They will only make him feel more of a failure or, worse, make him wish he hadn't mentioned anything to you in the first place. Instead, carry on tuning in with neutral statements like:

- *'That boy can be very intimidating.'*
- *'It must have been hard to know what to do.'*

***Zip your lip*** If he starts telling you what's happening or how he feels about it, for the time being stay quiet and do nothing. His feelings matter more than anything, so listen to them and keep yours under control.

It might be tempting to jump in and tell him what to do, say a bunch of nasty things about the perpetrator, contact the bully's parents, or even yell at his teacher, but you'll probably make matters worse. We aren't saying you shouldn't help him. But for the moment, the best way to do it is by staying quiet.

***Keep things in perspective*** Apart from providing an environment where your child can open up, there's another good reason for pausing when he is going through a tough time. It allows you to try to get things into perspective.

The vast majority of children's altercations are normal, and there's no point in holding long-term grudges over little mishaps and skirmishes. Try not to pass judgement until you have heard the other side of the story.

> *My son was kicked in the playground and I was so angry I called up the other boy's mother and shouted at her. How embarrassing. It turned out my son wasn't the innocent victim at all. She told me that he'd been kicking and pushing her son for weeks.*

But if your child says he has a problem, don't assume he's exaggerating. Try to find out what's going on, because it could be really serious.

> *My son mentioned that he didn't like going down to the lockers because three bigger boys hung around there. I wish I'd paid more attention. It turned out that they were beating up the younger boys,*

*giving them half nelsons and dead legs, and stealing their lunch money. They weren't caught until another mother reported what was going on.’*

## Try being a PHYSICAL PARENT 

**Just be there** Your child can't pour his heart out or come to you for advice if you aren't there. Even if you're stretched thin already, this is the time to temporarily readjust your priorities.

*‘I cancelled dinner plans last night. My son really needed me. He was terrified of going to school today because two boys have been picking on him. We didn't do much, but I'm glad I stayed at home. I can't remember him needing me like that since he was little.’*

**Be affectionate** Even if he won't talk about his problems, a good hug can help a lot if he's suffering.

*‘When my daughter was having trouble with two of her friends at school, she wanted lots of hugs. She said it felt like she was getting energy from me, which made her stronger.’*

But don't force it. He may not want affection, and it might make him feel too vulnerable or emotional. You can always try rubbing his back or giving him a foot or head massage instead. Or just sit with him and watch a video. And don't be too surprised if his sleep is affected and he appears in your room in the middle of the night.

## Try being a LAID-BACK PARENT

**Ask for solutions** If your child is having problems, he may have some good ideas about solving them. This will also boost his confidence, which is probably on the shaky side (see pp. 208–20 for more on confidence). After you've done lots of tuning in, simply ask him what he could do next.

*My son sat next to a boy who would pinch him and flick him every time the teacher's back was turned. He started saying he didn't want to go to school, so I thought, 'That's the final straw. I need to go in and sort this out.'*

*I asked him if there was anything he wanted me to say to the teacher. 'Yes,' he said. 'Could you ask Mrs Brown if I can switch desks?' I was quite proud of him for coming up with the obvious answer to the problem.*

Sometimes being a **Laid-Back Parent** works quite naturally after you've done a lot of tuning in.

*My daughter was best friends for years with Janie. But Janie started being nasty to her, and refused to be her partner. Eventually Janie dumped her completely and started turning other girls against her.*

*One day my daughter came home from school and cried her eyes out. I didn't know what to say, so I just sat and listened, nodded my head, and agreed how sad it was. She went on for ages. It was awful.*

*But what happened next surprised me. Suddenly she said, 'But I know what to do. I am going to try to make some new friends.' And she did.*

## *Try being a SORTED PARENT*

Though it would be great if your child could always solve his own problems, sometimes you need to get sorted and give him some strategies to cope with the people who upset him.

***Train them up*** If your child feels tongue-tied or emotional when he comes face to face with the perpetrator, help him work out in advance what to do. If he's prepared, he will feel more in control, and if he doesn't act like a victim, the bully might leave him alone.

## Strategies to Deal with Bullies

Get your child to practise responses so next time he'll know what to do.

### Think up replies to teasing, name-calling or nasty comments

For example, if the bully keeps calling him 'Big Head', he might say, 'That's right. Big head, big brain,' or 'Better a big head than no head.' Tip: Straightforward or humorous replies are fine. Avoid aggressive ones because the bully will know he's struck a chord, and keep at it.

Another way to go about it is to give the bully a taste of his own medicine.

> *A slightly overweight boy in my son's class was teasing him and calling him 'Mole-on-Mole' because of a mole on my son's face. My son decided to tell him that if he didn't stop, he would start calling him 'Fat-on-Fatso'. That did the trick and he stopped immediately.*

If someone makes little remarks like 'Charlie just told me that he's never liked you,' it can be hard not to feel hurt and even harder not to show it. Your child could try a neutral comment like 'That's interesting,' and leave it there. If he knows the tell-tale well, he could try 'Sounds like you're trying to hurt my feelings,' or 'I wouldn't pass on a comment like that, because friends should stick together.'

### Plan a strategy so he feels in control

Tell him not to wait for the bully to upset or exclude him. Instead, first thing in the morning he should say, 'Morning, Jim,' but keep on walking towards his own desk or wherever he is going. Have him practise this. If he's not unfriendly but keeps on walking, the bully has no chance to turn away from him on purpose, or try to get a reaction.

## Plan a strategy for the playground

If a bigger boy comes up to him and starts pushing him around, he might practise saying something like, 'I don't need this,' and turning and walking away. Or he might want to try standing up for himself.

> *One of the older boys kept telling my son he'd punch him if he put one foot on to the football pitch. We practised and practised what he was going to say. Next day the boy started giving him a hard time. So my son said, 'You are older than me and bigger than me, and if you hit me it is probably going to hurt quite a lot. But that is a risk I am ready to take, and I'm not moving.' The bully glared at him for a while, walked away, and never bothered him again.*

## Come up with a plan if his friends are excluding him

There's no point in your child standing around, looking forlorn, hoping for sympathy. He needs to take it upon himself to find someone else to play with. Help him practise how to ask another child to play.

## Work on his body language

Practise standing up straight, head up, shoulders back. If he looks defeated he will feel defeated, and the other way round. If he changes his posture, he's less likely to be picked on.

## Encourage children to stand up for each other

Bullies can't intimidate children who stand up for each other.

> *When my daughter went to a sleepover, one friend went straight to sleep. The dominant girl suggested cutting off part of her plait. The other three let her do it, because they didn't want to be the next victim. But before the next sleepover they made a deal to look after each other.*

Encourage your child to stand up for his friends or siblings, and thank any child who has stood up for him.

## Other Things You Can Do if Your Child is Being Bullied

Whether your child is being seriously bullied or having a hard time with friends, there are lots of other things you can do.

### Work with the school

Make sure that the right people at school know what's going on. A good teacher can help enormously. She can keep an eye on your child, put sanctions in place against bullying and change the atmosphere in the class. By laying down the rules to the entire group she can prevent further incidents without drawing attention to your child. She can also foster a culture where no one stands by and lets bad things happen to other people, by reinforcing that anyone can come and talk to her.

***'But my child won't let me talk to his teacher about it.'***
Your child may not realize that his teacher can help him without dropping him in it. If he insists you don't tell anyone, be sympathetic but don't make any promises. It can be very hard not to cave in to your child's pleading, but you may need to talk to someone at school, so be honest and don't say you won't.

### *Try being a COMMANDO PARENT*

#### *Give information*

- *'I can tell you are worried. The last thing I want to do is make things worse for you by embarrassing you or getting you into more trouble. But I'm not saying I definitely won't talk to your teacher. Depending what happens, we need to keep our options open.'*

- *'Bullies rely on people not telling. That is how they keep their power. But your teacher can sort this out without anyone ever knowing I spoke to her.'*
- *'If we tell your teacher, you are helping yourself as well as anyone else he picks on. We can't just do nothing and let him carry on.'*

You might want to go directly to the head. Don't feel embarrassed that you are wasting her time. A good head will have seen it all before and know exactly what to do.

If your child is being bullied, you can feel emotional and might get tearful when you talk about it. So write everything down before you go in. Then you'll have a road map to follow and won't forget the points you want to make.

> *My daughter came home with bruises on her legs. She said there was a gang of girls who were beating up the rest of the class. They'd kick them, push their faces in the dirt and pull their hair – all behind the trees so the teachers never saw.*
>
> *I asked a couple of other mothers if they knew about it. They admitted their daughters had told them, but they thought it sounded exaggerated. So they'd done nothing. I couldn't believe it!*
>
> *The next morning I went to see the headmistress. I was on the verge of tears as I told her who was in the gang, who was the leader, what they were doing, and my daughter's reaction – 'It makes me not want to go to school any more.'*
>
> *Well, the headmistress smashed that gang to smithereens. She found out exactly who was in it, and made each girl come to the front of the room and admit what they had done in front of her, the teacher and the entire class. She made it very clear that she didn't tolerate anything like that in her school, and anyone who did it again would be asked to leave.*

That week the bullies brought cookies into school for the others, to make it up to them. After that, the entire class was friends. This mother finished her story by saying:

*Every other girl in the class knew what was going on and either didn't tell their parents, or their parents didn't take them seriously. It made me realize that I have to listen and I have to act if my child needs me. I can't sit back and just let things happen.*

This headmistress was amazing, but other parents aren't so lucky. If your child is being bullied and the school is apathetic or doesn't know how to handle it, you are going to have to be proactive. Get as much information as you can from other parents and anti-bullying organizations. You may have to pressurize the school to call in an anti-bullying counsellor to train the staff and talk to the children. Try the internet for contacts and advice.

## Talk to the bully yourself

This is a definite no-no if you are full of emotion and convinced of your child's innocence. You can't talk to the perpetrator unless you are feeling calm, and are open to the possibility that there may be two sides to the story.

But if you can be reasonable and straightforward, you might be able to help.

*My daughter, Caitlin, and her best friend fell out. Caitlin was desperate to make it up. But her ex-friend wouldn't talk to her or even look at her. Then she started turning other friends against Caitlin. It was really bad.*

*One day, I spotted her ex-friend at a match, and I sat myself right next to her so she couldn't avoid me.*

*Of course I wanted to have a go at her, but instead I said, 'You and Caitlin don't have to be best friends any more. You don't even have to be friends. But it would be good if you could be nice to each other. Why don't I have a word with Caitlin and tell her the same thing?' She smiled and said it was a good idea.*

*Miraculously, after weeks of anguish, it was the turning point. Both girls realized it didn't have to be all or nothing; they could be friendly without being best friends.*

## Talk so the bully can overhear you

If engineered properly, this little strategy can work wonders.

> *My daughter was being pushed around by a girl called Mary. She refused to tell the teacher because she was afraid the bullying would get worse.*
>
> *I tipped off the teacher privately. Then later, when the bully was within earshot, I told the teacher in a loud voice that my daughter was being bullied, but didn't want to get her friend into trouble. I said that if it carried on, Lucy would have to tell me who it was.*
>
> *Her teacher said, 'You've done exactly the right thing because we don't allow bullying in this school ever, do we, Mary?' (turning to the girl who was the bully). Mary went absolutely white, and the problem stopped there.*

The teacher needn't be involved for this strategy to work.

> *Someone kept stealing my son's biscuits from his lunch. He worked out who it was, but was afraid to confront him because he was the toughest boy in the class.*
>
> *One morning when I dropped my son at school I said loudly, so the other boy could overhear, 'I respect your decision not to tell me who is stealing your biscuits. But if it happens again you will have to tell me straight away because the headmaster needs to know about it.' That was all it took. It never happened again.*

## Invite the bully over

This sounds such a lovely idea. If only the two children could see each other away from school, surely they'd get on and become friends. Unfortunately, it doesn't always work like that. It's a high-risk strategy that can go horribly wrong.

> *There is a girl in my daughter's class who keeps spreading mean stories about her. I thought we'd put an end to it by inviting her to play. The afternoon went quite well, and they seemed to have a great time.*
>
> *But the next day she was even fouler than ever before, and now she*

*had real ammunition. She even ridiculed the flowers on Annie's duvet cover. I wish we'd never invited her over.*

*One of the boys at school was throwing gravel at my son and pushing him around. His mother invited us over so the boys could play and get over their differences.*

*But it was a disaster. The other boy wouldn't cooperate. His mother was very embarrassed, and did everything she could to force him to play, but it just wasn't going to happen.*

Of course there must be times where everything has worked out, and sworn enemies have become best friends and soul mates. But don't try this one unless you are very sure of your ground.

## Talk to the bully's parents

On the face of it this also seems a great idea – be adult about it, have a civilized conversation and sort the problem out. Unfortunately, we know from our own experience, and the experience of many others, that talking to the other parents is usually a big mistake. If you think your child is being bullied you will be feeling emotional, and if you point the finger at their seemingly innocent little cherub, the other parents will get worked up too.

Before you know it, you might find yourself in the middle of an argument. The things that can come out of even the most respectable parents' mouths can be quite astonishing. So tread carefully.

*My best friend and I are very close, but when our children quarrelled, we each took our own child's side, and it got pretty ugly. We ended up making a pact that we will never discuss our children's fall-outs again.*

Our primal need to protect our children runs so deep that it is hard to stay rational, whether your child is being bullied or is accused of bullying. It's those protective instincts at work, ready to take out anyone who attacks our cubs. If the other parents won't accept your side of the story, you can feel indignant about it for years. Our advice? If it's a school-related problem, go straight to the school and let them handle it. They can talk to the other parents directly.

## Irritating children who get bullied

***'My child is the victim, but when I went to the school his teacher said that* his *behaviour has to change. She made me so angry. Surely she can't be right.'***

Children are often picked on for things they can't change – their colour, size, religion, eyesight, hair, dyslexia . . . the list goes on and on. The triggers for this kind of bullying aren't the victim's fault and the school should come down hard on the perpetrators.

But lots of cases are much less clear cut. You won't want to hear this, but if your child is the victim, you have to accept that his behaviour may be part of the problem.

> *Louis's mother was upset because some boys had been picking on him and calling him names. It's true. They have been. We can't tell her, but they hate him because he drives them crazy every day.*

Some children simply don't fit in very well with others, and this may be the case with yours. We are not talking about shyness, more about being irritating. If your child isn't naturally socially aware, it's not his fault. He may just be slightly immature compared to his peers.

Perhaps he doesn't pick up subtle signals about body language or tone of voice. He might lean in way too close when he talks, or shout, or burst out with inappropriate comments. He might tell a joke over and over again, even though no one else finds it funny. He might be the one still shuffling, talking or pulling faces when the teacher has told the class to settle down. He might be bossy, sulky, a tell-tale, or a fibber.

> *My son is so reactive that if someone accidentally bumps into him, he'll lash out and thump them back. He also shouts and screams when he's upset. Once he got so over-excited, he threw another child's hat out of the window. The teacher told me that he's a bully's dream. If the others are bored, they wind him up just to see what happens.*

Even if your child's behaviour is only slightly off, other children may start to get annoyed by it. Children are usually perceptive enough to notice when someone doesn't fit in, but they may not be mature enough to know how to deal with the fact that he's different. Irritating children can be rejected, called names, picked on mercilessly, or even used as a punch bag.

If your child is being bullied, it is far easier and less painful to blame the bully or the school for letting it happen. It's easy and normal to make excuses for him: 'It's not his fault. He's young for the class . . . The others are so unkind . . . His teacher is too inexperienced. The class is out of control.' But if you are in denial or busy blaming others, you run the risk of not helping him. He needs your support to change, and it won't happen if you keep justifying his behaviour and thinking of him as the victim.

> *My daughter was in tears because no one would play with her at break. I telephoned another mother in the class for advice. After a bit of prevarication, she told me the girls found my daughter annoying. When she lost in a game she'd sulk and try to make the others feel guilty. So they didn't want to include her any more.*
>
> *At first I was outraged. But eventually I spoke to my daughter about being a good loser and I have to admit, things seem to be going better for her.*

Some bullied children find they have even more to grapple with. Social problems often go hand in hand with behavioural or learning issues, like dyslexia, dyspraxia or mild autism. So your child may have a whole extra layer of frustrations to deal with.

If you suspect that your child may be irritating other children, there are a lot of ways you might help him. But there is no easy answer. You may need to reinforce the strategies in this chapter with the advice in Chapter Eight on changing difficult behaviour.

## When Your Child Is a Bully

***'I've heard that my child has been bullying other children. I'm so angry, I'd like to tear him limb from limb.'***

What do you do when you find out your child has been a bully? Parents' reactions are often quite extreme. They might feel rage and shame – how could their child be so stupid and mean? – or go into total denial – he isn't capable of such behaviour.

Usually the truth lies somewhere in the middle. Your child is both guilty and innocent. There's every chance your child did do something appalling, but there are almost always extenuating circumstances. Though there may be no excuse for what he has done, you may come to understand why it happened.

Some parents simply can't accept that their child has ever played a part in any problem. If you are convinced your child is completely squeaky clean, think again. It is a myth that bullies are always big tough kids from difficult families. Children bully for all sorts of different reasons. Every one of us has a good side and a bad side, and every one of us makes mistakes. Unless you recognize this in your own child, you won't be able to help him, and you can unintentionally put him under pressure. He may be so afraid of tarnishing your image of him that he'll do almost anything to cover up the truth. Even when he needs your moral support and guidance, he'll find it hard to be honest.

It's almost inevitable that your child will fall out with his friends, get into fights or hurt their feelings. Sometimes he will be the one to blame or the one who has caused the most damage. It is not pleasant when it happens, but it does.

### Reasons Why Your Child May Be a Bully

- ***Classic bullies*** throw their weight around because they think it's fun or they enjoy the power trip.
- ***Lack of social skills*** He may not be unkind, just tactless and heavy-handed.

- ***Reactive children*** lash out when people annoy them. He may not know how else to respond.
- ***Peer pressure*** Lots of children want to feel part of the group, and will exclude other children rather than be excluded themselves. It's risky to stick your neck out and stand up for the outsider, because the group could pick on you instead.
- ***Hormone surges*** These don't only happen during adolescence. Younger children get all sorts of pre-teen hormones which can make them feel bad-tempered and unsettled.
- ***Circumstances*** like divorce, peer pressure, a new baby, a new school or being bullied himself can make your child behave badly.
- ***Siblings*** If he is being picked on and bossed about by his siblings, he may treat other children the same way to feel more powerful.
- ***Parents*** Yes, it could be your fault if your child is a bully. It's hard, but look at your own behaviour.

**Are you:**

***Too authoritarian?*** If you shout, boss him around or compare him unfavourably to other children, he is likely to copy your example. When you hear your own words coming out of his mouth – in that same awful tone of voice – you know it is time to try something different.

***Too lenient?*** This is a hard one to accept, especially if you have reasons to worry about your child. You might feel extra protective because he's your youngest, or if he's had medical problems or learning difficulties. You might worry about him because you're moving house or getting divorced. It's your job to give him the benefit of the doubt. But if he never has to take responsibility for his behaviour, he'll never learn.

***Too distant?*** This, too, can be hard to come to terms with. Your child may be acting up because you are never around or there isn't a strong connection between you. He may feel angry, empty and desperate for attention.

If it's a classic case of bullying rather than a spat with a friend, the behaviour is more extreme and the feelings more intense, but the strategies to turn things around are the same. At both ends of the spectrum you need to help your child learn how to deal with his irritations without being aggressive or unkind.

### *'A mother phoned to tell me that my child has been bullying hers. What do I do?'*

Don't take sides. Don't agree with the other parent that your child is a demon, but don't start defending him or justifying his behaviour. Try:

- *'Thank you so much for letting me know. I'll go into school first thing in the morning to find out what happened and get this sorted out'*

or:

- *'Thank you so much for letting me know. I'll talk to him about it straight away.'*

Then you have a little time. Whether he made one snide remark or was caught beating up another child, your first job is to find out exactly what happened and hear his side of the story. If he can admit his part in it, you can help him to apologize and smooth things over. When this is all out of the way, you can work on a longer-term strategy so it doesn't happen again.

## Get him to tell you what happened

You need to hear his side of the story, but this probably won't be easy because talking about it means admitting what he's done. There are very few children who will willingly own up to something heinous.

## *Try being PAUSE PARENT* 

***Calm down fast and zip your lip*** If you feel consumed with rage or embarrassment, pause before you tackle the subject. It might be tempting to yell at your child, ground him or stop his pocket money, but it's important to listen before you pass judgement.

❛ *A neighbour complained about my children's behaviour in the communal garden. They'd cornered her daughter in the playhouse and barred the door. I was so angry. I had a real go at them the minute I picked them up from school.*

*Then I heard how this girl had been teasing and tormenting them for weeks – chanting 'Naa-na-na-naa-na,' calling them names and throwing their shoes into the bushes. Though they still had to apologize, I was secretly surprised they hadn't lashed out sooner.* ❜

You might get irritated if your child isn't forthcoming, but keep pausing.

❛ *My son's teacher reported that he'd hurt another boy in a fight and said I needed to talk to him. But when I asked him what had happened, he said he wasn't going to talk to me about it, not in a million years.* ❜

This shouldn't come as a surprise. It would be more surprising if your child owned up. If he's stonewalling you, take it as a good sign. Clearly he knows he's done something wrong, and silence is better than lying or denying anything happened. Once he goes down the lying route it is far more difficult for him to own up, ever.

❛ *My daughter's friend, who lives right round the corner, called her a sewer rat. When we went round to sort it out, the girl denied it completely. So her mother refused to believe anything had happened.*

*My daughter has refused to play with her ever since. She says she doesn't want a friend who's a liar. It's such a shame. It could have been patched up so easily with one little apology.* ❜

If your child is refusing to talk, count yourself lucky he's not lying, and leave it for a bit. Try again after a rest, a snack or some exercise, or he may be more receptive before bedtime or the following day.

## *Try being a TUNED-IN PARENT*

***Listen to their feelings*** If you want your child to tell you what happened, approach the subject in a calm, non-judgemental way. Instead of blaming him, go in with the attitude that he must have had his reasons and you are happy to hear them. Try:

- *'I know there are two sides to every story. I have heard the teacher's version. But I would like to hear yours.'*
- *'You must have been really irritated to have punched him like that. What happened?'*
- *'You seem pretty angry about something. I guess you've had a bad day.'*

Once he starts opening up, listen to him and accept his reasons without interrupting. By keeping silent you aren't giving him the green light to hit or hurt people. You are giving him the chance to let off steam. Once these feelings are out of the way he can think more rationally about his mistakes.

Children who are listened to tend to be more empathetic than children who aren't. After 'How did you feel?' has been talked through, you can more easily move on to 'How do you think the other person feels?' But it doesn't work the other way round.

## *Try being a COMMANDO PARENT*

If your child still won't talk, try stepping up the pressure a bit.

### *Give options*

- *'We need to talk about this. It's not optional. Do you want to talk now, or do you want to wait until bedtime?'*

### *Give information*

- *'Because your teacher has called me, we need to talk about this. Let's get it over with instead of making life difficult for each other.'*

If he still won't open up, there is no point in having a go at him. Instead, go back to tuning in. He is probably feeling ashamed or resentful and talking through what happened is the last thing he wants to do. He is far more likely to confide in you if he knows you are going to be sympathetic. But if he still won't discuss it, leave the subject and try again in the morning.

## Saying Sorry and Making Amends

The next stage is helping your child to say sorry and make it up to anyone he has hurt or offended. It is very important that he takes responsibility for what he has done. If it's a one-off incident, this is the quickest, most efficient way to end the whole blasted business, put it behind him and start again. If it is just the latest in a long list of crimes, he needs a chance to do something good, to prove to you and to himself that he is capable of being a decent human being.

It would be nice if you could persuade him to say sorry immediately. But even minor incidents are usually wrapped in layers of misunderstanding and animosity. You need time to calm down and so does he, and the tuning in may take longer than you think.

Don't force him to apologize straight away, unless you really have to. An unwilling sorry isn't worth much. You are aiming for a genuine apology and the following parent tools can help you achieve this.

### *Try being a LAID-BACK PARENT*

Even if it is perfectly obvious to you what your child should do next, don't drive him demented with a lecture. Start by asking him for ideas.

### Ask for solutions

- *'How can you say sorry?'*
- *'What could you do to cheer her up?'*
- *'What should you do about the things that broke?'*
- *'How can you be friends again?'*

He may have some good ideas, but help him adjust them if necessary.

> *My son said some nasty things, got into a row with his mates, and spent a friendless week feeling upset. I asked him what he could do. He said he wanted to buy them each a special toy. I thought that was a nice idea, and I told him so. But I suggested an easier solution: apologizing at break time and asking them if they'd like to play a game. He did, and that was the end of it.*

A simple apology is often all that's needed to be accepted right back into the fold. But if apologizing face-to-face is too much for your child, he might prefer it if you help him write a note. Then he can do several drafts, and the final version can be delivered so he doesn't have to see anybody.

> *My son and his friend were playing Ninjas, whirling their belts around. It was a stupid thing to do and the other child got hit in the face. Both children were partly to blame, but the other mother went ballistic and blamed my son completely. Talking made it worse. The situation only calmed down when we delivered a grovelling apology through their letter box.*

## Try being a COMMANDO PARENT

**Give consequences** Your child needs to understand the consequences of his behaviour, but that doesn't mean punishing him. Punishment can be too similar to bullying and give him the wrong messages. If you smack him, take away his toys or send him to his room, he is not learning from the inside that bullying is wrong; only that it feels better to be the person with power and it's not worth getting caught.

Some consequences are easy. If he has damaged someone's property, he needs to fix or replace it. But sometimes the consequences aren't so obvious. What if he has been excluding another child or hurt his feelings? If he has ruined someone's day, the natural consequence is that he needs to try to make that child's day better. Again, the first step is to apologize.

***Give information*** If he is still reluctant, try giving him information:

- *'It's difficult and embarrassing to say sorry, but we all have to do it because we all make mistakes.'*
- *'If you don't apologize, your teacher will carry on thinking the worst of you, which would be a shame.'*
- *'The quickest way to end this is by saying sorry. If you don't, this problem could go on and on.'*

If the other child is partly responsible, yours may not feel he needs to apologize at all, so you may need to explain why it is important.

- *'Saying sorry is hard, but at least you'll know you've done the right thing.'*

***Express your feelings*** Still refusing? You might get through to him if you tell him how you feel.

- *'It is embarrassing for me to have to stand next to Jim's mother every day outside the school gate when I know she is thinking bad things about you. I would be much happier if you said sorry. Then we could put this whole thing behind us.'*

Sometimes you may need to try being a combination of parent types before you get a result.

*‘Out of the blue, I got a phone call from the headmistress. My youngest son, my darling angel, had ploughed another boy's head into the sand, sat on him and made him cry.*

*When he came home, I badgered him all evening to tell me what happened. But he said, 'I'm not going to talk to you. Never.'*

*It was like he had slammed a door in my face and I felt like a complete failure.*

*But I got another chance two weeks later. This time someone called him names and he wrestled the boy to the ground. After dinner, I put him on my lap for a cuddle. Very lightly I said, 'I got a call from your headmistress. Sounds like you don't like being called names.' I was already resigned to the idea that he might not talk to me, so maybe he didn't feel any pressure. He poured out the whole story and I listened quietly.*

*Still keeping it light, I said, 'It sounds like this other boy wasn't happy about it. What could you do to make him feel better?' His face lit up. 'I could say I'm sorry.' His sister chimed in, 'And you could tell him you will never ever do that to him again.' He scowled. 'No,' he said. 'I'm not doing that. I'm only doing my ideas.'* ❜

### *'I've tried all of this, but he still won't say sorry. Maybe I should punish him until he does?'*

If nothing seems to be working, simply apologize on his behalf. You will feel less embarrassed and the situation will calm down faster. More importantly, it will be easier to work on his behaviour without so much bad feeling swirling around. You could talk to the teacher or write a note to the other parents.

- *'I just wanted to let you know that I am so sorry for what happened. I've talked to him, we're working on it, and we're trying to make sure that it doesn't happen again.'*

### *'But surely that's not right. He shouldn't get away with it like that.'*

As long as you don't ignore the problem, make excuses for him or discount what the victim says, you are not letting him 'get away' with bad behaviour. He still needs to take responsibility for what he's done.

But what you do next depends very much on the circumstances and your child's character. For some children, knowing that you know what happened is deeply embarrassing. Even if they are too ashamed to discuss it, let alone apologize, they learn their lesson.

With tougher children, forcing them to say sorry might be impossible until you have done a lot more work on their feelings and general behaviour. You will probably want to set up tough boundaries and consequences if your child re-offends (see below). Your ultimate aim is to help him learn from his mistakes and turn his behaviour around.

## Strategies to Stop Your Child Being a Bully

Saying sorry and making amends may stop your child from bullying again, but it might not be enough. There are always going to be other people who annoy him – parents, teachers, siblings, friends, co-workers and bosses – and he is going to have to learn to co-exist with them. So he has to find another way to respond. How to deal with his feelings without hurting others is one of the hardest things to learn. Here's how you can help him.

### *Try being a TUNED-IN PARENT*

***Listen to and accept difficult feelings*** The more you understand your child, the more you can help him. If he can unload his frustrations at home, he is less likely to take them out on others.

### *Try being a SORTED PARENT*

***Train them up*** Help him practise how to calm down and walk away when someone bothers him.

## *Try being a PHYSICAL PARENT* 

Whenever a child is having behavioural problems, a little red flag should go up – are sugar highs or lows, E-number overloads, or a lack of exercise or sleep the cause of his vile behaviour?

## *Try being a LAID-BACK PARENT* 

***Ask them for solutions*** and then ask how the other child might feel. His behaviour is more likely to change if the answers to these questions come from him rather than from you.

## *Try being a COMMANDO PARENT* 

He may not be able to come up with the answers or solve the problem himself. If not, it's up to you to tell him. You can also start setting some boundaries so he knows what's acceptable and what isn't.

### *Give information*

- *'Think how it feels when someone's mean to you. All you want is for them to be kind – not your best friend, just kind.'*
- *'She may be really irritating, but don't be nasty to her. Next week it could all turn around, and it could be you everyone is excluding.'*
- *'There are times you can rough and tumble, and times you can't. You can't at school. But wrestling at home with your dad or your brother is fine.'*
- *'You don't have to like Josh, and you are free to think whatever you want about him. But you can't punch him.'*

***Give consequences*** Your child may need consequences if he continues to misbehave. Tell him loud and clear what they will be, and stick to your word.

*❛ I'm ashamed to admit my son used to be a horrible bully. When he got frustrated he'd hit others, both at home and school. I did the best I*

*could, but nothing worked. Finally his teacher and I worked out a plan together. We both told him that people don't want to be with him if he hits them, so if he did it again, he'd be sent out of the room.*

*It didn't take long. That afternoon he thumped his little sister. Immediately I sent him upstairs. After a few more goes both at home and at school, he finally got the message and the hitting stopped.* ❜

If possible, make sure the consequence relates to the crime. If your child doesn't play nicely with the neighbours, then perhaps he shouldn't play with them for a week. If he hits a boy at a birthday party, perhaps he should go home.

## Helping Your Child Deal with Irritating Children

### *'There is a boy in the class who makes silly noises and drives my son crazy. Yesterday my son punched him. What should I do?'*

Your child is cooped up with all sorts of different characters in the classroom. It would be a miracle if he got on with all of them. Ironically, it's often sensitive children who act like bullies because they can't filter out annoyances. Even so, there's no excuse for your child to bully or exclude anyone.

### *Try being a TUNED-IN PARENT*

*Listen to their feelings* If your child finds someone irritating, your pleas for tolerance – 'Just ignore him' or 'Try to give him a chance' – are far more likely to work if you accept his feelings first.

- *'Yes. I can see how that noise would irritate you.'*
- *'It would bother me too if someone was giving me funny looks all day.'*
- *'How frustrating that you all missed break time because he was misbehaving.'*

Your tuning in will give him the chance to chew through his irritation in an appropriate way. The idea is to get it out of his system so he doesn't gossip or lash out at the other child.

The more he can understand his own feelings – 'Why am I feeling annoyed?' – the easier it should be to understand the other person's feelings – 'Why is he behaving that way?'

## *Try being a COMMANDO PARENT*

***Give information*** After you've tuned in, it might help if you explain what life might be like for the other child.

> *There was a new girl in the class from Romania. My daughter wasn't impressed: 'She's annoying . . . She's shy . . . She's strange . . . She doesn't look us in the face . . . She's got a funny accent.'*
>
> *I said, 'Are you surprised? In one week she's moved to a new country, moved house and moved school. No wonder she's a bit shy and doesn't fit right in.'*

Once your child has a clearer understanding, he might be more compassionate.

> *There is a girl in my daughter's class who is incredibly irritating. She's clumsy, she shows off and I'm pretty sure she has some minor learning difficulties.*
>
> *Well my daughter couldn't stand her, and was horrible about her. After listening to her moaning, I said, 'You know, Jo has a hard time with everything at school. She finds sport, schoolwork and making friends difficult. I think that's why she tries so hard to get attention and make everyone laugh.'*
>
> *After that, my daughter saw her in a different light. Instead of moaning about her all the time, my daughter has been her champion at school, sticking up for her and stopping anyone else from being mean.*

## *Try being a SORTED PARENT*

***Train them up*** Your child might be more allergic to irritating children than most. If teaching him compassion and understanding doesn't work, try giving him strategies to cope. The best thing to teach him is how to leave irritating people alone and stop getting involved. This usually means walking away from provocation.

Try getting him to practise strategies at home to help him stay out of trouble.

❛ *My son, Sam, kept getting into trouble with the same boy. Every day they wound each other up, back and forth, with small insults turning into bigger ones until they were scuffling and fighting.*

*We practised and practised what Sam should do if he was provoked, and finally one day he pulled it off. The other boy kicked his shin and Sam said, 'I don't care if you kick me,' turned around and walked away.*

*To his surprise the other boy got so annoyed he attacked Sam as he walked off. The teacher saw him do it and sent him to the headmistress. Sam was so delighted that he now does this at any sign of trouble. That's a huge improvement from kicking back.* ❜

### *Try being a LAID-BACK PARENT* 

***Ask for solutions*** Ask your child what he thinks he could do. Help him write down a list. Ideas might include: going off to the bathroom to calm down, going to the other end of the queue or playground, or finding someone else to talk to.

# Other Things You Can Do When Your Child is a Bully

No matter why your child is being a bully, it would be great if you could sort out all his difficulties at home. But you might need to get other people involved.

## Work with the school

If your child has been tormenting other children, you may be embarrassed about talking to his teacher. But be brave and do it. He needs to learn to get on with other children and his teacher probably has the experience and the tools to help him.

*When my son was being aggressive, his teacher got the whole class to suggest rules, ten specific things they could do and ten things they couldn't. For example: be kind, be helpful, no kicking, no name-calling. She printed out the whole set, and gave them to each child on a card. When everyone had coloured in their card, she laminated them.*

## Talk to the other child yourself

If you're trying to find out what happened or want to smooth things over, you might try talking to the other child directly. This might work, but take into account that the child who's been bullied may be upset and not really want to talk to you, or may feel uncomfortable talking to other adults about his feelings.

## Talk to the other parents

This sounds like the most civilized thing to do, but be careful. Rather than smooth things over, the atmosphere can become explosive, just as it can backfire when your child is the victim.

*I got a call from the other father in the school run. He was furious. He said, 'What's all this about your son bullying Hugo?' I was flabbergasted. I didn't know anything about it. As far as I knew the boys got along fine.*

*When my son got home from school he admitted that he'd kicked Hugo in the football match the day before, and had been sent off the pitch for it. I wanted to sort the problem out as fast as possible, so we went round to Hugo's house to apologize.*

*When we got there his parents wouldn't let us speak. In fact they shouted at us. These were two professional people, but they were out of control. After ten minutes or so I said shakily, 'I think we'd better go,' and we left.*

*The boys made friends again immediately but we parents still don't speak. And I am so angry. It turns out that Hugo has been sent off lots of times for kicking other boys. His parents made out that he was the victim, but the reality isn't like that at all.*

*The car pool ended, which is a real pain, and as we live so close we often bump into each other, which is excruciating. Hugo used to have seizures when he was a baby, so maybe they're extra-protective. I'm trying to see it from their point of view. But it's hard.* ’

Parents often feel grievances longer and more deeply than their children.

‘ *The headmaster phoned and said my son was bullying a new boy in his class. I was horrified. When I saw his mother the next day I went up to her to apologize but she refused to talk to me. Instead she hissed, 'I have nothing to say to you and I don't want to talk to you. Just go away.' I have tried to be friendly since, but she stares right through me, which is ridiculous because that was two years ago and the boys are good friends now.* ’

If your child has done something awful, you'll feel much better if you help him to say sorry or apologize yourself. But the other family may need days, weeks or months to calm down. If the other parents are very protective or have bullying issues from their own childhood, they may not be able to forgive your child or be nice to you. After you've done your bit, wait for them to make the next move – if they ever do.

Learning social skills is a long process. It might take your child many years to figure out the right way to behave, and it takes some children a lot longer than it takes others. Most of us have regrets ourselves, times when we wish we had treated people differently.

If you tell your child he has terrible manners or call him a bully, it will be harder for him to change. He is a child who has made some mistakes, just like all the rest of us. So once he's apologized, don't mention it again. Let it go. Even if he has done something outrageous, give him the freedom to learn from his mistakes, to change, and to move on; not to be remembered for them.

‘ *When I was ten, I got into a huge fight with my brother. I picked up a kitchen knife and waved it at him to make my point. I never had any intention of doing anything with it, but my mother started screaming in total hysteria, 'GIVE ME THAT KNIFE! Oh my God! GIVE ME THAT KNIFE!' I didn't hear the end of it for weeks, even years afterwards.*

*Last week my eleven-year-old did exactly the same thing. I found her arguing with her brother and waving a knife around. I know she's not out of control, she's not delinquent, and she's a good kid. I said, 'That's not what knives are for. If you slip, there could be an accident.'*

*'I wasn't going to do anything,' she said.*

*'I know,' I said, 'but please don't do that again.' And that was the end of it.*

# 5

# The Great Family Food Fight

## Courgettes *v.* Krispy Kremes

Wouldn't it be wonderful if our children filled up on healthy, nutritious food and there was always a pleasant atmosphere at the table – no junk-food addicts, no fussy eaters, no moaning and no complaining? But given that most children love the rubbish marketed as children's food, changing the habits of your household may be far from easy. If it means replacing junk with vegetables, you certainly aren't going to win any popularity contests. Even if you buy lots of delicious fresh food, there's no guarantee your children will eat any of it. In fact, it may well just rot at the back of the fridge.

Feeding our children should be simple: we put good, healthy food in front of them and they eat it. That's it. Job done. But the reality can be very different.

Some children hardly eat a thing.

> *My son picks at his food. Every meal is a battle. I plead. I threaten. I make deals. I get so angry with him.*

Some only eat a tiny range of food.

> *She only eats white things. She'll have pasta and grated cheese, mashed potato and white bread. That's it. She just refuses to eat anything else. I'm worried sick about it.*

Some flatly refuse to eat vegetables.

*He'll only eat peas. I don't bother cooking other vegetables for him. It's not worth it.*

Some throw a wobbly if their food isn't just right.

*My son can't stand it if his food is mixed up, like if the pasta sauce is mixed in with the spaghetti. Everything has to be separate or he throws a tantrum, refuses to eat it, and insists I give him something else. It makes me want to wring his neck.*

Having a fussy eater can be such a pain. But it can also be very frightening. You wouldn't be alone if you found yourself doing all sorts of crazy things just to get your child to eat.

*My son hardly eats. This morning he refused to have breakfast. So I gave him cheesecake with chocolate sauce. At least I knew he was getting some calcium.*

But picky eaters haven't cornered the food-issue market. Having an overweight child can be just as worrying. It's not uncommon for a child's weight to creep up slowly and take parents by surprise. Then they haven't a clue what to do about it.

*I didn't realize my daughter was overweight until she started getting teased at school. If I don't do something about it she'll just get fatter, so that's not the answer. But I'm afraid if I talk to her about it I'll just make her feel worse. And I don't want to give her a complex. Maybe I should put her on a diet? But she's only young. What do I do?*

Then there are the junk-food addicts.

*All the good stuff I put in my son's lunch comes home every day untouched, but he eats the KitKat and biscuits. Then, after school, he wants three packets of crisps. I am tempted to ban chocolate and crisps, but he'll go berserk and he's got to eat something.*

Even if your child isn't a total junk-food addict, the pestering can go on and on.

*I hate going to the supermarket with my daughter because she pesters me for junk. She wants white bread, chocolate fingers, Fruit Winders,*

*Cheese Dippers, Pringles and Haribo. How does she even know about this stuff?*'

Some parents worry because their child is underweight and others worry because their child is overweight, but it's remarkable how many get a double whammy and have one of each.

'*My oldest has a huge appetite. She's a big girl and she'll eat anything. Then there's my youngest, who is so skinny and hardly eats a thing. It's a nightmare. I try to encourage one to eat less, and the other to eat more to fatten her up. But it isn't working.*'

But regardless of what your family's food issues are, there is one simple **Physical Parent** formula that should help every member of your family, including you: aim for a healthier lifestyle that includes plenty of nutritious fresh food and exercise.

If your child is heavy, you will see the benefits of her eating healthier food and exercising more almost immediately. Though her appetite may increase once she starts doing more exercise, it's pretty hard to stay overweight if you are exercising and not eating a bunch of junk. Your goal is not to get her to eat less, but to eat better and move about more.

If she is thin, stuffing her with cheesecake and chocolate isn't the answer. Again, focus on nutritious, healthy food and plenty of exercise and you are likely to see the benefits almost immediately. Her appetite is likely to increase from the exercise and you'll be happy because you'll know that she is getting the nutrition she needs.

If she is somewhere in between, count your blessings, and aim for her to become healthier by – guess what? – doing the same things: giving her plenty of nutritious, fresh food and making sure she gets plenty of exercise.

Even if you have one chubby and one skinny child, the same holds true. Your job is to consider the health of your entire family, not restrict the calories of one while bulking up the other. Your aim is to make sure they both get plenty of nutritious fresh food and plenty of exercise.

Our goal in this chapter is to help you solve your family's food issues. If you are feeling anxious because your child isn't eating enough, is eating too much, or is eating the wrong things, we'll show you how to make changes and stop worrying. If she is manipulating you by arguing over food, we will show you how to get back in charge. If the atmosphere at your dinner table is terrible and mealtimes have become a battlefield, we will show you step-by-step how to transform them. And if your child eats so much junk she could be classified as malnourished, we'll show you how to turn things around.

## Handling Your Family's Food Issues

Most parents worry at some time that their child isn't eating properly. Some are quite good at providing decent food, but find they have to coax, plead and negotiate to make sure it's eaten. Once your child starts getting lots of attention for being fussy or not eating, the dining table can easily turn into a combat zone where food is used as a weapon by both sides to gain control.

> *I always have to coax her to eat – three bites of this before she can have pudding, two spoonfuls of that before she can get down. I'm sick of doing it.*

Many other parents think they are doing all they can to get their child to eat properly. But for one reason or another, they cave in and let her eat more junk than they would like.

> *I gave my son porridge and he said he hated it. I told him he couldn't go to school without breakfast, but he refused to eat. I got more and more desperate, and finally I piled cream and golden syrup on top.*
> *'You can't say you don't like it now,' I said.*
> *'I'm not going to admit I like it,' he said. 'I've got my pride.'*
> *He went off to school with a chocolate muffin.*

If their child refuses to eat the food on her plate, these parents tend to worry and bend over backwards to make sure she eats something. Though they might feel they've done their best and it's not their fault, they are ultimately responsible if she ends up eating a bunch of junk.

Other parents know they have a problem on their hands because their child is overweight or eats a very restricted range of food. But for one reason or another (see pp. 166–8) they don't commit to doing anything about it.

If any of this sounds familiar, don't beat yourself up for being too controlling or caring too much, and don't feel guilty for giving in too easily or being too much of a softy. Lots of parents have found themselves in similar situations, and it is possible to turn things around.

If you want to make some changes to your family's eating habits, it might help to understand why you are worried or why you can't get to grips with their food issues.

## Why We Worry About What Our Children Eat

- ***We want them to be fit and healthy***
- ***We want them to be confident and fit in*** If a child is skinny or overweight she can get teased or bullied.
- ***Our survival instincts*** For more than 99 per cent of our evolution, food was scarce and parents had to be vigilant to keep their children alive. Now, though food is abundant, we're still programmed to worry.

  If your child had trouble feeding, lost weight or was seriously ill as a baby, it wouldn't be unusual if you were still worrying about her eating enough, even ten years later.
- ***Alarming media reports*** Although historically we've never had better access to such a wide range of good, healthy food, there are so many frightening food issues it's hard to ignore them: obesity, anorexia, salmonella, BSE, nut allergies, pesticides, trans-fats, additives – the list goes on and on.

## Why We Avoid Getting To Grips with Food Issues

It can be hard to get your children to eat properly. Though you may have been thinking about making changes for a while, you may still be avoiding the issue. Why bother buying and cooking healthy food if all they are going to do is complain bitterly and refuse to eat it?

It's not as though any of us consciously go out of our way to make our lives easier at the expense of our children's health. But we are often chronically tired or short of time and money. So we go for the fastest, easiest or cheapest options – using the car for the school run, letting the kids watch TV in the afternoon while we get on with other things, giving them a packet of crisps to keep them going until supper, and heating up ready meals instead of cooking proper food.

> *I feel guilty. I know I shouldn't buy ready-made meals, but I work, and at the end of the day I'm tired. I can pop one in the microwave, and seconds later – ping! It's all ready. No mess. No hassle. No washing up. And they eat it.*

Here are some of the most common reasons why you might be procrastinating:

### Fear of a backlash

What parent in their right mind would relish the idea of making unpopular changes to their child's diet? Just the thought of it is enough to put anyone off. It's no surprise so many parents stick to food they know their children like.

You want your child to think of you as a nice, kind parent, not an ogre. If you yourself were forced as a child to eat food you hated, you might feel particularly strongly that you don't want your own child to suffer the same way.

If the thought of confrontation is holding you back, we've got a whole section on minimizing your child's hostility and getting her to go along with the changes you want to make (see pp. 181–3).

## Lack of time

You may feel like giving up before you have even started, overwhelmed at the thought of the effort it's going to take to get your child to eat properly. Never mind the time wasted arguing, what about planning, organizing and preparing the meals?

Apparently the average Briton spends a measly thirteen minutes a day preparing food. We want to reassure you that it's possible (though not easy) to produce fresh food in the same time. The key is to keep things simple. It takes five minutes to put a chicken and vegetables in the oven, and you can peel an orange or a banana or wash an apple in about the same time it takes to get out a chocolate yoghurt and spoon.

It might help to remember that you don't have to prove you're a wonderful parent by giving your child perfect food. The historical biographer Elizabeth Longford was asked how she managed to bring up eight children and write so many books. She thought for a moment and said simply, 'Baked potatoes with everything, and fresh fruit afterwards.'

If you're concerned about how long it's going to take to get proper food on the table, we will give you plenty of ideas how to provide it quickly and easily.

## Lack of money

Fresh food doesn't have to be more expensive than ready-made food – in fact it can often cost less. A piece of fruit costs no more than a chocolate bar, a baked potato is cheaper than chips, and tap water costs nothing compared to fizzy drinks or juice. The question to ask yourself is – how can processed food be so cheap when you factor in the cost of manufacturing it?

### Lack of confidence

You simply might not know where to start.

### Inertia

You'll get round to it one day, maybe.

### A battle of wills

You may feel you are already doing everything you can to get your child to eat properly, but nothing seems to be working. If this is the case, we will show you how to make a breakthrough.

## Making Changes

Ideally our children would grow up to like healthy food without much effort on our part. But in reality, it's up to us to seize the initiative. Preparing healthy, home-cooked meals is a hassle, it takes time and your child may complain like crazy. So why not give her the food she likes, even if it's a fizzy drink and chicken nuggets?

We don't believe children have to stick to a perfectly balanced, organic, sugar-free diet, and we don't believe that guilt or anxiety help. But despite the attractive child-friendly packaging and manufacturers' bold claims, food aimed at children is often the lowest-quality food you can buy. You know the stuff we mean – the endless ready-meals, dippers, sausages, chips, crisps, biscuits, sweets, drinks and breakfast cereals, loaded with fat, sugar, salt and additives. You may assume that as they're produced for children it's OK to eat them, but if you looked closely at the ingredients, you might think again.

The trouble is, kids love the stuff. It is cleverly packaged, specifically targeted at them with millions of pounds' worth of sophisticated advertising, and then bulked up with foul things to hide the lack of quality.

As author Annabel Karmel puts it, 'It is shocking that at a time when diet is most crucial to health, the label "children's food" represents some of the worst-quality, most unhealthy food on offer.'

Children know what's out there and are desperate to have it. But your child doesn't buy her food – you do. She is too young to know what's best for her, and shouldn't be expected to make the right decisions. As the chef Jamie Oliver pointed out, we don't send our children off to school and then ask them to choose what they want to do there: 'They'd say they didn't want to do maths and then run around poking each other's eyes out with compasses.'

You may be putting it off, but there are a lot of benefits to cutting down on the junk. Fresh, unprocessed food is far better for your child and less likely to make her overweight. There have been numerous studies which link consumption of junk food to learning and behavioural problems. If she is rude, lazy, hyperactive, unfocused or has learning difficulties, it is definitely worth checking out her diet.

In his television series about school dinners, Jamie Oliver persuaded a family to substitute fresh food for their usual junk food. The results were staggering: within days the children's tantrums and mood swings had stopped; within a week, their whole family life had changed for the better. Changing your child's food may or may not be the answer, but you'll lose nothing by trying.

## What to Watch Out For

- ***Additives*** In general, the longer the list of E-numbers, flavourings, colourings and preservatives, the less likely it is that the food is good for your child.
- ***Sugar*** Watch out for sneaky labelling – glucose, fructose, corn syrup and high-fructose corn syrup are all forms of sugar. Too much sugar can lead to blood-sugar highs and lows and obesity, increase your child's chances of

developing diabetes and will almost certainly ruin her teeth. If products boast that they are sugar-free, they are often full of artificial sweeteners instead.

- ***Glycaemic load*** Try to avoid quick-release carbohydrates like white bread, white pasta and white rice. These are converted rapidly into sugar, which goes into your child's bloodstream too fast and can leave her feeling tired and grumpy.
- ***Bad and good fats*** Try to avoid hydrogenated fats and partially hydrogenated fats altogether, as they are linked with all sorts of health problems. Stay away from fried and deep-fried foods. Keep saturated-fat intake fairly low and stick to lean meat. Monosaturates (like olive oil) and polyunsaturates (like sunflower oil) are fine. The essential fatty acids found in nuts, seeds and oily fish are considered to be very good for brain development and behaviour.
- ***Intolerance*** Try to avoid giving your child too much of one staple food. It's so easy to serve cereal for breakfast, a sandwich for lunch and pasta for tea. But that's three meals based on wheat. A variety is much better. Overeating a particular food can lead to intolerances which, in turn, can lead to all sorts of behavioural issues including hyperactivity, tantrums and tiredness. Ironically, lots of fussy eaters have food intolerances, and crave the things to which they are sensitive.
- ***Organic*** Just because ice-cream, biscuits or crisps are organic doesn't mean they are good for you. And even if something is labelled organic, it isn't necessarily additive-free. Most organic producers have their customers' health and best interests at heart. But some food corporations will add pesticides and artificial additives into their products where legally possible, perhaps thinking we won't notice.

We all know healthy food is good for our children. Saying it is easy; the problem is getting them to eat it. So where should you start?

## Unhook Yourself Emotionally

Before you do anything:

### *Try being a PAUSE PARENT*

*Zip your lip* If you are worried about your child, stop nagging, pleading or coercing her to eat properly. And don't make her feel guilty because of the trouble you took to cook the meal or because of the starving people in Africa.

If she isn't eating properly, we aren't saying you should give up. But you need to untangle yourself from any dramas about food. You want her to fill up on healthy food of her own accord and stop eating when she is full. At some point you are going to have to stop micro-managing what she eats, and it might as well be now.

#### *'But if I don't make her eat, she won't eat a thing.'*

The hardest time to pause is when your child is super fussy or refuses to eat. Picky eaters tap right into our primal fears. It's hard not to panic – it's innate. From the moment she was born, your overriding responsibility has been to make sure she survives, and to do so she's got to eat. But these primal fears can get out of hand, especially if your child is small or slight. If she doesn't eat as much as you think she needs, alarm bells start ringing and you can get caught up in caring too much. It's not uncommon for otherwise sane parents to obsess about what their child is eating, forever keeping a mental tally of what's going into her mouth, and making constant comments about it.

- *'Come on. Have one little sausage. You need some protein.'*
- *'You're so skinny. You've got to eat something.'*
- *'You don't want it? Aren't you feeling well? Shall I get you something else?'*

Before you know it, mealtimes have turned into a vicious cycle:

Child refuses to eat.

Parent gets wound up and uses any means possible – bribes, threats, rewards, 'Here comes the little choo-choo train into the tunnel' – to get child to eat arbitrary amount parent has decided is right for child.

Child enjoys attention, so doesn't eat again at next meal.

> *Of course I'd prefer not to have to force the issue, because I don't want to give her a food complex. But I've got no choice. She's tiny and she's so picky. I've got to coax her to eat. If I don't, there's no way she'll eat enough.*

We've even known a couple of families where parents were still spoon-feeding their school-age children.

> *When my daughter started in reception, the headmistress called me in and said she was scooping up her shepherd's pie with her fingers. I was embarrassed to admit she had never fed herself. I'd always fed her because I was worried about her. If I didn't feed her she wouldn't eat a thing.*

One parent we know follows her plump four-year-old around the kitchen, shovelling chocolate biscuits into her mouth to ensure she eats enough.

These parents may seem to have lost the plot. But you can't blame them. They feel they are only doing their job. The problem is that your child's eating, or not eating, can so easily end up becoming a power struggle between the two of you. If you're not careful, you can end up getting locked in a continuous battle which, in the long-term, can screw up her relationship both with food and with you.

Regardless of whether your child is fat or thin, you can find yourself negotiating over food.

- *'Go on, be a good girl. Three more mouthfuls of carrot and then you can have your pudding.*

  *OK, then, two more mouthfuls of carrot and a slice of courgette.*

*No, that doesn't count as a mouthful. If you want that pudding you need to put more on your fork.*
*You don't want pudding? Well you have to eat your carrots anyway.'*

Suddenly you can find yourself in the middle of a big hoo-ha, with your child getting all sorts of attention for not eating. But try to remember your aim is for her to eat properly without any coaxing. So the next time you feel the urge coming on, zip your lip and resist all temptation to negotiate. She isn't going to shrivel up if she doesn't eat her carrots. You might think it's impossible to keep your thoughts and feelings to yourself, or to stop tallying up what she is eating. But if you really want to help her, you need to keep your own concerns and emotions away from the table.

## *'My child refuses to eat what I give her and you want me to ignore it?'*

*Keep things in perspective* Yes, we know it's a major pain in the neck when you provide decent food and your child turns her nose up at it. It's even more irritating if she fills up later on cereal. But we are still only taking baby steps here, and working on damage limitation. A lot of minor blips only become problems in the first place because you start focusing on them. So do what you can to keep the problem in perspective.

*'When I was a child I went through eating phases. One holiday I refused to eat anything except hard-boiled eggs and strawberry ice-cream with wafers. My parents were quite sensible and didn't make a big deal of it. They knew I wouldn't starve in a week and once we got home I ate normally again.'*

If your child starts throwing a wobbly over food, just pause. Say nothing and ignore it. You may not need to say another thing about it.

*'My son recently went through a phase of refusing to eat. A friend told me I should relax and ignore it, and he would be just fine. So I put a*

*variety of food on his plate, carried on eating my own meals as though nothing was going on, took away his plate after a reasonable amount of time, and didn't say a word. It only lasted a couple of days, and we haven't had a problem since. Well, not about food, anyway!*'

If you don't keep quiet, it's easy to make things worse: apart from enjoying the attention, you don't want to encourage your child to think of herself long-term as a bad eater or a picky eater. So instead of trying to control what she puts in her mouth, back off, pipe down, sit on your hands, do whatever it takes to think about something else, and stop watching what she is eating out of the corner of your eye.

If she doesn't eat a meal, try to accept that she isn't going to eat it and move on. If she is hungry later and you don't mind, she can eat her meal then. But don't fall back into the coaxing routine, don't offer alternatives and don't allow her to raid the snack cupboard.

### 'But my child has a serious problem, and you want me to ignore it?'

Start with a reality check. How severe is her problem? Is she actually anaemic, malnourished, obese, or anything close? If so, take her straight to the doctor. If not, are you worrying unnecessarily?

'*My son had a terrible case of the runs, so I took him to the doctor. The doctor said he had to eat easily digestible foods – only chicken, rice and bananas – for a week. A week! I was petrified. 'But won't that make him ill?' I asked.*

*The doctor reassured me, 'Your son is perfectly healthy. A week won't hurt him, but it will give his stomach a chance to settle down. You'd be amazed what other children in the world survive on.'*'

Of course, temporarily ignoring the problem is going to be much easier if your child is tall, strong, red-cheeked and energetic. But even if she is skinny or overweight, if she is doing OK at school, playing sports and games, and seems generally healthy and happy, keep things in perspective. We know one thirteen-year-old who literally hasn't eaten a single piece of fruit since she choked on a satsuma when she was two. But she is fit and healthy, and one of the brightest girls in her class.

It's also important to take a look at your body shape and your partner's. If your child is small and slender, or muscular and stocky, were either of you the same as children? Or are other members of your families built like her? As one Jamaican health visitor put it, you don't get bananas from a mango tree, or the other way round. So don't be unrealistic about your child's shape.

### *'You're telling me to be calm? But my daughter will only eat jam sandwiches on white bread. And I mean only!'*

*Calm down fast* This situation deserves an entry in the parent's-worst-food-nightmare hall of fame. Staying calm is going to be difficult, but you've got to do it. The more you worry about her eating, the more she will pick up your stress. However anxious you feel, you have to trust that this is a problem that can be solved in time.

*'Our daughter refused to eat anything but white bread and white pasta. It was a desperate situation. Her face was translucent and we were panicking. I took her to the doctor, who said she was anaemic.*

*He said I was making everything worse by worrying, and I should just serve her normal food. I was furious with him. What did he expect me to do, sit back and let her starve? But nothing else was working, so I followed his advice – though I put a bit of pasta or bread out for her alongside our regular food. At first she refused to try anything new. I calmly said she didn't have to eat anything she didn't want to. There was no pleading, no coercing, no watching her every spoonful. To be honest, it was agonizing, but after only a couple of meals she started to help herself. What a relief.'*

### *'What if I ignore the problem and nothing changes?'*

But something *has* changed – you aren't making the problem worse. You've stopped bringing your own anxieties to the table and stopped putting pressure on your child to eat. Ignoring her behaviour (what she is or is not eating) does *not* mean you are ignoring the problem. Your goal is to get her to think for herself and eat proper food, whether you are there or not. Removing yourself from the equation is essential.

Sometimes refusing to get drawn in is enough to break the cycle. Without all the stress at the table, your child may feel more confident and relaxed about eating.

If you also need to change the kind of food you are serving (more vegetables, for example), pausing is still a good place to start. It will give you time to think through your strategy, and once you've unhooked yourself, you may find it's much easier to make changes than you think.

## *Try being a SORTED PARENT*

***Sort your systems*** If you haven't had the time or energy to make sure your children get good food, don't feel guilty about it. Those who have already managed this feat tend to be either naturally **Physical** or **Sorted Parents**.

For **Physical Parents** this issue is so important it automatically floats to the top of their list of priorities. But **Sorted Parents** are the ones to watch. If there's something they want to achieve, they organize it instead of hoping they'll get round to it one day. They notice what they need to change and work out how to do it.

Here are some of the kinds of problems you might be facing:

- *No time in the mornings for breakfast, so your child gets into the car with a cereal bar or a muffin.*
- *She comes home from school starving, wolfs down biscuits and won't eat supper. Then later she says she wants cereal.*

If you want to set up some new systems, there are no hard and fast rules. If your children are hungry when they get home from school, maybe they could eat their main meal straight away instead of snacking. Or they could have a healthier snack by swapping fruit salad for biscuits, and a late dinner when they are hungry again.

## Get Your Cupboards Sorted Out

If you want your child to eat healthier food, it's up to you to provide it. There's no point expecting her to snack on fruit or rice cakes when there are loads of crisps and biscuits in the cupboard. It all comes down to clearing out the rubbish and only buying food you're happy for her to eat. Then when she reaches for a snack you know you don't have to worry, and whatever she eats at mealtimes, you know she is getting something nutritious.

It might help to spend an extra hour at the supermarket having a good look at the labels and finding alternatives. These days there are healthier, usually tastier alternatives to almost everything. You can buy tinned sweetcorn without sugar, all-natural organic children's bio yoghurt, and wholemeal biscuits without additives or hydrogenated fats. By reading the labels, you can cut back on a lot of junk quite painlessly.

## Get One Step Ahead of Meals

The next part of getting sorted is accepting that mealtimes are going to keep coming round, and you may as well be ready for them. If you are perpetually caught off guard it's very hard to come up with healthy food. If you find you're often cobbling together pre-packaged or makeshift meals when everyone is screaming for their supper, here is how you might make changes.

### Simple Tips from Naturally Sorted Parents

- Put baked potatoes or a chicken in the oven ahead of time, instead of last-minute oven chips and microwave dinners.
- Make a rotating fortnightly menu planner. This may sound too organized to be true, but it can be worth trying. The meals don't have to be elaborate (baked beans on toast or ham and salad is fine). A planner cuts out the mental slog of

thinking of different things to cook every day, and makes it obvious what you need on your shopping list. If you can't think of anything to put on the meal planner, there are plenty of books out there that will help you. When you do cook, cook in bulk. Make three shepherd's pies at a time and freeze two for later. Keep a large casserole or cooked ham in the fridge to eat over several days.

- Keep a stock of healthy ingredients. Put portions of meat and fish in the freezer instead of ready-meals, and remember to defrost in the morning, instead of serving last-minute nuggets.
- No more emergency dashes to the supermarket. Get on the internet and do your grocery shopping. Once you get going, your weekly shop will take you less than half an hour, and be delivered to your door.

### *Try being a PHYSICAL PARENT*

***'I can go out and buy all sorts of good food, but how on earth am I ever going to get her to eat any of it?'***

*Feed them well* There are all sorts of clever ways to encourage your child to eat the healthy stuff. Here are some simple practical ideas. For overcoming more difficult hurdles, see How to Minimize Your Child's Hostility, p. 181.

## Easy Ways to Get Your Child to Eat Fruit and Vegetables

The simplest way to get your child to eat healthy, nutritious food is to keep putting it out, ready to eat, in an obvious place. Don't force her to eat any of it. If you say anything, just casually mention it's there: 'There's fruit salad on the table.'

- *Slice fruit first thing in the morning and put it on the table. Your child will be hungry when she comes down for breakfast and it will be the first thing she sees.*
- *Leave a fruit salad out on the table with a bowl and spoon so she can help herself when she gets home from school.*
- *Leave sliced raw vegetables out in the afternoon or before dinner. Try cherry tomatoes, carrot and cucumber sticks, coloured peppers, sugarsnap peas or raw peas. That way when she comes mooching around the kitchen looking for something to munch on, they're easy to grab.*
- *Leave hummus or guacamole out to use as a dip. Your children will have no idea it's actually good for them.*
- *Plain, boring vegetables are plain and boring. Take the time to learn to cook them with garlic, lemon, herbs, soy sauce, or even a bit of butter. Children are also more likely to eat salad if they like the dressing.*
- *At mealtimes, serve the less nutritious food later.*

> *At weekends we love going to the café in the park. But they serve chips with everything, and once our kids fill up on them they refuse to eat anything healthy. It took us a while to figure it out, but the answer was so simple. We ask for the chips to come afterwards. By then they're so full they can't finish them.*

One father told us that he used to nag his son to eat vegetables, but nothing worked until he took off the pressure.

> *Our two daughters ate vegetables quite happily, but our son simply refused. We talked to him for hours about the importance of vitamins and fibre, we tried the 'No pudding unless you eat your vegetables' rule, but he refused point blank to touch them. The more we nagged, the more entrenched he became.*
>
> *So we finally changed tack. We put dinner on the table and said, 'We aren't going to tell you any more. You decide how many vegetables you need to eat.' He looked at us as if to say, 'You mean it's up to me now?' Then he helped himself to a bit of everything. He still does.*

Don't be disappointed if some of these strategies take a bit of time to work.

> *I tried putting vegetables out on a plate for my children, but they wouldn't touch them. I tried a week later and still had no luck. A friend of mine said not to worry. She cut up vegetables for two months, put them out on the table and left them there. She and her husband would always end up eating them, so they never got wasted. Then, literally two months later, her children started helping themselves. Now they eat platefuls.*

## Getting Your Child Moving

Making sure your child gets enough exercise can be as important as changing the food on her plate. Once you are making progress at mealtimes, it's time to start thinking about how to encourage her to be more active.

Children used to go out to play when they were bored. Now they are more likely to sit in front of a screen. Even if your child isn't overweight, she won't be as healthy as she should be if she doesn't get enough exercise.

If she's sitting around on her backside most afternoons, you may have to help her find other things to do. Yes, this might mean organizing play dates and activities. If she isn't moving around enough, you have to take responsibility for doing something about it.

She won't have as much time to sit in front of the computer or TV if she is cycling in the park, playing football, ice skating or swimming. If you normally drive her to school, or take the car to the shops, try walking or scootering at least part of the way. Lots of exercise means lots of endorphins, which will make both of you feel fitter and happier. See pp. 43–4 for more tips.

## Eating in Front of the Television

Another way to encourage healthier habits is to sit round the table at mealtimes rather than eating in front of the television. Of course, there is nothing wrong with the occasional TV dinner. But if that's where your child eats most of her meals, here are some reasons why you might want to make some changes:

- *Family meals are a good time for children to chat and interact with you.*
- *Vegging out in front of the TV won't get your child moving.*
- *It is easy to snack mindlessly while watching TV. When you are distracted you don't notice what you're eating or how full you are. Your child can get through a lot of junk this way.*

Cutting back on time spent in front of the TV or computer is a tough one; for tips on how to accomplish this particular miracle see Chapter Three, p. 85.

## How to Minimize Your Child's Hostility

It's easy making these changes if your child is cooperative. But you'll be reluctant to throw away all the junk food and sign her up for lots of after-school activities if you know she'll kick up a fuss about the new regime. So what do you do?

This is where **Sorted Parents** come in. They know that the best way to make changes is to lay the groundwork first. It takes time to get organized, overhaul your larder, and think through meal plans. So while you're busy working it all out, start telling your child what is going to happen and why, and ask her for ideas about what healthier food or sports she'd like to try. It will also help enormously if you let her moan about the changes before you implement them. If you do enough preparation, it won't be as much of an ordeal as you think.

## *Try being a SORTED PARENT*

***Give advance warning*** Even if your children are quite easy-going, you have a better chance of getting them away from the computer screen and eating proper food if you warn them what's going to happen. Otherwise they'll see the changes (like your refusing to buy any more chocolate breakfast cereal) as a violation of their basic human rights.

Preparing your child in advance is especially important if you have drastic changes to make. Here's how one mother, the type who dreads confrontations, got her children off a juice habit and on to drinking plain water:

> *'I hated giving my children juice, but they refused to drink anything else. Against my better judgement, I used to cave in and buy it in bulk. Finally, I told them I wasn't going to buy any more juice because it was expensive and bad for their teeth. I said we'd water down what we had left, bit by bit, until the last carton was gone.*
>
> *I told them our stocks would last about two weeks. We started diluting the juice and a week later I reminded them when we'd run out. Finally they got down to the last carton and they watered it down very carefully to make it last. I haven't bought juice since, and now they drink water quite happily.'*

This mother said that, to her astonishment, there was no whinging – no moaning at all – and once her children were in the habit of drinking water the occasional juice didn't threaten her system.

***Set up rules*** Setting up rules gets rid of ambiguity so everyone knows what to expect. If your child makes a habit of refusing to eat dinner, but then demands fluorescent-pink Barbie yoghurts instead, setting up a rule should take care of this.

When you prepare your children for new rules, what you say depends on what you want to achieve, but here are some suggestions:

- *'Dad and I have decided it's time for a few changes. We all need to be healthier and that means better food and more exer-*

*cise. Starting from next week we are going to cut out sweets and cakes and limit TV time to an hour a day.'*

- *'I'd like us to eat healthier snacks. Next time I go shopping, I'm going to buy fruit instead of biscuits and plain popcorn instead of crisps.'*
- *'I notice you don't eat your tea, and then you want snacks at bedtime. For the next two weeks let's try having tea later, at six thirty, and see if that works better.'*
- *'I know you all love chocolate spread, but it's not good for you. So once we finish this jar, I'm not buying any more. What do you think you'd like in your sandwiches instead?'*

Set a start date and, as the day looms closer, remind everyone what changes are going to take place and when.

If you have one child who is heavy or out of shape, don't single her out. Her siblings will hate her for it if they even get a whiff that she is the reason why they are giving up ice-cream and oven chips. It works better to propose changes for the good of the whole family – which they should be.

### *Try being a COMMANDO PARENT*

**Give consequences** If your children won't stick to the rules, you may have to set consequences. In one family we know, the children kept refusing to eat their dinner and demanding pudding. So the mother stopped buying puddings altogether and that was that. They didn't have any puddings – no biscuits, no ice-cream, nothing – for six months. The surprising thing was that when there was no sweet stuff in the house, everyone completely forgot about it.

## No-guilt Ways to Cut Down on Junk Food

We all like giving treats to our children – taking them to the café after school for a cake, buying ice-creams in the park, and letting them choose a little something from the shop. None of this is a problem if the majority of your child's diet is nutritious. But if she eats sugary breakfast cereal in the morning, a questionable lunch from the school canteen, biscuits for a snack, skips dinner and eats pudding, spends her pocket money on sweets and is living it up on the birthday-party circuit, something's got to go.

You might find it very hard to deny your children biscuits and sweets because you want to make them happy. One full-time working mother told us:

> *If she wants ice-cream for a treat, I find it really hard to say no. I want her to be happy because I love it when she is smiling and enjoying herself. I want her to think of me as a kind, loving mother in the free time we have together.*

If your first inclination is to be kind, being firm feels cruel and unnatural. The minute your child starts fussing or demanding treats, you might start to waver. And if she sees that she's getting to you, she'll probably carry on.

But our job as parents is to think about our children's long-term health and happiness, as well as their short-term pleasure. If you wrestle with this, one of the best ways to cut down on junk food without feeling guilty is to set up rules.

- *'We need to cut back on ice-cream in the house. Instead let's have a treat every Saturday afternoon at the park.'*

Once you've set the rule up, you'll find it easier to say no and your child will be less demanding because she'll know what to expect.

Another good way to cut down on the junk is to give rewards for good behaviour that include spending time with you, instead of offering sweets. Popular options include: a trip to the park, ice-skating rink or cinema; time together out gardening or preparing dinner; a mock wrestling match; reading a story; renting a film; or even kicking a ball back and forth.

## Try being a TUNED-IN PARENT 

If you give plenty of warning, your child may not grumble about the changes. But what do you do if she does? Tuning in is usually your best option.

**Listen to their feelings** This part can be the hardest. When your child starts moaning, it might be your cue to get drawn back into an argument. Or, if you're the soft-hearted type, you may feel like giving in. But by tuning in to her feelings you can hold firm and reassure yourself that you're being kind. Listen, and confirm in a matter-of-fact voice that you understand what she's saying:

- *'I don't like sweetcorn.'*
  *'You don't want to eat it.'*
  *'I hate it.'*
  *'You wish it wasn't on your plate.'*

You don't have to do or say anything else. Nor should you take away the sweetcorn. Just keep eating your own meal. Your child may be so surprised she drops the subject altogether.

## Try being a LAID-BACK PARENT 

What else can you do if your child is kicking up a fuss? Try letting her solve the problem for herself, and incorporate any sensible suggestions she has.

**Ask for solutions** If she has helped choose the food, she is more likely to eat it when it shows up on her plate.

> *After spending hours in the kitchen, the last thing I wanted to hear was whinging about the food. I was getting frantic, so I said, 'We need to eat proper food. You tell me what you would like.'*
>
> *In the end we reached a compromise. I cook what they request, within reason, three nights a week (boring things like pasta with grated cheese) and I try something new on the other nights. They don't have to eat it, but they can't bug me to make something different. It's not a perfect system, but it's better than before.*

If your child often makes a fuss, you might be worried about asking her opinion. What if she says she only wants hot dogs? But it's worth a try. She may be more cooperative and creative than you think. If she refuses to give you any sensible ideas, tell her this is her chance and if she doesn't want to take it, you'll keep making the decisions.

Still complaining? You can very casually give her some options: 'Tuna or ham with your salad?' 'Corn or carrots tonight?' 'Mashed or boiled potatoes?' Or you can take things a stage further and look through menus and recipe books together.

***Allow them to do more*** You can also try getting your child to do some of the cooking. Children are usually more inclined to eat the food if they've helped prepare it.

> *My son used to refuse to eat onions. Then one day I was chopping them and he said he wanted to help. I warned him that the onion juice could hurt his eyes and make him cry. 'I know what to do about that,' he said. He ran off and came back wearing his swimming goggles! He was so proud of his idea. Now he always wants to chop the onions, and he eats them.*

If you don't mind, you could also let your child choose something different to eat.

> *About once a week my daughter refuses to eat what we are having for dinner. Instead, she helps herself from the refrigerator, having either leftovers or a piece of fruit and cheese. So what? As long as she chooses something decent I don't think it's worth getting worked up about it.*

If your child is used to dinner-table conversations revolving around what and how much she eats, she may be puzzled by your new laid-back attitude, and she may still keep trying to get your attention. If she keeps asking, 'Do I have to eat this? Have I had enough?' don't get sucked back in.

Ask her, 'What do you think?' Then accept whatever she says in reply and carry on eating your supper. Whatever answer you get is fine. You are aiming for long-term victory here, not constant little skirmishes.

# Improving the Atmosphere at the Table and Around Food

If you can improve the atmosphere at the table, mealtimes will be far more pleasant. This section looks at various ways to encourage friendly conversation and reinforce good table manners, so everyone is happy to sit together.

## *Try being a TUNED-IN PARENT*

*Listen to their feelings* Try to make an effort to listen to your child at mealtimes and find out what's going on in her life. It's a nice way to give her attention. If there is any kind of food issue, listening can make her feel more relaxed. In an ideal world, conversation is what family mealtimes are for.

Try veering it towards something that interests your child or that she wants to discuss: her day at school, an irritating teacher, her netball match, what she would like to do at the weekend. Try:

- *'You said your teacher really bugged you today. What happened?'*
- *'Elliot scored an own-goal? I can't believe it. How did that happen?'*

If she still doesn't want to chat you could talk about what you've been doing, or have a quiet meal and say nothing at all. The more comfortable she feels at the table, the happier she will be to sit there. Almost anything is better than criticizing her or commenting on what she's eating.

*'I'd been at it so long I simply couldn't stop trying to get my daughter to eat. I finally broke myself of the habit by focusing on conversations about other things. It wasn't easy. I had to force myself to listen instead of perpetually looking at her plate. But I got there in the end.'*

## *Try being a CHEERLEADER PARENT*

*Give specific praise* If you want to start creating a better atmosphere around the table, praise your child and give her positive attention at mealtimes, but for something other than what she is eating. So instead of:

- *'Well done eating your carrots'*

try:

- *'Thank-you for passing the peas.'*
- *'Well done pouring the water so carefully.'*

## *Try being a SORTED PARENT*

*Give advance warning and set up rules* It can be tough getting children to sit at the table and eat properly. Having a set of rules will make your life easier and your mealtimes more enjoyable. Set up whatever rules work for you and give your children plenty of time to get used to them so you don't ruin the atmosphere at the table by nagging. Here are some suggestions:

### No toys at the table

It's irritating when your child is more interested in her Pokémon cards than dinner. A little bouncy ball can be even more of a wind-up: thump . . . thump . . . thump. You might set up a rule that no toys are allowed at the table. If necessary, ban books and homework, and newspapers and mobile phones for adults.

### No rude comments about the food

Your child needs to know that unkind comments are very bad manners – especially if she is at someone else's house.

## No lavatory humour

Some children find it hilarious to talk about the loo, what you do there and other related subjects. Even if you find some of it funny too, you might want to put an end to it at the table because it can put everyone off their food and if you don't crack down, it can go on for years.

## Everyone needs to sit properly

If your child can't sit still or keeps tipping her chair, getting up out of her seat, sitting on her knees or putting her feet on the table, it might be useful to have a rule that she must sit properly – or she may have to leave the table altogether.

## Everyone needs to help

If you want your child to lay the table, clear the dishes or load the dishwasher, set up specific rules beforehand so she knows what to expect. There's no point nagging her at the table and souring the atmosphere.

### *Try being a LAID-BACK PARENT* 

*Let them get on with it* We don't think it's a coincidence that some of the happiest, most relaxed meals are at the houses of **Laid-Back Parents**. They put the serving bowls in the middle of the table and let their children help themselves. These parents feel they are in control because they've chosen what they are going to serve and how it is prepared. The children feel in control because they're able to choose what they eat and how much.

It goes without saying, however, that if you've been too laid back and your child helps herself to cereal and ice-cream instead of dinner, then giving her more control isn't the answer. But if you've done your bit and put healthy options on the table, it shouldn't matter what she chooses. As long as you know what she likes and offer a bit of choice, she should be able to find something she wants.

Part of letting your child get on with it is letting her deal with the consequences if she chooses not to eat. If she says she isn't eating because she isn't hungry, then that's her decision. If she is refusing to eat what you serve because she says she doesn't like any of it, tell her she doesn't have to eat anything she doesn't want to. But don't jump up and cook another meal. If you do, you are setting a dangerous precedent and could find yourself pandering to her for years.

If you tend to worry about what your child eats, this may go against the grain. But always telling her what and how much to eat messes up her confidence and judgement. She may need to feel for herself what it is like to be hungry or over-full. This is where it helps if you have already sorted out your cupboards. Skipping dinner doesn't mean she can mow down crisps or biscuits, but you might not mind too much if she finds a reasonable alternative. It shouldn't be a problem if most of what she's been eating all day has been healthy.

## How You Can Help Your Picky Eater

Lots of picky children are skinny, but some are overweight because they refuse to eat anything except junk. The following section should help if you want to broaden the range of food your child eats – whatever her body shape.

If she is particularly fussy, follow the advice above: unhook yourself emotionally, clear the junk out of your cupboards and make healthy food available instead. It will help if you warn her about the changes, listen to her complain and give her some responsibility for what she chooses to eat. But if all this isn't working as well or as quickly as you'd hoped, here are some more suggestions:

### *Try being a TUNED-IN PARENT* 

***Listen to their feelings*** There are plenty of reasons why your child might be picky. Make a big effort to listen to her and you may be able to help her.

# Why Your Child Might be Fussy

## She doesn't like the food

There may be a lot of food she simply doesn't like. If she is making a big fuss, the best thing to do is acknowledge how strongly she feels:

Child: *'I said I* hate *broccoli!'*
Parent: *'Oh, you absolutely hate it. You wish it wasn't on the table, and you don't want to eat it.'*

As before, don't rescue her by whipping it away and substituting something else. Just leave it there.

If you've been forcing her to gag down broccoli every night, this reaction alone is going to surprise her. You've heard the feelings. You've accepted them. Amazingly, this is often enough. She might even surprise you by eating some.

But don't start panicking or giving orders if she doesn't. Even if she doesn't eat any vegetables for a week, or a year, keep putting a variety of them out on the table. Lots of children grow to like things as their taste-buds mature. Others only become confident about new tastes when they have seen and smelled the food a dozen or so times. So even if your child doesn't like something, don't stop putting it out. Just don't force her to eat it. If you tune in and accept that she doesn't like something now, she is less likely to have an issue about it in the future.

## She wants more control over what she eats

How would you like to have someone plop a great glob of food on your plate and expect you to eat it? Lots of children prefer to help themselves.

> *My son was never much interested in food and I spent years trying to get him to eat and worrying about his weight. I finally asked him why he didn't like eating. He said he hates it when other people dish up his food.*

## She wants your attention

Though she wouldn't be able to put it into words, fussing over food could be her subconscious saying, 'I want your attention, and irritating you over dinner is one way I can get it.'

If you suspect this is the case, give her lots of attention by tuning in and listening to her. It's far kinder than nagging her to eat.

## She is feeling stressed or out of control

She might not be eating properly because she is anxious. Some people turn to food for comfort at times of stress, others lose their appetite. Maybe a teacher, friend or sibling is getting to her. Tuning in will help her process her feelings.

- *'You've really had it with your sister.'*
- *'You are angry with me because I couldn't come to your concert.'*
- *'This exam is hanging over you like a dark cloud, and you're worried you won't do well in it.'*
- *'I can understand it annoys you when I tell you what to do. Do you have any suggestions how we could change things?'*

Mealtimes themselves can be stressful. If your child is sensitive she may not feel like eating if there is too much rush and panic (this is particularly true of breakfast), too much bickering or if you are barking orders.

*I could never eat Sunday lunch. I used to feel sick with dread. I realize now it was because my father was always snapping at us. 'Sit up straight . . . You are holding your fork like a caveman . . . Eating with you is like eating with a bunch of pigs.' Usually one or all of us would end up in tears.*

If you suspect your child finds mealtimes stressful, pick a neutral time and have a chat with her. Tune in, be as receptive as you can be, and ask her for ideas about how to make them better for her.

Many anorexics say their eating disorder started because their body was the one thing they could control in a chaotic world. Try to accept your child's feelings in all sorts of areas, not just those related to food. Bringing them into the light means there's less chance they'll affect her appetite.

## Food Phobias

Some toddlers show signs of being food phobic and go through a stage of refusing to try new food. As long as you don't panic or force her to eat, your child will probably grow out of this phase and new food won't seem so scary.

Other children become fearful after a bad experience. If they choke on a particular food or are sick after eating it they won't go near it in the future.

*I choked on a lump in my mashed potato when I was five. I'm forty-five now and I can't look at mash without feeling cold and sweaty. Roast potatoes and chips? Not a problem.*

Some people can't eat food they associate with strong emotions.

*There were so many arguments at Christmas. I still feel sick just thinking about roast turkey and mince pies.*

For some children the link is less obvious. They just feel apprehensive or uncomfortable, perhaps because their food is all mixed up or has a funny texture, or they find something they weren't expecting like a mushroom in their shepherd's pie.

If your child is frightened of a certain food, there's no point in forcing her to taste it, or telling her she's being silly. The kindest approach is to tune in and listen. Once she feels understood, her fears will seem less overwhelming and she may be able to overcome them on her own. If not, at least she'll feel understood.

Provided that nothing deeper is going on, familiarizing your child with the food by growing it, picking it or preparing it might help her. Or you might offer a tiny taste, without any pressure.

> *My son refused to eat gravy for years, though I knew he had never tried it. I think he hated the thought of it flowing all over his food. One day I suggested he might like to taste a tiny bit of mine on the end of his little finger. After all that time he found he liked it.*

Start small and don't push your child any further than she wants to go. If she is very apprehensive about eating fruit, for example, with her permission start with one drop of orange juice in her water, and work up from there. Over time she might get used to proper fruit juice, then juice with pulp and even smoothies. From there she might try yogurt with bits, and eventually eat a piece of fruit. This might sound slow and laborious, but if it helps it's better than leaving her with an unnecessary fear.

## *Try being a CHEERLEADER PARENT*

***Be open-minded*** Labelling your child 'a bad eater'or 'my fussy one' gives her attention for the wrong reasons and makes it hard for her to see herself in any other light. So don't put a value judgement on whether or not she is hungry and don't hand out criticism or praise for eating.

Even if you don't say anything out loud, watch what you are thinking. The labels we give our children can be out of date or just plain wrong because they have more to do with our own fears than what is really going on.

> *My daughter didn't eat well as a baby and lost weight, so the doctor classified her as 'failing to thrive'. After that I never stopped worrying*

*about how much she ate. In my mind I've always thought of her as a fussy non-eater, and been anxious that she wasn't getting the right nutrition.*

*It wasn't until she was ten that I realized how strange this was. Of course she's an eater, otherwise she wouldn't be alive. She is also one of the tallest and smartest in her class. I finally realized she is absolutely fine. Her food issue all these years has been my issue, not hers.* ❞

## Practical Tips if Your Child is Fussy

- Your child's poor appetite could be down to a simple zinc deficiency. You can buy Lambert's Zincatest from health-food shops, which will tell you if she is zinc deficient. You might feel more confident that she is getting the vitamins and minerals she needs if you give her a daily supplement. There are pleasant-tasting chewable ones, or try vitamin drops in her juice.
- If your child sits around all day and never does any exercise, she won't work up much of an appetite. But if you can get her outside to play in the fresh air, healthy food will suddenly seem much more attractive.
- Give her lots of affection. Whether she is overweight, under-weight, or neither, don't forget the power of a good hug. The more loved and physically comfortable with herself she feels, the easier it will be for her to deal with difficult feelings about food. Heavier children can be sensitive about being hugged around their tummies, and lots of children of all shapes and sizes feel uncomfortable with outright affection. If this is the case, try rubbing her back, giving her a head or foot massage or a mini-manicure, cuddling up together to watch a video, or lying with her in bed to read her a story.

## *Try being a LAID-BACK PARENT*

***Be a good role model*** If you don't want your child to be picky, try and set a good example. If you eat properly and get plenty of exercise, you may not need to say or do anything at all to get your child into healthy habits because she will pick a lot of them up by osmosis.

***'I'm always thinking about my weight and I talk about it all the time. Do you think this will affect my children?'***
You bet. If this sounds like you, do whatever it takes to keep quiet about your own food issues. Don't even mention your weight, dieting, calories, how much you've eaten or what you shouldn't have eaten. Your child will take it all in, and can easily end up with skewed attitudes towards food.

*' I couldn't believe what came out of my daughter's mouth. She looked at the label on the carton of milk and said, 'Oh, I didn't realize milk was bad for you.' I asked her what she meant, and she said, 'It's got calories in it. Calories are bad for you.' I was so surprised. She must have picked that up from me, always carrying on about dieting and how many calories I'd eaten.*

*I realized that mentally I was like Bridget Jones, always tallying up my calories and disappointed that they didn't come to zero. I'd completely forgotten that calories mean energy and we need them.*

*I decided right then to stop talking about it in front of my children. '*

***Get help*** If you can't stop worrying because your child is super-fussy, try hanging out with families who are relaxed at mealtimes.

*' My son was such a picky eater, and I always had to persuade him to eat. Then we went to stay with a noisy bunch of cousins. At teatime he started looking sorry for himself and said he wasn't hungry. 'No problem,' said his cousin. 'Nobody here has to eat anything they don't like.'*

*He didn't know what to make of this. Then he saw his cousins arguing over who was going to get his share. It was clear that if he didn't eat, the food would be gobbled up, so he launched right in.*

*He's still not going to win any eating competitions, but it was a major shift at our house. If he's not hungry, I don't worry about it. If he doesn't want to eat what I've cooked, I don't offer alternatives. I realized we'd got into a power struggle that he'd been winning by acting feeble and refusing food.* ❞

Sometimes it works even better if you can leave your child with another family, without you. If you can't take her to someone else's house to eat, try getting out of the house yourself and letting someone else take over. Just make sure your stand-in doesn't make an issue out of food either. And don't ask for a run-down of what your child ate afterwards. Just leave it.

If she's been used to getting attention for being fussy or has been at it for a long time, don't be surprised if she keeps trying to draw you back in. She may feel, subconsciously, that being picky is one of her defining characteristics, and she may not want, or know how, to give it up. Just keep giving her as much attention at mealtimes as you can for other things.

Once she finally does start eating healthier food it's incredibly tempting to praise her and tell her how well she is doing. But this is one of the few times when praising is more likely to make the situation worse, not better. So don't chime in with, 'Well done for eating your courgettes,' or 'You are such a good eater.' Resist the temptation to give her attention for eating or not eating.

If your previously picky eater starts trying to impress you by listing all the things she has eaten, a simple smile from you will suffice. Ditto when she tries something new. Don't congratulate her or say something patronizing like, 'See. That wasn't so bad,' or, 'I knew you'd like it if you tried it.' Worst of all, don't try and force her to eat another three mouthfuls, 'Now that you like it.' You'll irritate her and risk heading right back to square one.

If you really feel it's necessary to make an appreciative comment when your child tries something new, then we suggest that you do it later, perhaps at bedtime, so it doesn't backfire and cause trouble to flare up again. 'That was brave of you to try that tomato at dinner.

Now you know whether you like it' will do. Then leave it. It is up to her to decide whether or not to have a tomato again next time.

# How You Can Help Your Overweight Child

It's no coincidence that the British are the fattest nation in Europe: we eat the most junk food, watch the most television and do the least exercise. It's estimated a whopping 25 per cent of children in the UK are clinically obese, never mind those who are just too heavy. Unfortunately, fat children usually have a tough time of it. They are more likely to be teased and bullied than other children and to have low self-esteem.

*'Sports Day is horrible for us. Last year my daughter came last in every race. I watched her from the sidelines, doing her best not to cry. It wrenched my heart. I don't see any point in going and making her suffer again, so this year I think we'll skip it.*

*I think because she's heavier than the others she's lost all her confidence. She refuses to play any physical games unless she is forced to, and she does anything she can to get out of swimming because she is ashamed to wear a swimsuit in front of the others.'*

Sedentary habits and a poor diet can lead to all sorts of behaviour issues and health problems. If your child is overweight, your main goals should be to get her to eat better quality food and do more exercise (see pp. 163–4). If she is fussy, and insists on eating junk food, you could also try to broaden the range of food she will eat. But if these strategies don't seem to be working, here are some additional suggestions.

### *Try being a PAUSE PARENT*

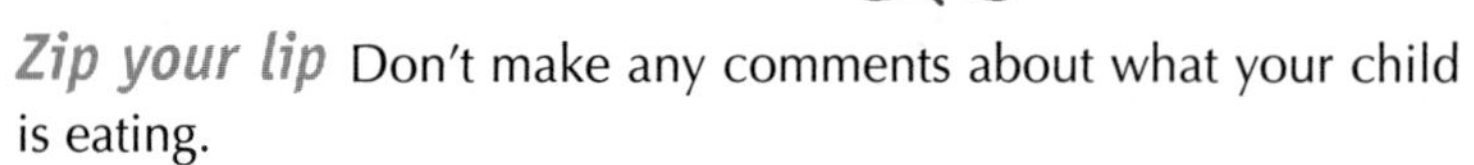

***Zip your lip*** Don't make any comments about what your child is eating.

*I just can't help it. I keep finding myself repeating the awful things my mother used to say, like, 'More chocolate cake? I don't think that's a good idea. You are heavy enough as it is.' I know from experience how hurtful it is when your own mother says you're fat. But what am I supposed to do?*

Keep quiet and concentrate on providing healthy food. If it is fresh and unprocessed, it doesn't matter how much your child eats. As long as there are no puddings or crisps to guzzle down, she'll be fine.

***Keep things in perspective*** Pausing and getting some perspective on the problem will stop you saying or doing anything which might hurt your child's feelings and make the problem worse. She didn't become overweight overnight, and she won't become healthier or fitter overnight either. This is going to be a long-term project.

## *Try being a CHEERLEADER PARENT*

***Be open-minded*** Parents of overweight children often want to motivate them to lose weight by pointing out that they are too heavy, greedy or lazy. But bite your tongue. Labels hurt, they stick, and they can easily end up becoming self-fulfilling prophecies. Even labelling your child a 'good eater' can be a problem. Do you really want her to have an image of herself as someone with a big appetite? It certainly won't be helpful when she gets older if, like many adults, she has to work at keeping her weight under control.

## *Try being a TUNED-IN PARENT*

***Listen to their feelings*** If your child is overweight, instead of trying to get her to cut back on food, put your energy into listening to her. At the table – or anywhere – talk about things that interest her. It's kinder and can help boost her self-esteem.

*I feel so guilty I can hardly talk about it, but I used to use all sorts of tactics to stop my daughter eating so much. I'd move the potatoes off the table, or dish her up tiny portions.*

*Once I stopped focusing on her weight and started taking an interest in her, her whole personality changed. The stress I put on her and the unhappiness I caused – I feel terrible about it.* ❜

If she complains when you try to get her into healthy habits, tuning in will help you to stand your ground. Try:

- *'I know. It's such a shame we aren't having croissants and waffles for breakfast any more, because I know they're your favourites.'*
- *'You'd prefer it if you could go back to watching TV in the afternoons. I can see you're missing the programmes you liked. It's hard getting used to doing something different.'*

***Accept difficult feelings*** It can be hard to tune in if your child has painful feelings about her weight. If she is unhappy about the way she looks, if she is being teased at school, or if she is doing badly at sport, hearing her talk about it can be upsetting.

It's difficult to judge whether to bring up the subject at all. It's a sensitive issue and you don't want to make her feel any worse. To be on the safe side, don't mention it unless she does, and accept that she may never mention it at all.

If she does, just listen and sympathize, even if you find it uncomfortable. Although you might want to try to cheer her up – 'That's not true. Don't be upset. Those children are just nasty' – denying the problem exists won't truly comfort her or make her feel any better about herself. By far the best thing to do is to acknowledge that her feelings are hurt. You might try:

- *'I can see you are really upset. Those are hard feelings to bear.'*
- *'She called you a fat pig? That was so unkind. No wonder you're unhappy. I'd be unhappy too.'*

If you can't think of anything to say, just stay quiet and nod. Don't rescue her, and don't deny how she feels. She needs you to listen and understand.

## Practical Tips if Your Child is Overweight

- As long as her diet is healthy and she is exercising, it shouldn't matter how much your child weighs or whether she actually loses weight. Over time, she'll grow into her weight.
- The only way to change her weight in the long run is for her to eat healthier food and move more. So don't ever mention the word diet. If she raises the subject, explain that diets are short-term attempts to lose weight which aren't good for you and don't last. Talk instead about healthier long-term habits which will help her feel fitter and happier.

  One of the reasons your child may be eating so much might be that the chips and nuggets she is so fond of aren't giving her the nutrients her body craves. If you provide healthier food, she'll get the vitamins and minerals she needs so she may not feel so hungry.
- Try and get her to drink plenty of water. Lots of people snack when they're actually thirsty because they misinterpret the signal their body is giving them.
- Do everything you can to cut back on screen time. The more she sits, the less she moves. It's also easy to hoover down a zillion calories without thinking when sitting in front of the TV.
- Don't make excuses to make her feel better. It won't do her any favours. If you say, 'She's just like me. She takes after my side of the family,' or 'She can't help it, it's her glands,' you may think you are being kind because you are taking the blame for her size. But if you give her the message that she can't do anything about her weight, she may end up feeling even worse. The vast majority of overweight people are overweight because they eat too much junk and do too little exercise.

- If she already feels embarrassed about her body, it may be hard to get her to do more exercise. But even if she refuses to go swimming or jogging in case someone sees her, you could get her to walk or cycle to school, do exercise videos with you at home, or find a sport like judo where size isn't such a problem.

## When Food Is No Longer an Issue

By now you should be seeing some improvements. Healthy food is being served, you're not forcing your child to eat it and she's not complaining or trying to manipulate you.

When the subject is no longer emotionally loaded, with no undercurrents from either side, you can be quite direct if you want to make further changes.

### *Try being a CHEERLEADER PARENT*

When food isn't an issue, of course you can talk about what your child eats or doesn't eat – no problem. Go ahead and praise her for trying a Brussels sprout or a green olive if you feel like it.

### *Try being a COMMANDO PARENT*

***Give information*** You are finally in a good position to give your child important information about food without sounding bossy or desperate.

With so much advertising and peer pressure out there, she needs to know what food is actually good for her and why eating rubbish isn't. We aren't saying she will always make the right choices, but at least you can provide information to balance the junk-food lobby. The more she understands about it, the more likely she is to make good decisions, even when you aren't around.

As long as there is no power struggle still going on, go right ahead and give information.

- *'Courgettes are full of good vitamins.'*
- *'Different-coloured fruit and vegetables have different antioxidants. So it's good to eat a wide range.'*
- *'It's important to drink some water in the morning to keep yourself hydrated, especially with your big football match today.'*

One mother stopped having to nag her son to drink water after his teacher gave the whole class information.

*His teacher was great. She told them all to check the colour of their wee when they went to the bathroom. If it was colourless or very pale yellow they were doing well. But if it was dark yellow, orange or brownish they needed to drink more water. I still put out water at every meal, but now I never need to remind him.*

Teachers can often give out this kind of message quite easily. The trick is to say things matter-of-factly, in a non-threatening way, without that toxic desperate edge to your voice. Yes, of course you want your child to eat vegetables, choose fruit and drink water. But if you put the pressure on, you can put her right off them. You need to be able to give her the facts without getting her back up.

*I got a huge shock when my daughter said she wanted to skip tea and go on a diet. Goodness knows where she picked up that idea. From her friends at school, I suppose. So I told her that food is our main source of energy, and we need that energy to do all sorts of things, like thinking, running, jumping – even playing the piano. She was fascinated by this. I also reminded her how awful we can feel without it – tired and really unhappy. I've noticed she hasn't skipped a meal since.*

Once you can give information, you can start to genuinely enthuse about food. You can point out that it tastes and smells good, and you can casually make suggestions that will help your child enjoy it.

- *'Apple with cheese is one of those great combinations.'*
- *'Prawn and cress is my favourite sandwich.'*
- *'Doesn't this lasagne smell amazing?'*

If she is reluctant to try something new, you can help change her mind if you present her with information, as long as you make it clear you don't mind whether she tries it or not. Presented purely as exploration, she might take the leap.

> *I said to my daughter, 'I'll never force you to eat anything, but do yourself a favour and try it. Then you'll know if you like it or not.'*

Sometimes she is going to taste things and not like them. That's fine – don't make a big deal of it. But you can always praise her for having a go.

***Express your feelings*** When you can keep your tone casual without pleading or sounding desperate, you can also speak your mind.

- *'I expect each of you to have some vegetables.'*
- *'Please eat a piece of chicken with your rice. You need some protein to help you grow.'*
- *'No more ice-cream. One bowl is plenty.'*

You can even speak your mind and say outright how irritating it is when she doesn't eat what you prepare.

By this stage we hope you'll have reached your goal, or at least made some progress towards it. Your whole family should be fitter and filling up on healthier food, and you should have a much more pleasant atmosphere at the table. However, if nothing seems to be working, here is a wonderful piece of advice that was pinned up on the noticeboard at the Great Ormond Street Children's Hospital:

> *Some children won't eat anything except mashed potatoes. If your child is a fussy eater and won't eat anything but mashed potatoes, don't worry about it. This phase won't last for ever.*

# 6

# Surviving School

## Building Confidence and Coping with Tests, Teachers and Homework

Is there a parent out there whose children have never had any trouble with school? Some parents are lucky and get away with only a couple of minor blips, but for others there's no end to the dramas. Your son's been disruptive in class, your daughter's upset because she didn't make the netball team, or you're fretting that neither of them is working to their full potential and won't get great exam results. Then there are those who worry because their child doesn't seem very happy at school.

Of course you're concerned, but what on earth are you supposed to do? These problems are school-related, so why can't they be solved at school? When you've got ten thousand other things to do in the evening, school problems are frustrating, and doubly so because you have to sort them out from a distance.

If your child is having trouble at school, we are going to show you how to get him back on track and, with any luck, keep him there. If you can give him some support behind the scenes, he will be more likely to be able to cope with whatever school throws at him. If his problems are to do with other children, see Chapter Four.

# General Problems with School

The most common worry parents have is that their child is struggling and losing confidence. The classic complaint from children is that school is boring. Either way, if your child is fed up with maths, PE, his teacher, or the entire school day, he won't engage in what's going on.

If you can boost his confidence, he may find school a lot less intimidating and a lot more interesting. But if you don't feel that confidence is the issue, go straight to the section on Boredom (pp. 220–3) for advice.

## Lack of Confidence

Though your child might insist he hates school, it's astonishing how often school-related problems come down to confidence issues. He could be sensitive and easily crushed by criticism, or panic if he can't understand something first time round. He might be comparing himself to other children in his class who are more sporty, musical or academic. The cause doesn't matter, but it can affect his whole outlook. Once he thinks he isn't good at something he may slip further and further behind, and perhaps even give up trying altogether.

Confident children, on the other hand, aren't so sensitive to setbacks. They can take criticism from teachers without being reduced to tears or becoming defensive. Even when something does upset them, they can bounce back. They don't mind so much if they aren't good at something, because they know that if they try a little harder, they'll improve. So they'll go for it and put in the extra effort to get higher marks or make it on to the team next time.

Don't worry if this doesn't sound like your child. There is quite a lot you can do at home to boost his confidence, even if his problems do mostly relate to school. And though the focus here is on school issues, you'll see all-round benefits.

### *Try being a PHYSICAL PARENT* 

Start with the basics: if your child isn't feeling confident, try to send him to school in good physical shape, because he will find it easier to cope. **Physical Parents** make sure their children:

- *Get plenty of sleep*
- *Have a proper breakfast, which usually includes fruit and some sort of protein or slow-release carbohydrate, rather than sugary breakfast cereals*
- *Have a glass of water every morning*
- *Walk, cycle or scoot to school to get their bodies moving and blood flowing to their brains.*

If your child is having a problem, it can be easy to overlook these things. But the better he feels physically, the less daunting school will seem.

## *Try being a PAUSE PARENT*

***Zip your lip*** It's impossible to boost your child's confidence if he is feeling persecuted and self-conscious. So pause, think before you speak and don't criticize him. Try to keep quiet when he isn't doing something exactly right, even if you feel you ought to set him straight. Half the time we don't mean to be critical. We only want to help by correcting our children's mistakes, improving their essays or working on their ball skills. But well-meaning advice can backfire. If your child isn't feeling confident or already knows he has messed up, your comments can make him feel worse.

## *Try being a CHEERLEADER PARENT*

***Notice the good, ignore the bad*** Instead of picking up on mistakes, look for something he's doing right.

> *'My son was chosen to read a poem in assembly, and he brought it home to practise. I listened carefully and told him how he could improve it by pausing between phrases and using his voice more expressively. But he refused to read it again. On the day, he sounded flat and boring, and I know he could have done a lot better.'*

Children are sensitive and can interpret advice as criticism. If you want your child to listen, don't tell him where his poem needs to be improved, but praise him for the things he is already doing well. For example, even if he gabbles through the verse, notice the one time he pauses and compliment him on it.

- *'I liked the way you slowed down after the first line and took a breath. It made me want to know what happens next.'*

Similarly, if he mostly reads in a boring monotone, mention any part that sounded different.

- *'That bit when you suddenly got louder was good. That made it sound exciting.'*

If you tell him what you like, he will probably have another go, concentrating on pace and inflection. Then you can keep praising him for getting better at it in other parts of the poem too.

***Be specific*** Nebulous praise like 'Wonderful! Well done!' is friendly, but if your child isn't feeling confident he won't believe you mean it. But specific praise, given in a matter-of-fact voice, will help him start building up a little repertoire of things he knows he can do and do well. Though you are aiming to improve his confidence in the classroom, the compliments don't all have to relate to school.

- *'Good job – packing your school bag by yourself.'*
- *'You found some great pictures on the internet for your project.'*
- *'Thanks for remembering to feed the rabbit and change his water.'*

The best thing about zooming in on specifics is that your child will believe the nice things you say.

*‘My daughter has always been at the bottom of her class in English. But her teachers have been absolutely incredible at keeping up her confidence by focusing on how creative she is and what wonderful ideas she has. So even though she struggles to get the words on paper, she thinks she's quite a good story-writer and keeps plugging away.’*

## Point Out Achievements

If your child is feeling really low about something at school – perhaps he's struggling in maths or thinks he's a terrible swimmer – he might not want to discuss it. So don't. Instead, sit down together and come up with a list of all the wonderful things he *can* do. Tally up everything you can think of together.

A younger child might be able to:
- Hop on one leg
- Stay the night at Granny's on his own
- Draw an intergalactic superblaster
- Undress himself
- Walk the dog

An older child might also be able to:
- Work the washing machine
- Scramble eggs
- Cycle to the shop
- Sleep in a tent
- Keep an eye on younger brothers and sisters

And he will almost certainly understand all the baffling gadgets in the house. Can you download music on to your mobile phone or programme Sky Plus without him?

You will both be amazed at how long the list gets. He should start feeling better about himself. After making such a list with his parents, one boy said, 'Wow! I really can do lots of things, can't I?'

## Helping Your Child to Read

If your child is struggling to read and losing heart, focus on the parts he's getting right and he's more likely to try again:
- *'Well done, it does start with a B. Have another go at the next sound.'*

- *'That was a good guess. It does sound like "bees". Let's take another look.'*

Even when his reading is becoming more fluent, it's worth keeping up the praise:

- *'Nice expression. That ogre sounds mean.'*
- *'You worked out some pretty difficult words.'*

If you are listening to an older child read out loud, you don't always have to make detailed comments, nor should you if he finds them embarrassing. By paying attention and briefly mentioning that he's read well, he'll know you've noticed.

## *Try being a TUNED-IN PARENT*

Listening to your child is vital if you want to boost his self-esteem. Just letting him unload his feelings at the end of the day and accepting whatever he has to say – good, bad and mundane – can go a long way towards making him feel that you love him unconditionally and he's an OK person.

Listening is also important because going to school can be a stressful business. So much of what children come up against is unexplored territory for them. Learning can be fun, but it can also be frustrating and downright difficult.

> *At an open evening at my daughter's kindergarten, the teacher held up a sheet of Persian writing. It was all swirls and squiggles and none of it meant anything to any of us. She said, 'I wanted to remind you all how hard it is for these four- and five-year-olds to learn to read. We know what A, B and C mean. These children are decoding symbols that are completely new to them.'*

When children can't do something well at school, it can knock the confidence out of them. Fear of failure, especially public failure, is a powerful emotion and our children have to deal with it constantly.

> *I never learned to ride a bicycle and my husband took me to the park to teach me. I was wobbling along and kept having to put my foot down so I wouldn't topple over. A gang of teenagers strolled past and one of them started pointing and laughing at me, saying, 'You can't even ride a bike!'*
>
> *I was so humiliated. Tears smarted in my eyes and I gave up and went home. In the end it took me five years and two days to learn. Five years to get over my hurt pride, and two days of practising until I could do it on my own.*

When your child has a problem, it's natural to want to give advice immediately. But if you listen sympathetically and accept his feelings, you'll be in a much better position to help him deal with it.

> *My daughter used to cry because she hated going to school on swimming days. I gave her all sorts of advice about using a float and staying in the shallow end until she got used to it.*
>
> *But that wasn't the problem. Eventually she told me that the swimming part was fine, but she was afraid of going down the steep hill to the pool in the school bus.*
>
> *Once I knew that, I could help her. Her teacher agreed to sit next to her until she wasn't frightened by it any more.*

If you want your child to confide in you, try to get into the habit of tuning in and listening non-judgementally when he tells you about his day. If he knows you'll listen, the chances are he'll come to you when he has something more major on his mind.

If he comes home unhappy, it's tempting to stop listening and start talking. You'll probably feel desperate to cheer him up or tell him what to do. But there is absolutely no point doing so until he has talked it through.

***Accept difficult feelings*** Sometimes tuning in can feel subversive, if you find yourself agreeing that maths can be horrible or that teachers can be unfair.

- *'You're upset about that maths. It's awful when you try and you still can't work it out.'*
- *'I can tell you're dreading that French test tomorrow.'*
- *'Doing ballet with the girls must have been really embarrassing.'*
- *'You're worried because you've got no idea how to even start your project.'*
- *'You weren't the only one messing around, so you felt it was unfair that you got told off.'*
- *'It must have been humiliating when Mrs Adams shouted at you in front of everyone.'*
- *'You don't feel like going to school this morning. It's cold and dark and you'd rather stay in bed.'*

But you're not undermining the school's authority or letting your child off the hook. You aren't saying he can be rude to his teacher or that he doesn't have to do his homework. And even if it is cold and dark, he still has to go to school. You are simply accepting his feelings. Try to resist the temptation to say 'But . . .' and get preachy. Just listen to him and let him know you understand how he feels.

## *Try being a COMMANDO PARENT*

**Give information** Once you've tuned in and he's calmed down and feels understood, of course you can go ahead and give him advice. In fact, if he's feeling unconfident at school, it's very important to give him some perspective on his problems.

- *'You'll feel better in the morning.'*
- *'You don't have to come top.'*
- *'I know you wanted to be in the team, but I am proud of you for trying.'*
- *'Maths isn't optional, so for the time being you've got no choice but to get on with it.'*

These are things he needs to know. But timing is everything. If you want to help him feel better, you can't go straight in with the common-sense advice. Tune in first or you could make him feel worse, and the two of you could end up arguing.

## *Try being a LAID-BACK PARENT* 

*Allow them to do more* Another way to improve his confidence is by letting him do more for himself, so he feels proud of small daily achievements. What these things are and how much supervision he needs will depend on his age, but suggestions range from letting him choose his own clothes to letting him cook or make short journeys on his own.

If he's sure of himself in some areas, he may not take it so hard when he doesn't do well in others.

*Ask for solutions* Instead of always trying to solve your child's problems, ask him for his own suggestions and solutions. If he asks you a homework question, try saying:

- *'That's a good question. What do you think?'*
- *'That's interesting. How would you solve it?'*

Your aim is to get his brain working, and it's great training for problem-solving. He will gain confidence by thinking round problems himself or knowing how to look things up on the internet.

But judge it carefully. If all he wants is a simple answer to a simple question, it can be incredibly irritating for him if you make him look it up. And there may be times when he really needs your help.

## *Try being a SORTED PARENT* 

**Sorted Parents** build confidence by making sure their children are well prepared for school. Rather than dropping them in at the deep end, they try to give lots of help.

*Train them up* **Sorted Parents** expose their children in advance to things they know will come up at school. These can range from teaching the alphabet, to doing some minor addition or taking a couple of swimming lessons. Their children feel more confident when they encounter these things at school because they aren't totally unfamiliar with them.

If you show a small child how to weigh and measure ingredients when baking, he'll be familiar with weighing and measuring when he does them in maths and later in science. If you allow him to hold money and hand it to the shopkeeper, he'll feel more confident when his teacher starts talking about coins. The same holds true if he has had some exposure to telling the time, or passing a football. Similarly, you might take an older child to the museum to see the mummies before he studies Egypt or to an Elizabethan house before he does the Tudors.

This strategy is particularly helpful in areas where you know your child lacks confidence. Over time you can gradually expose him to things until they're no longer a big deal. Literally or metaphorically, hold his hand and take it slowly. For example, if he's scared of swimming, let him get used to wetting his hair in the bath, then playing in a paddling pool, then dangling his feet in the shallow end of the baby pool. But don't put any pressure on him. The more relaxed he feels, the more likely it is that he'll begin to enjoy it.

Whether it's school work or sports, regular practice boosts confidence because it helps your child to improve over time. If he gets better he may make the team and get even more coaching at school. The more he plays, the better he'll get.

But if your child hasn't yet developed sufficient interest or skills, the cycle can become a negative one. If he doesn't think he's any good at football, he may feel discouraged and not want to play at all. It's so easy to drop further and further behind. He may end up giving up altogether.

*'I can't believe it. My daughter didn't get on to any team at her new school. The atmosphere is so much more competitive than at her primary school and it has completely destroyed her confidence. Now she thinks she's so rubbish she says she hates sports.'*

Children need to know that if they keep having a go at something they will slowly get better at it. As Lloyd Gordon, a martial arts teacher, told us:

*If a kid isn't naturally sporty I tell him not to worry about it. Anyone can learn if they put in the time and the practice. Things usually have to be broken down into simple steps and practised separately before they come together. I tell my pupils that there is no point in getting upset if they can't do something the first time. Your body often has to practise something hundreds of times before it becomes natural and automatic.*

Showing your child how to do things step by step can help him in lots of areas. A big school project won't seem so daunting if you show him how to break it up into small, manageable pieces. He might be putting it off because he doesn't think he can handle it.

*My son had six weeks to do a big science project, but he never settled down to it. On the last weekend he was hysterical with anxiety, and we stayed up until midnight, painting ping-pong balls to look like planets and gluing them on to bits of wire. I vowed, never again.*

*Next time round it was a project on pollution. He didn't even want to talk about it, but we sat down and worked out a plan of what he needed to do and when. It wasn't too bad in the end. He did a bit every week, handed it in on time with no stress, and ended up getting a merit for it.*

Going to a new school can be particularly intimidating. Try to take your child to visit it beforehand so he isn't so overwhelmed on that first scary day.

*My son was changing schools and was quite nervous about it. He liked the playground and games pitches, so we spent time looking and talking about them over the holidays. By the time term started he couldn't wait to get there.*

If the school is happy to give out telephone numbers, invite some other children round so he has a chance to meet them in advance and will know people when he gets there.

***Sort your systems*** Though teachers do their best, in a large class they may not always be able to work out what makes each child tick, or have the time to help each one individually. If your child gets left behind, he can lose confidence. **Sorted Parents** realize their child might do better with a different approach.

*‘My daughter thought she was no good at English, because she found it so hard to write stories. So I taught her how to do it in a very formulaic way, which has helped her a lot. She asked me why no one had ever shown her before. I told her I was sure her teacher had tried, but not in a way she could understand.’*

*‘My son’s school used a phonetic method to build up words and teach the children to read. He couldn’t get the hang of it. He was unhappy because he was miles behind everyone else, and it broke my heart. When I bought a more traditional method and worked with him at home, he picked it up quite easily.’*

If your child isn’t doing well at school, helping him find a hobby or an interest outside might help him. It doesn’t matter if it’s mainstream or obscure – singing, trampolining, even stamp collecting – as long as he enjoys it. Perhaps he is more creative than academic, better at building things than conceptualizing, or perhaps he excels in a sport that isn’t offered at school. It will be an added bonus if he becomes good at it and makes new friends.

*‘I took my kids to trampolining lessons at the sports centre, and I noticed that a chubby teenage girl was nearly always there. She said she wasn’t much good at anything at school, but trampolining was something she could do well, so she came almost every day.’*

*‘I signed my daughter up for some drama lessons on Saturdays. School’s not her thing, but she looks forward to them all week.’*

## Your Own Expectations

*It's great to try to build your child's confidence at school by coaching him, but it's worth thinking about your motives. If you were very sporty or academic, you may want him to be the same. Or if you weren't, you may want him to have more opportunities. But don't forget that he may not be particularly interested in these things, or very good at them, and too much pressure can put him off altogether.*

*Try to keep your own feelings out of the equation and accept your child as he is. Not being able to live up to your expectations can damage his self-esteem.*

*It's worth keeping an open mind about your child and his abilities. We know adults who say they were no good at maths until they went to secondary school, and then it suddenly clicked. And children's fine motor skills develop at different times, so he might get better at sport as he gets older.*

## *Try being a LAID-BACK PARENT* 

**Get help** However good your intentions, sometimes you aren't the best person to help your child. This is particularly true if he has a real block about something, refuses to cooperate, or if you aren't that confident with the topic yourself. If this is the case, maybe his other parent can help.

> *My son was phobic about swimming. I tried to take him a couple of times, and he refused to go near the water. But while we were on holiday last summer he hopped into the pool with his father, no problem.*

Or you may have to find another teacher.

> *I tried to teach my daughter the piano. But she drove me mad when she wouldn't concentrate and fiddled around with the keys. We struggled on getting nowhere, and I got so angry I'd sometimes reduce her*

*to tears. The unhappier she got, the more mistakes she made. Eventually I could see that I was grinding down her confidence. So I found a piano teacher instead.* ’

# Boredom

***'My son says he doesn't like school because it is boring. What can I do?'***

There are any number of reasons, other than lack of confidence, why your child might say he is bored. He may be super bright and catch on after the first two sentences, he may be the type who gets the big picture very easily and isn't interested in the detail (this is often true of dyslexics), perhaps the subject doesn't sing to his heart and he doesn't see the point, or he could simply have a boring teacher.

First, find out what's going on.

## *Try being a TUNED-IN PARENT* 

***Listen to their feelings*** When your child starts complaining, let him talk. We know how hard it is to listen when he moans about being bored at school, especially when you know he wouldn't be if he just paid attention. But your pep talk will go in one ear and right out the other if you don't listen first and show that you understand.

- *'I know you think she's boring. It must be torture to have to sit there and listen to her all day.'*

Your hope, of course, is that you can solve this one quickly. With any luck, once he airs his grievances, he will let them go and move on. But sometimes it's a slow process, so keep listening. He needs to unburden himself, and the more you understand, the easier it will be to help him.

## *Try being a LAID-BACK PARENT*

**Ask for solutions** Once you've tuned in, ask him what it would take to get him interested. If he comes up with a solution, there's more chance of it working.

This can work quite well for bright children who whiz through their work and then get bored and disruptive.

*'Maths lessons aren't streamed in my son's school, and he found the work so easy that he was being a nightmare in class. He asked me to ask the teacher if he could have extra worksheets. They've been keeping him busy, so his behaviour has been much better.'*

It's not always easy to change the school curriculum, but you can try.

*'My son kept complaining that his science lessons were boring and that he wished they could do more experiments. I had a word with the school head, who was amazing and made sure there were more hands-on things for them to do.'*

Even if the school won't cooperate and your child is still bored, at least he'll feel that you understand him, and that you both did your best to try and change things.

### Ways to Interest Your Child in School Subjects

Once you know why your child is bored or switched off, you need to find a way to get him motivated. One day he will be able to drop the subjects he doesn't like, but it probably won't be until he is fourteen and starting his GCSEs. Until then he's going to have to sit through endless hours of history, geography and modern languages. If you can help make the boring bits fun and relevant, he might engage and see the point. Really good teachers are brilliant at this. They know that once a child is interested, he'll be much more able and willing to learn.

**Here's how some parents have tackled the problem:**

*My daughter found the Victorians excruciating. Her teacher is obsessed by Victorian engineering and went on and on about bridges and railways, which isn't her thing at all. So we checked the internet and looked at fashion instead, and corsets and what happened to women's insides when they wore them. She found it really interesting.*

*My daughter kept complaining about maths, saying she didn't see the point. So I suggested we make chocolate-chip cookies, and double the quantity so she could take them to school for her class.*

*We worked out how much of each ingredient we needed to buy, and measured everything out. After baking them we counted them out. I never let on about my motives, but at the end I complimented her on all the great maths she'd done.*

**More ideas include:**

- ***Maths*** Most children are fascinated by money. So let your child handle it and teach him to compare prices, add up bills and count the change.
- ***Reading*** Spark his interest in books with bedtime stories. You don't have to stick to the conventional ones. He might be happier with *Guinness World Records* or the Captain Underpants series.
- ***Singing*** Sing along to the radio in the car, so he doesn't think singing is just for girls.
- ***Performing arts*** Take him to a show to inspire him to take up dancing, acting or music.
- ***Sports*** Kick a football around with him, hit tennis balls against a wall, go cycling or play games when you go out on walks, so he sees what fun it is.
- ***Science*** Lots of museums have hands-on experiments. There are also some fun kits you can use at home, like making volcanoes and growing crystals.

### *Try being a CHEERLEADER PARENT*

***Be open-minded*** It's important to look at your own attitude. If you thought school was boring, never took to reading or maths, or thought drama was a waste of time, it is easy to influence your child. If you are trying to keep him interested in school, it's best not to cloud his views with your own.

> *My son had always sung in the school choir. But when he moved on to senior school my husband put him off by telling him it wasn't cool. So he refused to audition. His three best friends did join the choir, and they all went off to New Zealand on a choir trip. What a waste.*

# Specific School-Related Problems

## Getting to School on Time

For many of us, the first job in the morning is getting our children to school. Easy – until you factor in making sure they're fed, dressed in the right gear, with hair and teeth brushed, bags packed with gym/swimming/sports kit and instruments, forms signed, snacks and lunches organized and homework finished.

It's complicated no matter how many children you have, and the more you have, the more complicated it gets. If you also have to clean up the kitchen, feed the baby or get yourself off to work, you need to be organized or you don't stand a chance. This is where **Sorted Parents** come into their own.

### *Try being a SORTED PARENT*

***'Getting out of the door in the morning is a nightmare. How can I avoid that last half-hour of hell?'***

Getting sorted in advance is the key to everything. If you aren't naturally sorted and don't have some sort of system in place, it's a perpetual wind-up.

*I loathe those smug, organized parents who always seem to get their children to school early. But underneath it all, I wish I knew how they did it.*

Getting organized might not be as hard as you think. Try a few of the following ideas and see if they work for you.

***Sort your systems*** It's completely obvious to **Sorted Parents** how to get organized, but it can take the rest of us years to work out how to get out of the door on time – if we ever do. The trick is to get as much done as possible the night before, so you don't start running late and panicking at the last minute. **Sorted Parents** also train their children to help.

- *Put homework and reading books in school bags.*
- *Put school bags by the front door.*
- *Pack sports bags/instruments so they are ready to go, also leave by the front door.*
- *Put gloves, hats, coats, shoes, scooters and helmets in one obvious place.*
- *Put uniforms in separate piles for each child.*
- *Pack snacks or lunches and put in the fridge.*
- *Lay the table for breakfast and set out whatever you can the night before.*
- *Figure out how long everyone needs to get washed and dressed, eat breakfast and leave, then set the alarm.*

***Bite the bullet*** Unbelievable. Do you really have to do all this before you go to bed? No, of course not. But otherwise you might have to get up at dawn to run round the house and find everything. Take your pick. If you and your children are suffering morning after stressful morning, you might as well accept your fate and set up some good systems. Otherwise it's impossible to avoid that last half-hour of hell. Set aside half an hour before bedtime instead so everyone can help get things organized.

## When Your Child Doesn't Want to Go to School

For some parents, the problem isn't getting organized, it's motivating a reluctant child.

> *My son hates school. He drags his feet every morning. He doesn't want to get up or get dressed, he refuses to eat his breakfast and complains of feeling ill. It's a major production just getting him out of the door.*

### *Try being a TUNED-IN PARENT*

If your child is refusing to go to school, your best strategy, by far, is to tune in. There could be all sorts of reasons behind his behaviour – he could be nervous about a test or ground down by weeks of bullying. He might be having trouble with friends or with his teacher. If you're going through a tough time (a messy divorce, for example), he might feel worried about leaving you at home.

Once you've taken the time to listen, you can start working on a solution.

### *Try being a PHYSICAL PARENT*

If your child is slow in the morning and reluctant to get out of bed and get ready, don't necessarily assume he's having a problem with school. He might be exhausted by mild anaemia or glandular fever, or simply too many late nights. Some children just aren't morning people and they don't feel alert and ready to face the day.

You might try putting him to bed earlier, but he may be a night owl and won't fall asleep. This is a problem that often gets worse for teenagers, because their body clocks can change.

Here are some things that might help:

- *Start by getting him a good alarm clock – he may even need two.*
- *You may not want to provide room service, but try bringing him some juice or a rice-cake. After a whole night without food,*

*he might feel better immediately after a small sugar boost.*

- *Open his curtains. The daylight will stimulate his melatonin levels.*
- *Check he is doing enough exercise. If he isn't, he will feel much more tired in the morning than a child who exercises regularly.*

### *Try being a COMMANDO PARENT*

You can't allow one child to hold up the entire household when you're running against the clock to get everyone to school on time. As long as there isn't actually anything wrong with him, school isn't optional and there simply isn't time to argue or negotiate. This is when you need to go straight to consequences.

> *'When my daughter holds us up in the morning, I tell her the others can't be late because of her. So if that means she goes to school in her pyjamas or without her books, so be it.'*

## Disorganized Children

### *'My son is so disorganized. He's late, he's forgetful, his stuff is a mess. Why can't he get himself together for a change?'*

Organized children just seem to know instinctively that they need to be at school early on Monday, they need their trainers on Tuesday and their library book on Thursday. Disorganized children haven't even clocked what day of the week it is. They are the ones mooning around in a world of their own, amazed every morning when it's time to leave for school. Their homework, if it came home at all, is scattered all over the house, their school shoes have disappeared. By the time they've found everything, they've missed the school bus. And later, to top it all off, they call you from the school office asking you to bring in their swimming bag, which they left on the back seat of the car.

Disorganized children create a lot of stress for themselves and their parents. But scolding them doesn't help. Many of them simply aren't capable of changing on their own and need your help.

## *Try being a CHEERLEADER PARENT* 

Start by praising your disorganized child as often and as specifically as you can. He is probably used to causing a lot of anger and being criticized. The way to begin turning things around is to start noticing the good.

***Notice the good, ignore the bad*** Try to give him attention for being organized instead of constantly reminding him of his failures. You might be thinking that we don't know your child and just how scatty he is. But we guarantee that if you start looking, you will find something to praise him for, no matter how small. You want to start helping him to see himself as an organized, helpful person instead of a disorganized, irritating one.

- *'Two of your books are in your book bag. Well done.'*
- *'You're right. When you have football I do pick you up late. Thanks for reminding me.'*

## *Try being a SORTED PARENT* 

It's so tempting and far more efficient to organize a disorganized child by packing up his bag for him and stuffing it in his hands as he goes out the door. But if he expects you to do everything for him, he'll never start learning to do things for himself.

But leaving him to fend for himself is cruel. Most disorganized children simply wouldn't be able to cope. When there are things to be done, they don't have a sense of structure or timing, and it is hard for them to prioritize their thoughts. Without a clear mental map, they can easily become overwhelmed or distracted.

***Train them up*** The situation isn't hopeless. Help your child to come up with ways to remember what's happening when. You might help him draw up a chart so he knows what he needs to take to school on which day, and another for his desk at school so he knows what to bring home. Then you can teach him how to pack up his school bag himself at night when he isn't rushed and there's time to find everything.

At first you might feel you can't spare the extra time to explain everything and supervise him. But as he becomes more self-reliant (and there are fewer last-minute disasters to deal with) you'll start to save time.

**Sort your systems** It's worth remembering that your child may be disorganized because of the way his brain works. For example, he may be better at taking information in visually than being told what to do.

> *My son can't take in too much at once. If I ask him to do more than two things at a time, he covers his ears with his hands and shouts, 'Stop giving me so many things to do! It's too hard for me!' But if I write him a list, he will happily work his way through the whole thing more quickly and efficiently than anyone else in the family.*

Some children are better with oral instructions, while some need to be shown what to do and practise doing it themselves before it clicks. Your child may need a combination of approaches.

## *Try being a LAID-BACK PARENT*

**Ask for solutions** You can encourage responsibility by asking your child for ideas, especially in areas he finds difficult.

- *'We need to find a way to stop your mouthguard getting lost again. Where would you like to keep it so you always know where to find it?'*

## *Try being a TUNED-IN PARENT*

Some children are disorganized because they find school – or life in general – complicated and overwhelming. They would rather tune out and think about something totally different. Sometimes troubles at home can affect behaviour and concentration at school.

As one school head told us:

*I always know when parents are getting divorced, long before they tell me. I can see it in the child's behaviour. He is not quite there, not quite with us here at school.*

Tuning in and listening is the best thing you can do to help him.

## Homework

### *'Getting my son to do his homework absolutely ruins my day, every day. How on earth can I persuade him to get on with it?'*

After six to eight hours at school, most children just want to switch off and chill out when they get home. It's tough for them to rev up their brains again and tackle a pile of homework. It can be tough for parents, too. If your child doesn't do his homework willingly, coaxing and nagging is a horrible task. It can be a total nightmare, a massive time-waster, and mess up your whole evening.

Some children will do anything and everything under the sun to avoid the inevitable, from sitting for hours sucking their pencil to claiming – yet again – to have forgotten to bring their work home. You may find yourself negotiating deals and threatening punishments until you both end up angry, defiant, or in tears.

*Unless I'm on his case, my son will find any excuse to avoid his homework. Yesterday he insisted he had to look something up on the computer, and I caught him playing Club Penguin again.'*

*Getting my daughter to do her homework is torture, and it can take hours to finish it. If I get angry, she sits staring at her paper in tears.*

If he would only sit down and polish his homework off quickly and efficiently, you would both have more time for other things.

We are going to show you how to make this happen. If you are only having minor homework problems, you might find the right piece of the jigsaw puzzle first time. We will talk you through the easiest options first, in the hope that one of them will work.

But if you have a serious time-waster who holds out until you force him or gets away with doing no homework at all, there may not be an instant fix. To get him into good homework habits will probably take time and a combination of parent skills.

## *Try being a PAUSE PARENT*

*Zip your lip and wait until later* If the homework saga is driving you crazy, take a deep breath, stop whatever you are doing, and don't get sucked into the drama. If your strategy isn't working, whether it is nagging or ignoring the problem, you need the space to think your way through another one.

## *Try being a PHYSICAL PARENT*

**Physical Parents** know there are simple ways to improve their child's concentration. He may need a snack to raise his blood sugar, or to run around after being cooped up at school all day. Or if he's exhausted, he may need some down time before he can face his homework.

All these things will also improve his mood. If he's foul and argumentative from the minute you pick him up, don't take it personally. He probably just needs food, exercise or a bit of peace and quiet. Once you sort these things out he may not only be prepared to do his homework, but he'll be a lot nicer to be around.

*Just be there* **Physical Parents** also know the power of simply being there. Some children work well on their own, especially as they get older. But the majority of primary-school children feel happier if someone else is nearby. If your child is small, sit him on your knee for early reading practice or simple sums. As he gets bigger, you can sit next to him, watching and helping, or doing your own paperwork at the table. In time you'll be able to get on with your chores in the same room. Lots of children do their homework at the kitchen table while their parents make dinner. Plenty of others sit right in the middle of the living-room floor to be near the action rather than going off to their own rooms.

If you have a problem giving him your undivided attention, put your answering machine on and switch off your mobile phone during homework time.

## *Try being a TUNED-IN PARENT*

***Listen to their feelings*** If your child says he doesn't want to do his homework, try listening to him to find out why. The more you can understand what lies behind the laziness and defiance, the easier it should be to untangle. Once he feels understood, he's more likely to get down to his work.

- *'It must be awful having to sit here and work when you can hear your sister playing outside.'*
- *'I get it. You don't want to learn French vocab because you don't see the point.'*

You aren't agreeing that he doesn't have to do it. You are only showing that you understand how he feels.

## *Try being a CHEERLEADER PARENT*

***Notice the good and be specific*** Once he does *anything* that has to do with homework, give him positive instead of negative attention for it. If you're desperate you could even start with:

- *'Thanks for turning off the television.'*

If he's begun his homework, but is irritating you by dawdling, try to motivate him by finding something positive but specific to say:

- *'I see you've written your name at the top. That's a good place to start.'*
- *'You've copied out the first problem so it's all clear. Good idea.'*
- *'I can tell you've been thinking about what to do next.'*

If your child hates doing homework, one of the best things you can do is try to help him feel good about it. Start by pointing out everything he is doing right. This isn't always easy. When checking over homework, the wrong answers are the ones that leap right off the page. What's the first thing you notice about this sentence?

The black catt sat on the mat.

You may not be able to take your eyes off that double 't'. If your child wrote it, it would be nearly impossible not to home in like a hornet and correct him; he needs to know how to spell.

But if you can manage to hold back and show him what he has done *right*, he will often work out for himself what he has done wrong.

You may be baffled at this point. What has he done right? What can you possibly say? How about noticing the nice clear handwriting, the good spacing that separates the words, the capital letter at the beginning of the sentence, the full stop at the end, or the fact that six out of the seven words are spelled correctly?

You don't have to ignore that double 't' for ever. But if you want to teach your child how to spell 'cat' properly, make sure he is receptive by picking out something positive to mention first.

Even when you come to correct the mistake, it works well to notice the letters that are right. You could say:

- *'In this word you've got every letter right, and they are all in the right order. But there is one letter too many.'*

If you don't give him the answer but he gets it right, you have yet another chance to praise him.

Of course, you won't need to go through this whole routine every time he makes a spelling mistake. But it's a good way to help him without being over-critical. If he has a longer homework assignment, try tapping each correct answer with your pencil, and keeping up a flow of nice comments. When you get to one that's wrong, don't say anything at all. Just skip over it. At the end of the page, tell your child he can be proud of himself for getting so many right. With luck, by this point he'll be bursting to tell you that he's worked out for himself where he went wrong.

- *'I know, I know. That one is two times eight so it should be sixteen.'*
- *'I thought I got question six wrong. I couldn't work out how to do it.'*

If he doesn't know the right answer, it's no big deal at this point to help him figure it out. If you've noticed the ones he got right, he won't be feeling stupid or defensive about the others.

If he is on to more difficult maths problems, try praising him for individual steps, starting with the way he's set the work out on the page. If he's writing an essay, pick out a couple of things you like before mentioning any part that could be improved.

## *Try being a LAID-BACK PARENT*

***Ask for solutions*** Try asking him how to sort out the homework problem. He's more likely to follow through if the ideas are his own.

> *'My children always wanted to play in the garden straight after school. But after running around, then eating dinner, they were always too tired to do their homework. We tried catching up in the morning, but there was never enough time.*
>
> *So I asked them how to get it done. To my surprise, they suggested starting their homework the minute they got home, so they could do whatever they wanted for the rest of the day. We tried it, and they've stuck to that system ever since.'*

If your child always expects you to do his homework for him, try answering his questions with questions:

- *'That's really interesting. What do you think?'*

or:

- *'How would you find that out?'*

***Let them do more*** You might also try backing off completely. You can tell your child it's his choice whether he does his homework or not. It sounds like a risky strategy – maybe he'll choose not to do it at all.

But knowing you won't be nagging him any more might be enough to get him to take responsibility for it. If not, mention he'll have to face the consequences with his teacher. The mere threat of getting her involved may get him moving. If he knows he'll have to explain missing homework personally, it may suddenly seem worth getting on with it. Discuss this with his teacher first, so you can work together. Your plan will backfire if she doesn't notice it's missing.

***Accept help*** You may have to accept that you're losing the battle and need help. Try getting other adults in the house to oversee homework, find out if there's an after-school study period where he can finish it off before coming home, or if you have to, hire someone else to help him.

> *I pay my neighbour's daughter, who's thirteen, to come once a week and help my children with their spellings. They look forward to it because they think she's cool.*

## *Try being a SORTED PARENT*

**Sorted Parents** are good at thinking up new ways to tackle problems.

***Sort your systems*** If your child is younger, look around for ways to make homework more interesting. You can work on times tables in the bath or while walking to school, stick spelling words on the fridge, make flash cards, or work on adding and subtracting using chocolate buttons.

***Give advance warning and set up rules*** With an older child, you may have to get tougher and make a concerted effort for a few weeks to change his homework habits.

Lots of children are reluctant to get down to homework because they've drifted into the habit of playing on the computer, watching television or messing around instead. And lots of parents are inconsistent about making sure homework gets done because they're busy or don't want to create a bad atmosphere by nagging.

The idea of setting up a new routine can seem daunting, especially if your child is stubborn or if you feel ambivalent about homework and wish he could play in the garden all afternoon. But if you warn him in advance and are clear about what's going to happen, the process may not be as difficult as you think.

- *'Starting next week, as soon as we get home, we'll have a snack and then it's straight down to homework.'*
- *'From next Monday, there will be no television, computer or Game Boy until homework is done. So it is worth getting on with it as quickly as you can.'*

You may also have to clear your diary to focus completely on the homework issue for the first week or so to make sure he doesn't bend the rules.

## *Try being a COMMANDO PARENT* 

While you are reinforcing the new rules, a couple of **Commando** approaches might stop the foot-dragging.

Giving options might help:

- *'Do you want to do your homework down here or in your bedroom?'*
- *'Do you want me to help you or do it on your own?'*

Or promising rewards:

- *'Once you've finished your homework your time is your own and you can do whatever you want for the rest of the day.'*
- *'If you finish your sums in the next fifteen minutes, I'll have time for a quick game before I start dinner.'*

If your child is still fussing, you may have to get tough with consequences:

- *'You know computer games aren't allowed until your homework is finished. I'm taking away the laptop until you have done it.*

*If I catch you fooling around again, there'll be no screen time today at all.'*

### Dealing with Chronic Offenders

In difficult cases, establishing good homework habits can take a concerted effort and you might need to combine several parent skills.

*'Trying to get homework done was awful. For months it was like a dark cloud hanging over the house. I did my best. I nagged, I left him to do it on his own, I tried star charts, but nothing helped.*

*In the end I spent two weeks focusing on establishing a routine. I made the rules as simple as I could – no treats, football or TV until homework was finished. Then I'd sit with him at the table and tried to give him lots of encouragement. I also asked his teacher to praise him for anything he handed in.*

*It was very hard going, and it took a lot of my time and energy enforcing the new rules. But after two weeks of insisting he stuck to them, he stopped arguing. Finally homework wasn't such an issue, and he started doing much better at school, too.'*

This mother did a great job of being a **Sorted Parent** by organizing a new regime, a **Commando Parent** by sticking to her rules, and a **Cheerleader Parent** by praising her son's efforts. Part of her genius was also getting the teacher involved. Very few children can stand up to a coordinated parent–teacher pincer movement.

## Perfectionist Children

If your child is a perfectionist, you may have the opposite problem. You won't need to nag him to do his homework; he'll work hard and make a good job of it on his own. But if he doesn't meet his own high standards, the emotional fall-out can be disruptive and exhausting for everyone.

*My daughter spends hours obsessing over her homework. She will rip it up and start all over again because of one little ink spot, and work herself up into a total state if she doesn't think she's done her best work. True, she gets high marks. But you can't imagine the scene when she doesn't.*

If your child thinks it's a tragedy if he only gets 19 out of 20 in a spelling test, sucking you and everyone else into the drama, you might want to tell him to keep things in perspective, lighten up and get over it. But start by pausing.

## *Try being a PAUSE PARENT*

*Zip your lip* If you find you are getting dragged into a scene, don't get involved. While your child is caught up in his frustration and disappointment, he won't listen to reason. Pause and let him calm down. He'll be more rational later.

## *Try being a TUNED-IN PARENT*

*Listen to their feelings* Tuning in to a perfectionist child can be hard, especially if he has been driving everyone demented. If you feel he is fussing over nothing, you may not feel very sympathetic. But if you want him to listen to you later, tuning in is the place to start.

- *'You like to hand in homework that looks perfect. You've been working hard and you want to impress your teacher.'*
- *'You were very disappointed with that mark. It annoys you when you don't do as well as you'd like.'*

The more sympathetic you can be, the faster he will calm down.

## *Try being a COMMANDO PARENT*

*Give information* Once you get the sense that your child feels understood, then you can help him put his problem into perspective.

- *'It's frustrating to spend a long time on your homework and still not be happy with it. But it's bedtime. You'll feel much better about it in the morning. Leave it for now, and have another look tomorrow.'*

- *'I know you're disappointed, but you can't always get everything right. Getting 19 out of 20 is a great result, and shows you worked hard learning all those words. I think you can be very proud of yourself for the work you put in.'*

## Dealing with Disappointment

Although perfectionists particularly hate disappointment because they drive themselves so hard, everybody has to learn to deal with it.

*My daughter was so looking forward to the school play. But when she was cast as a tree (no singing, no dancing, no lines) she cried for weeks.*

So what do you do?

Do lots of tuning in until your child calms down and then you can give information.

- *'There will be more school plays in the future, and if you want a better part next time, let's sign you up for singing and drama after school so you can practise.'*

If he's still feeling demoralized from the disappointment, see p. 208 for ways to boost his confidence.

# Peer Pressure

### *'My son is goofing around because he wants to be part of the cool crowd. I could throttle him.'*

On one level, you can't blame him. Even in the most well-run, academic schools, children can be picked on for being a nerd or the teacher's pet. But it's so disappointing if your child doesn't try. It's also a shame if he wastes the teacher's time and disrupts the entire class. Either way the following parent skills will help:

## *Try being a TUNED-IN PARENT* 

*Listen to their feelings* Though this might be one of those times when you want to tell your child to stop being such an idiot, hold back if you can. If you've got this far you're ten steps ahead of many parents, because at least your child is talking to you about it. Instead, try tuning in:

- *'You don't want to look like a geek by being good at maths, so you haven't been trying.'*
- *'I can understand how you feel. You want to keep your friends.'*

## *Try being a COMMANDO PARENT* 

*Give information* If you try to give him advice immediately, he may write you off as a sad loser who doesn't understand anything. But if you do enough tuning in, he's far more likely to accept what you say.

- *'You think you can't be part of the cool crowd and do well at school. But the coolest ones are the ones who do both.'*

## *Try being a LAID-BACK PARENT* 

*Ask for solutions* It might also help if you ask him for ideas or come up with suggestions together.

- *'That's a great idea. If you ask Mr Woodward if you can sit at the front, you won't get distracted by the others messing around.'*

If your child is still desperate to fit in with the crowd, see the sections on confidence (pp. 119–23) and making friends (pp. 115–19) for more ideas.

## Trouble with Teachers

If your child doesn't get on with his teacher, you can have a big problem on your hands. He probably spends more waking hours with her than with you, and their relationship can have a big impact on his level of effort and his confidence.

Good teachers naturally do lots of praising, reinforcing your child's good habits by noticing the things he does right, and taking the time to tune in and understand the reasons behind what he does wrong. But with so many children packed into a classroom, even the best teachers can struggle.

As we know, it is only too easy to forget the times when our children behave well. It's the bad behaviour, the shuffling, wriggling, ignoring us and rudeness that get our attention. Imagine multiplying this kind of aggravation by twenty or thirty.

If your child is good at handling criticism, a grouchy teacher isn't the end of the world. He might be able to see her as an unpleasant but inevitable part of school life. He may be able to develop strategies to avoid her or stay on her good side, or realize that her comments aren't personal.

But often children don't like their teacher if they suspect their teacher doesn't like them, and find it hard to cope. A sensitive child can pick up signals that he isn't one of his teacher's favourites, or assume she hates him weeks after an incident she's completely forgotten. The trigger could be quite small, even run of the mill – being told off for a bad test result, missing a ball or messing around.

If he takes her comments personally, he can slip into a downward spiral. The worse he feels about himself, the more sullen or disruptive he can become. The less he tries, the more likely she is to criticize him.

### Helping your child

If the relationship goes wrong and your child's teacher thinks he's badly behaved, disruptive, sloppy, lazy or stupid, you might need to step in.

So what do you do? You can't shield him from his teacher's criticism; you aren't there. You may be tempted to go straight in and have it out with her, but there's plenty you can do behind the scenes.

When he presents himself as the victim, it can be hard to admit that he may actually be part of the problem. But if his attitude or behaviour needs to change, you can help him to work on it. Even if he is blameless, but stuck with a foul teacher, you can help him find ways to cope. If you eventually do go and talk to her, we will show you ways to make the discussion as productive and angst-free as possible.

## *Try being a TUNED-IN PARENT* 

***Listen to their feelings*** Start by listening. This might give your child the strength to go back in and face another day. Being stuck in a classroom or sports hall with someone he dislikes, who has power over him and makes him feel anxious, can stir up strong emotions. So let him talk and show you understand.

- *'Mm, that sounds bad.'*
- *'So he shouted at you and it wasn't even your fault?'*
- *'What a boring lesson. It sounds like torture.'*

***Accept difficult feelings*** You may be shocked by the way he talks about his teacher and find it difficult to listen. But he doesn't need to like everyone, and he is entitled to his feelings. You aren't saying he can be disrespectful or disobedient, just accepting that he finds it hard to get on with her.

## *Try being a LAID-BACK PARENT* 

***Ask for solutions*** When your child is feeling better, he may come up with a solution to his problems. If not, ask him for some ideas.

*Though three boys were noisy, my son was the only one getting told off. Finally he decided to talk to his teacher about it.*

## *Try being a COMMANDO PARENT* 

**Give information** If your child can't come up with a strategy on his own, there's nothing wrong with giving him advice. One of the nicest stories we've heard was good advice from a sibling.

*James was really unhappy when he came home. He hated his swimming teacher, and said he'd been made to stand by the side of the pool freezing for most of the lesson because he'd been caught talking.*

*His older sister listened sympathetically and then she said, 'Oh I know that teacher. He's awful. His lessons are so boring. He never lets you have any fun. He just shouts his head off. I bet you hated it today.'*

*Then she added, 'I used to get through by thinking the lesson is only half an hour and it's a whole seven days until the next one.'*

*James brightened up. 'I guess,' he said, 'I could survive by thinking that at least I'll be getting strong arms and legs.'*

**Give orders that don't sound like orders** Sometimes your child needs to know that unless he pulls his socks up and starts behaving, the teacher isn't going to stop telling him off. If he is still feeling upset and resentful, you've got to be subtle about it. Tough talk or nagging can drive him into a corner. Friendly advice is usually much more effective.

If his teacher is irritated with him, the likely cause is that he's being irritating. One of the best things he can do is to lie low for a while. One mother suggested this to her child:

*If you want to get back in her good books, try staying quiet when you are supposed to be working. Then she'll start focusing on someone else who is being badly behaved, and you will no longer be on her radar. It might take a little while before she notices the difference, but if you keep it up for a little while, she will probably start being nicer to you.*

## *Try being a SORTED PARENT* 

*Sort your systems* If your child irritates his teacher because he is disorganized, you can help him stay on her good side by getting him sorted.

Here are a couple of suggestions that might help, or see p. 224 for more:

- *Get him a watch so he can get to class on time.*
- *Help organize his homework so it gets handed in.*
- *Make sure his school bag gets packed with the right kit so he isn't missing anything.*

# Talking to the teacher

Some teacher problems can be solved from the sidelines. But sometimes you can't just patch your child up and send him back into school. If he can't handle the problem on his own, you may have to get involved. Even great teachers blow it sometimes, and if your child is in trouble, you may need to mediate between them.

Sometimes it is up to us parents to work out what's behind our child's bad behaviour and then explain it tactfully to the teacher so she can help him get back on track. Or if he isn't mature enough to work out how the teacher wants him to behave, she can explain it to us and we can help to set him straight.

If the problem is a small one and you have built up a good relationship with your child's teacher, of course it's no big deal to go in and see her. But if you feel she's picking on him, you might be surprised by the strength of your reaction. The more upset he is, the more upset or angry you're likely to be. It is natural to want to protect our children if we feel someone is attacking them, even if that someone is a teacher.

*My son came out of school in tears. The teacher's assistant said he was being a baby because he couldn't tie his shoes. It was lucky it was Friday afternoon and the school was closed by the time he told me what had happened. I felt like marching in and giving her a piece of my mind. How dare she embarrass him in front of the others? Besides that, how the hell does she expect him to be able to tie his shoes when he is only five?'*

Some parents feel defensive or ashamed, as though they're the ones being criticized.

*'The headmistress called me in for a meeting about my daughter's sloppy attitude. In her office I was shaking. I felt like I was the one being hauled in and told off. It brought back old memories of my primary school. It was so hard to get the right words out, and the meeting went badly. I am sure she thinks I'm a terrible mother.'*

Other parents feel out of their depth.

*'My son doesn't like school and it shows. I don't want to go in and hear he's done this, he's done that. What am I supposed to do about it?'*

When your child is having a problem at school and you've got to go in and meet the teacher, how can you best help your child? By making sure the atmosphere is friendly and productive.

## Preparing to see the teacher

### *Try being a PAUSE PARENT*

***Calm down fast and wait until later*** If you are full of emotion, the very first thing to do is to pause, especially if you think the teacher is picking on your child and you're feeling confrontational. Have a bath, go for a walk, or sleep on it. Things may be clearer in the morning, or you may need to wait a few days. Often it helps to chew over the problem with your partner or a friend.

Put the meeting off until you can string a rational sentence together. Your job is to improve the relationship between your child and his teacher, and you can't do it if you are angry or upset. If you feel his teacher doesn't like or understand him, your natural reaction might be to dislike her. Though it could take a little while to calm down, wait until you can go in with the attitude that you are both on the same side.

It is also worth preparing yourself for a couple of nasty surprises; the teacher may tell you things about your child's behaviour that you don't expect or would rather not hear. If you are too defensive to listen, you won't be able to help him.

If you think you might get emotional or forgetful in the meeting, write down a list of the things you want to discuss and take it in with you.

## During the meeting

### *Try being a CHEERLEADER PARENT*

***Be positive*** Try to open the discussion on a friendly note. It doesn't really matter what you say, as long as you can pick out something you genuinely appreciate.

Compliment the teacher on the way she has displayed the class artwork on the wall. Thank her for giving up her time to meet you. If you're really struggling, you could mention something she has done for another child.

- *'I heard how kind you were when Emma got a nosebleed.'*

If you go in with a positive attitude, the meeting is more likely to go well.

### *Try being a TUNED-IN PARENT*

***Listen to their feelings*** Next it helps to tune in to the teacher to understand her reasons and try to see the situation from her point of view.

So instead of being confrontational:

- *'Why do you keep picking on my son?'*

try:

- *'I'm so sorry to hear that Adam's been bothering you.'*

Then brace yourself for some unpleasant truths, and let her talk.

> *My son was given a detention by his teacher. He said Mr Black was unfair, and often yelled at him for no reason.*
>
> *I spoke to Mr Black about it, and he said that James talked all the way through lessons, disrupted other children, and got the detention for throwing a paper aeroplane across the lab.*

Even if you still feel that the teacher's complaints are unfair or utterly ridiculous, you haven't lost anything by listening. The reason you are there is to help your child, and if you and the teacher can be open with each other, you'll have a better chance. By letting the teacher go first and unload some of her frustrations, she is more likely to listen to you.

## *Try being a COMMANDO PARENT*

***Give information*** Teachers aren't mind-readers. They don't necessarily know that your child is sensitive or dyslexic or that his pet rabbit just died. If you give the teacher some background information, she may find his behaviour more understandable and be sympathetic about it.

- *'Matilda might not show it at school, but underneath she's very sensitive. She was in tears last night after being told off in front of the class.'*
- *'I don't know if you realized, but Jim is mildly dyspraxic. This sometimes makes him seem quite clumsy and handwriting is a big struggle for him.'*
- *'Jane used to mess around in maths at her last school too. They thought she was slow, but it's the opposite. She actually needs harder work to keep her busy.'*
- *'Tim finds it hard to stand up to his friends. He knew it was wrong to climb on the shed, but he didn't know how to say no to the others without losing face.'*

Sometimes a plain misunderstanding can give the teacher the impression that your child is naughty. Once she knows what's going on, the problem can be cleared up.

> *My six-year-old's problems with his teacher started because she kept asking him to tuck in his shirt and he never did it. Then, when he asked if he could choose his own reading book, she got angry with him for being wilful. After that she felt he was being deliberately slow to line up for lunch just to annoy her.*
>
> *Finally, when he refused to tuck in his shirt again, she spoke to both of us when I collected him. He reluctantly confessed that he didn't know how to tuck it in. Once she knew this, she stopped assuming the worst of him.*

If the teacher has a faulty image of your child, their relationship can go askew. If you can help correct the misconception, things should improve.

> *My daughter tries hard at school, but she was losing heart because her teacher never seemed to notice. So on Monday morning I said, 'I wonder if you can help me with Alice. Even though she does quite well, she feels she's not very clever.'*
>
> *'Oh,' she said, 'I never realized. She always seems so sure of herself. Of course I will keep an eye on her and do everything I can to help her.'*
>
> *After that she was so much more supportive. Alice has been much happier and now I think her teacher is great.*

## *Try being a LAID-BACK PARENT*

***Ask for solutions*** After you and the teacher have had your say, it's time to come up with solutions. Start by asking her for ideas:

- *'I would love your advice on how we can sort this out.'*
- *'What can he do to change things round?'*

Then make suggestions of your own:

- *'When you mark her homework, perhaps you could point out a couple of small things she has done right? I think it would make her feel better.'*

- *'As he finds it so difficult to read out loud, I wonder if you could give him an easy passage if you know one is coming up?'*

## *Try being a SORTED PARENT*

**Sort your systems** The last step is to get sorted and make a plan of action. After you've batted ideas between you, you could decide on this together.

- *'Great. So you'll check he's written everything down in his homework diary, and I'll check that the diary and worksheets come home.'*
- *'Thanks for being gentle with her for the next couple of weeks. It's not a great atmosphere at home, with everything that's going on between me and her stepfather.'*

If you can't see the teacher informally at the beginning or end of the day, it's a good idea to take her email address to keep in touch, or book another appointment for an update.

If the meeting doesn't go as well as you hoped, you might worry you've made things worse for your child. But most teachers are reasonable people, and unless you've behaved appallingly, give yourself credit for trying your hardest.

## After the meeting

If you are lucky, you won't have to do anything else. Any misunderstandings can be cleared up and your child and the teacher can carry on quite happily without you.

But it's more likely that there will still be work to be done with your child. It can be hard to accept this, but your teacher may have some legitimate complaints. If your child has some unappealing habits – whether it's being rude, disruptive, disorganized or whatever – you need to work with the school to sort him out, or he'll carry on getting into trouble.

*When Edward was naughty and disruptive at school, I had no idea what to do, until the teacher and I worked out a strategy. If he behaved, she would give him gold stars and lots of praise for good behaviour, and she would let me know so I could continue with the praise at home.*

*By working together, his behaviour improved. He's not a problem at school now, and he is a lot more cooperative at home.*

## But My Child Won't Let Me Talk to His Teacher

What do you do if your child begs you not to discuss anything with his teacher? If you want him to confide in you, it's tempting to promise that you won't. But she may be the best person to sort out the problem, and if things get worse, she'll summon you anyway.

If he thinks you've gone back on your word, he won't trust you, so don't make any promises and keep your options open. Here's how:

Start by listening and show that you understand.

- *'You don't want me to talk to your teacher. You're worried that I might make things worse for you.'*

Then give information and negotiate from there.

- *'I can't promise never to talk to her, because if you've got a problem, that might be the best way to help you. But I can swear to keep some things secret. For example, I promise I'd never, ever tell her that you hate her.'*

Opening the discussion gives your child the chance to get used to the idea.

## Disliking a teacher

What do you do if your child's behaviour isn't the whole story?

There are plenty of inspiring, wonderful teachers out there, but your child may not have one of them. His teacher might have very old-fashioned, strict views about discipline. She might have been ground down by years in the job. She might not know how to control a classroom except by making threats and shouting.

Sometimes it's not even as straightforward as this. What if he is stuck with a teacher he simply doesn't like? Not everyone in the world gets on. Your child and his teacher may both be perfectly nice people, but if there is a bad fit or the wrong chemistry between them, they can rub each other up the wrong way.

If your child is trapped with a teacher he dislikes, besides feeling angry he is probably feeling sorry for himself. So first tune in to his feelings as much as you can, praise him for the good things he does at home, and ask him what he can do to get along better with his teacher.

### *Try being a COMMANDO PARENT*

***Give information*** If he still can't work out the best way to handle a grumpy teacher, give him some advice.

- *'If you want her to be nicer to you, try being nicer to her. When you arrive, why not smile and say good morning.'*

Sometimes you have to make information explicit, because your child can't work it out on his own. You may need to tell him, 'This is the way it is, and this is why.' Even if the teacher seems unfair, he has to accept what she says or does and try to get along with her.

*My daughter's Year Five form teacher wanted absolute silence while she taught and hated being interrupted. The other girls in the class knew how to adapt, but my daughter kept getting into trouble.*

*I spoke to the headmistress about it, who kindly but firmly spelled it out. 'Mrs Edwards is focused on one thing: preparing the class for the 11+ exams. She doesn't like interruptions and she won't stand for people messing about. While Caroline is in her class, she needs to sit properly, pay attention and be quiet until Mrs Edwards asks if anyone has any questions. When it's break time she can talk and giggle all she wants.'*

*I relayed this information to Caroline, who finally got the point.* ❞

You could also remind him that teachers are people, too. If a teacher is grumpy, children can take it personally. But the cause of her bad mood might be something entirely different.

❝ *Last term, one teacher was so mean that my daughter dreaded her lessons. Then I heard the teacher was in the middle of a messy divorce. I had a long chat with my daughter about it. It's important for her to understand that people have their own problems which can affect their moods. She was happier once she knew it didn't have anything to do with her.* ❞

If your child's teacher is clearly unbalanced, you can take it up with the head or the board of governors. No child should have to put up with a bully. But if she's just a bit difficult, learning how to cope with her can be a valuable life lesson, and at least your child has your support.

## Exams

### *'Oh my God! My son has exams this year. I'm sure I'm supposed to be doing something to help him, but what on earth is it?'*

It's hard not to get worked up when your child has exams. The worst ones are the competitive entry tests for a new school, particularly if there is intense pressure for places. A couple of hours inside the exam room will affect so much over the next few years of his life.

Even if he doesn't have entry exams, Year Six SATs can also be stressful, as the results will be passed on to his new school. Some parents also worry about the SATs in Years Two and Nine, not to mention music and ballet exams, judo gradings, drama auditions or whatever their child is into. We will concentrate on crucial academic exams, but the basics are the same for all of them.

*It's ridiculous. My son failed his first entry test at four. The best local kindergarten is so oversubscribed that mothers around here get obsessed about it. They coach their children, if you believe it, to make animals out of Play Doh instead of worms, and bridges out of blocks. I thought they were being pathetic, but guess what? Their children got places.*

Depending how important they are, looming exams can create constant low-level stress for weeks, and if they are taking place in January they can cast a shadow over the Christmas holidays. Many parents have sleepless nights worrying about them.

As a parent it's hard to get the balance right. On the one hand you need to be relaxed so you don't stress your child out. If he does badly, he needs to know that in the big picture of life, you'll love him regardless and it doesn't matter. But on the other hand, you might want to be proactive and give him lots of support in the run up to the big day, so he is well prepared and has the best possible shot at it.

Different children need different kinds of support. The key is working out the best way to help him.

If he is a perfectionist, highly motivated or seems completely on top of his revision, it might be better to hang back and not get too involved with his exam preparation. Leave it to his school. Ditto if he isn't responding well to the stress of exams or kicks up a fuss at the prospect of doing any extra work. Instead of piling on more pressure, a trip to the park or a film might be what he needs instead.

Most children, however, will benefit enormously if you help them. Focus on the basic knowledge and techniques he'll need, and do what you can to boost his confidence (see p. 208). If he is also feeling well, he will find it easier to revise and he will perform better on the day.

## *Try being a PHYSICAL PARENT* 

Academic exams are a test of mental skills, but **Physical Parents** understand the link between a sharp brain and a healthy body.

*Get them to bed* It's hard to function well if you don't get enough sleep. If your child is over-tired he will find it hard to concentrate. So cut back on sleepovers, television and computer time, and get him to bed promptly until the entire process is over.

*Feed them well* Try to make sure he's eating properly well in advance. This can boost his immune system, so he's less likely to come down with a bug at exam time. Good food will also give him a chance to concentrate and focus for long periods of time by minimizing mood and energy swings. One of the best ways to do this is to cut down on processed foods (full of quick-release carbohydrates, E-numbers and hydrogenated fats) and increase servings of fresh fruit and vegetables, whole grains and protein. Try encouraging him to drink plenty of water, too.

As a little insurance policy, months in advance you might also start giving him oily fish a couple of times a week or fish-oil supplements. Some studies show that they are good for brain function and can stabilize moods.

*Get them moving* Exercise is a great stress-buster. **Physical Parents** make sure their child gets plenty of it, and plenty of time to play. Both are essential for keeping up energy and endorphin levels.

*Be affectionate* Never underestimate the comfort of a good hug, hand-holding or a simple kiss goodnight. Your child needs to know that whether he passes his exams or not, you're going to love him just the same. Affection can give him the extra strength and support he needs.

*Just be there* He may have questions and want to chat, or he may not. Either way, he is likely to feel calmer and more contained if you are around. If he is older, he may no longer want as much affection as he used to, but he may still like knowing you are there.

Very few parents have the luxury of putting their life on hold for exams. Nor do children expect it. But if you can shift your focus even slightly, you'll find extra time from somewhere to help your child.

One working mother we know hired an au pair for six weeks so she could help her dyslexic daughter with her revision.

> *Normally I can answer questions about homework while I cook and pay bills and load the washing machine. But uninterrupted time every evening? Impossible, until I hired someone to help me.*

## *Try being a SORTED PARENT*

***Train them up*** To help prepare your child for exams, it helps to find out what he knows, where the gaps are, and then spend time filling them in. **Sorted Parents** have a huge advantage because they'll have worked this out, and what to do about it, months in advance. But don't be put off. There is a lot you can do to help your child even if his exams are only a few weeks away.

> *I only realized my daughter needed help during the Christmas holidays, and her 11+ was in January. My husband worked with her on maths and I worked with her on English. Between the two of us we boosted her scores in the practice papers by at least 10 per cent.*

Find out what your child needs to know by looking through his work and talking to his teacher or the school head, who might keep a stash of appropriate practice papers. If not, you can find excellent year-specific workbooks in bookshops and newsagents.

Though it would be nice to sit your child down with a workbook and let him get on with it, you might need to be actively involved. The workbooks will highlight areas where he needs help. If you can, go over some exam techniques too, like structuring time, planning essays and checking for mistakes.

***Sort your systems*** Some parents trust that exam revision will happen naturally on its own. **Sorted Parents** get organized and set aside plenty of time to work with their child. Even if you are not naturally sorted, it is well worth making some sort of revision plan. As we said before, the key is balance. Do what you can, but don't turn up the pressure so much that he ends up hating you or his schoolwork.

## Get Involved

Reports show that parental interest and involvement are very important indicators for how well your child does at school. They can make more of a difference than whether you dropped out of school yourself, whether you are rich or poor, or whether or not you are in a stable relationship.

## Interviews

Most children won't need to do interviews yet, but if yours is trying to get a place at a popular grammar, faith or private school, they may be part of the application process. Help him with some gentle practice beforehand so he isn't lost for words on the day. Here are the sort of questions he may be asked.

**About himself:**
- *'What are your favourite books?'*
- *'What are your hobbies?'*
- *'What is your worst fault?'*

**About school:**
- *'What is your favourite subject?'*
- *'Why do you want to come here?'*

**Current affairs:**
- *'If you could be prime minister for a day, what would you do?'*

There are no right answers. On the whole, the interviewer is just trying to see how interactive and thoughtful your child is. Practise with him so he can chat away quite confidently. Interviewers won't be impressed by grunts or monosyllabic answers.

In case the interviewer asks 'Have you got any questions?' he needs to have one up his sleeve, so he doesn't feel like an idiot.

## Try being a LAID-BACK PARENT 

**Get help** Many parents start with good intentions, but become frustrated if they can't get their child to cooperate. Some don't feel confident about teaching the material and others find that they care too much and make their child anxious. If you can't work with him, get help. The first place to turn is to his other parent.

> *My son refused to do any exam preparation with me. But when my husband worked with him, he enjoyed it.*

If neither of you can help him and the exam is a crucial one, try finding someone else who can.

## Try being a TUNED-IN PARENT 

**Accept feelings** Tuning in is critical around exam time because your child has so much extra work and anxiety to cope with. Though you might be tempted to nag him to work harder, tuning in is actually much more effective.

- *'I know you're fed up with homework and you'd much rather play.'*
- *'I couldn't agree more. These tests are a real pain, and it would be so nice if you didn't have to do them.'*

It will be much easier for him to get back to his work and concentrate if he feels understood.

## Try being a CHEERLEADER PARENT 

**Be specific** One of the nicest ways to boost your child's confidence is to praise him specifically for work he's doing right. Even if he is feeling nervous and overwhelmed, he will know that you appreciate his efforts, and this will help to keep him motivated.

- *'You've been concentrating so hard. And now that page is finished.'*
- *'You got a lot of answers right on this comprehension, and they're difficult.'*

Show that you appreciate him, whether or not he is doing his revision, by complimenting him for other things too.

- *'Thanks for coming down to dinner when I called.'*
- *'Well done, that was a great goal.'*

## *Try being a PAUSE PARENT* 

***Zip your lip*** You want to get the balance right and motivate your child without overwhelming him. But if there is a lot riding on the exam, revision can be stressful. You know time is running out and he needs to focus and work hard. But if he doesn't have that same feeling of urgency, he might start goofing around, or pick up on your anxiety and start behaving badly. So even if he is annoying you, bite your tongue. It isn't helpful to say:

- *'If you don't buckle down right now and do your work, you'll never pass.'*
- *'No. That answer is wrong! Don't you ever listen? We've already been over this twice.'*

Instead, wait until you can say something positive to help him.

***Keep things in perspective*** It's important not to push your child beyond his capabilities to satisfy your own ambition. There is no point manoeuvring him into the school of your dreams if he is going to be out of his depth once he gets there.

> *I'd like to send my daughter to a very academic school nearby, but from the test papers, she'd barely scrape through the exam. Even if she got in, I think she would always struggle, and that could really affect her confidence. What kind of a life would that be for her?*

These exams aren't a matter of life and death. Even if he doesn't get into your first-choice school or the top maths stream, or pass his piano exam with distinction, it doesn't mean he is going to be a failure in life. The very worst that can happen is that he will have to learn to deal with disappointment a bit younger than you would like.

## Learning Difficulties

If your child is diagnosed with learning difficulties it can be a mixed blessing. On the one hand, it's nice to have a diagnosis because it explains so much. He isn't stupid, lazy or wilful; he has an identifiable problem. On the other hand, finding this out isn't what you want to hear.

### Learning and Behavioural Disorders

**The big four are:**

- ***Dyslexia*** Difficulties in learning to read or write.
- ***Dyspraxia*** Difficulties in coordinating movement, which often means clumsiness.
- ***ADHD*** Attention Deficit Hyperactive Disorder – lack of attention and/or hyperactivity.
- ***ASD*** Autism Spectrum Disorders – difficulties understanding other people, a restricted range of behaviour and interests.

When their child's behaviour is given a label, parents can react in all sorts of different ways. Some panic and fear the worst. Some try and ignore it and pretend it isn't a problem. Some feel overwhelmed and want to leave it up to the school or other professionals to sort out. Some just want to cry. For parents who have had learning difficulties themselves, it can bring up all sorts of uncomfortable feelings of their own.

But above all, parents usually feel sorry for their child. In a school system largely based on academic success, children with learning difficulties struggle. They have to work harder to do things that their peers take for granted. When they don't keep up, they can lose self-confidence. Some get depressed. If behavioural issues are part of the mix, they can also be aggressive and uncooperative, which means that they tend to get told off a lot. If their self-esteem is low, they're also more likely to be bullied.

But there is a lot you can do to help your child. Start by doing everything you can to build his self-confidence (see pp. 208–20), and make sure he knows you love him and are on his side. Many parents find it helpful to join a support group, meeting informally with people whose children have similar problems. They'll understand how you feel, will be a good source of information about specialists and therapies that might work, and can warn you against the expensive, rubbishy ones.

Read up as much as you can – the internet is full of information – because an umbrella diagnosis like 'dyslexia' covers a huge range of difficulties, and every child's brain works in a different way.

> *My daughter is dyslexic. We saw all sorts of experts and tried all sorts of things: coloured lenses, coloured cellophane, a special diet, making letters out of clay. But the breakthrough was a book about right-brained children. It has helped us so much to help her.*

Here are some more ideas that might help.

## *Try being a PHYSICAL PARENT*

**Get them moving** There are a surprising number of physical therapies for children with learning difficulties. Many see a big improvement just by doing basic coordination exercises, like juggling, standing on one leg, standing on a wobble board, or touching each finger in turn with the thumb of the same hand. Yoga or martial arts might help. Your child could also try brain gym exercises to make the left and right side of his brain work better together (see internet). Some people swear by body brushing (brushing their child every day with tiny paint brushes). Other children improve with the DDAT system of physical movements to stimulate the cerebellum at the base of the brain (see Resources pp. 369–71).

**Feed them well** There is evidence that food sensitivities (including wheat, for example) and sensitivity to E-numbers are associated with some learning difficulties. So it may be worth reading up on these and finding out if your child can't tolerate something.

Studies suggest that cutting down on transfats and upping your child's intake of essential fatty acids can help his brain to work more efficiently. Drinking lots of water can also help.

*Be affectionate* A hug and a cuddle go a long way, and that's especially true if your child has a problem.

## *Try being a SORTED PARENT*

*Bite the bullet* **Sorted Parents** are fantastic because they are so proactive. Getting enthusiastic about potential remedies isn't enough; it takes time and lots of dedication to put them into practice. **Sorted Parents** actually factor the time into their schedule, and get on with it.

*Train them up* It's tempting to help your child with the things he finds difficult. If he's dyspraxic, you can tie his shoelaces in thirty seconds, and it seems kinder than watching him struggle. If he's dyslexic he may be exhausted after a day at school, and you might let him off responsibilities like packing his own school bag.

But though he has a harder time than the others, he still needs to learn to do as much as possible for himself. You can help him by being a **Sorted Parent** and taking time to work with him and train him up one step at a time.

## *Try being a LAID-BACK PARENT*

*Allow them to do more* Once you've taught him how to do something, it's important to let him do it. Being able to do things for himself will increase his confidence.

*Get help* If homework is torture, you might both want to give up from sheer frustration. Don't be ashamed if you feel you need help. Instead of compromising your relationship with your child, it might be better to get some support from his school or hire someone else to oversee homework.

## *Try being a TUNED-IN PARENT* 

***Listen to their feelings*** If your child is frustrated, let him talk. It might take a while. If his feelings of frustration or inadequacy have been building up, it will take time before they start to dissipate.

But tuning in won't help if he is so ashamed he doesn't want to talk about his difficulties at all.

> *My son has ADHT. He finds it hard to concentrate and gets told off a lot at school. It also affects his work, so he's not keeping up and I know he feels stupid in front of his friends. I want to make things better for him, but he doesn't want to talk to me about it.*

## *Try being a COMMANDO PARENT* 

***Give information*** It may not be easy to talk to your child about his learning difficulties. He might be resistant, and it might be emotional for you. The more he knows about his condition, the more he'll realize that it is not a character weakness on his part. As one dyslexic teenager put it:

> *I realized that I wasn't lazy or thick after all. I just had dyslexia. It made me feel better and more confident that there was something I could do about it.*

Most children with learning difficulties already know they are different. But the more they understand, the easier it will be to accept and adjust to the world. You can help your child see this by discussing it openly and honestly.

You could tell him there's a long roll-call of famous dyslexics, including Einstein, Leonardo da Vinci, Walt Disney and the Olympic rower Steve Redgrave. The list goes on and on. Einstein and da Vinci are also claimed by the dyspraxic and ADHT community, which just goes to show how the symptoms and syndromes can overlap. Many autistics have remarkable focus – Satoshi Jajiri spent six years dreaming up the entire world of Pokémon – and some are exceptional at maths.

### *Try being a PAUSE PARENT* 

***Keep things in perspective*** There are no easy answers to learning and behavioural difficulties, and you can struggle along for years. But whatever your child's particular issue, there's no need to despair. His brain may work slightly differently to the majority, but this could even turn out to be an advantage. You may wish you had a less complicated child, but he may have all sorts of talents that other people never develop.

The BBC2 programme *The Mind of a Millionaire* interviewed three hundred self-made millionaires. The surprise result was that 40 per cent of them were dyslexic. The theory is that children with learning difficulties have to form their own strategies to cope with life. If they survive the system, they tend to have many more resources than other children because they have had to work much harder and they see things from a different perspective.

7

# Getting Your Child to Sleep

## When You're So Tired You Can't Think Straight

On TV it works like this: mother tucks child into bed, gives child quick kiss, turns out light and closes door. Cut to the next scene. Child falls asleep straight away or stays quietly in bedroom. Adults get on with the plot.

If this is how things work in your house, congratulations – you can skip this chapter. But what happens if your child doesn't follow the script? Where is: 'Child refuses to turn TV off'? 'Child screams for forty minutes because she doesn't want to go to bed'? 'Child bursts out of bedroom to bug sister'? 'Child follows you back downstairs begging for drink'? and 'Child still up at ten o'clock, driving you demented'?

Don't imagine for a moment you are the only tired, grumpy, unsympathetic parent who gets stretched beyond your limit at bedtime. By that hour of the day there is usually someone past their sell-by date, and if it's not one of your children, it's you.

When bedtime doesn't work, it can be like lassoing wild pigs. It's a mystery why such simple steps – bathtime, teeth and pyjamas – can be so difficult and take so incredibly long. If you are already tired it can be hard to think of the right things to do or say. But nagging and shouting is such an unpleasant way of ending the day.

There are lots of things you can do to make the whole process easier. However, if getting your child ready for bed is difficult, the thought of making changes might seem overwhelming. But don't feel bad, because you aren't alone. Several mothers in our parenting group put off dealing with bedtime for weeks. They would leave the group mentally prepared to tackle the chaos, and sheepishly admit the following week that they'd bottled out.

You could give up and wait until your children are old enough to put themselves to bed. But calm bedtimes for children of all ages really are possible. Here's how to make them happen.

### *'Do we need to have a bedtime routine?'*

When you have a baby all anyone seems to want to know is whether she's sleeping through the night or whether you've got her into a routine. For some parents, organizing a routine is the natural thing to do; others prefer to go with the flow. But by the time you have a couple of children to get to bed every night and, more importantly, to wake up for school the next morning, even the most flexible parents tend to get themselves into some sort of pattern.

*'I preferred to think of myself as a relaxed kind of person and mother. The word 'routine' made me think of Victorian orphanages and nannies with stopwatches. I never wanted the pressure of sticking to a timetable.*

*But now, shattered at the end of the day with three children to get up for school in the morning, I don't think I could cope without some structure. I have to know roughly what time they need to get ready for bed and roughly what time the lights are turned off or it all takes too long.'*

Whether or not you set up a routine is totally up to you. If bedtime at your house generally works and you're happy with it, even if you do something different every night, then why mess with a good thing? But most of us do have some structure to our evenings, whether we realize it or not. It's generally some combination of the usual steps: homework, tea, tidying up, washing, teeth, pyjamas and bed.

Having spoken to hundreds of parents, we've found there is no magic right way to do it. Just find whatever works for you and your family.

*'I am a morning person, up at six a.m. no problem, but exhausted in*

*the evening. If my children aren't completely ready and in bed by eight o'clock, I find I can't control my temper.*'

'*I'm hopeless in the morning but fine at night. I honestly don't mind if it takes hours to put my children to bed. We potter about chatting, cooking, watching television, reading stories and getting everything ready for the next day.*'

So much of getting children ready for bed is about getting cooperation. However, we've given bedtime its own chapter because it's such a big issue for so many parents. Try what we suggest here, and if you're still having problems, see Chapter Three.

# The Run-up to Bedtime

***'Getting my children ready for bed takes so long I get frustrated and lose it. What can I do?'***

## *Try being a PAUSE PARENT*

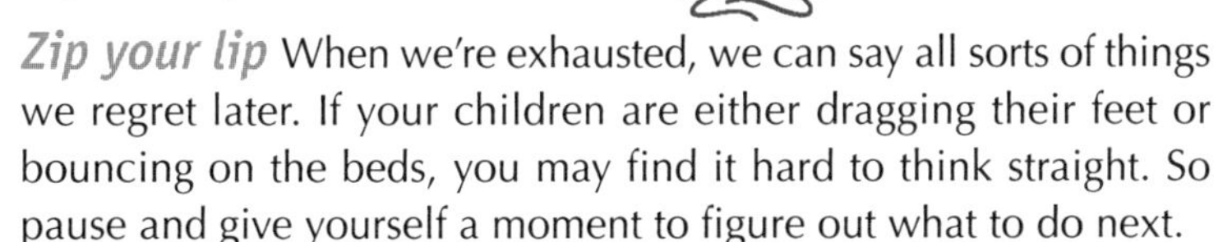

*Zip your lip* When we're exhausted, we can say all sorts of things we regret later. If your children are either dragging their feet or bouncing on the beds, you may find it hard to think straight. So pause and give yourself a moment to figure out what to do next.

## *Try being a CHEERLEADER PARENT*

### *Notice the good, ignore the bad*

'*Trying to get my daughter to bed is impossible. She faffs about until I can't take it any more and get hysterical, and she ends up in tears. After she finally goes to bed, I end up feeling guilty all evening.*'

So what do you do? Start by ignoring as much of the bad behaviour as you possibly can and focusing on the good. Noticing the one thing she is doing right can snap things round and she might start being surprisingly cooperative. It can also help you feel more in control and put you in a better mood.

*My son would take ages getting undressed and ready for bed. The more I harassed him, the slower he got. Then I decided to try doing it differently. Instead of saying, 'For goodness' sake, I can't believe you've only got one sock off,' I'd say, 'You've got one sock off already. Well done.'*

*Things move along at a much better pace now, which I am happy about. But more to the point, the whole atmosphere is better.*

If bedtime is chaos and you can't think where to start, try focusing on one aspect at a time, and praise every little step she makes in the right direction.

*I realized I couldn't change everything all at once. So I decided to stop nagging and concentrate on just one thing at a time. I started with getting the television turned off.*

*For a week I ignored the mess they left in the kitchen and the toys strewn all over the sitting room and focused only on turning it off, and praising them for being cooperative.*

*When that was no longer a problem, I could work on getting them to tidy up.*

## Try being a TUNED-IN PARENT

When your child starts being resistant or complaining that she's the only one in her class who has to go to bed so early, try tuning in.

***Listen to their feelings*** Instead of getting sucked into an argument, or worse, let her know you understand how she feels.

- *'You really don't feel like going to bed now. You wish you could lie in front of the TV until you fall asleep.'*

You aren't saying she doesn't have to get ready for bed, you're only acknowledging that she doesn't want to. If you've been arguing about it every night, your reaction alone will catch her off guard and she might get up and get on with it. This can work surprisingly well, and it is much less stressful than forcing her to go to bed.

## Try being a SORTED PARENT 

**Sort your systems** Quite a lot of bedtime hassle can be avoided if you can find a way to get one step ahead of the chaos by keeping things organized. For example, if everyone knows where to find hairbrushes and pyjamas and there is one consistent place to put their dirty clothes, the whole process will run a lot more smoothly.

## Try being a LAID-BACK PARENT 

**Ask for solutions** Try asking your child how to solve the problem.

- *'It really bothers me when you don't get your pyjamas on. What can we do about it?'*

Write down her suggestions, no matter how silly, and together choose a way forward.

**Allow them to do more** Try stepping out of the fight and letting your child experience things for herself.

> *My daughter refused to put her pyjamas on night after night, and I got so sick of arguing. It was winter, and I knew she would be cold without them. But I told her if she wanted to go to bed without wearing any, that was her choice.*
>
> *She kept it up for two nights. Now she puts her pyjamas on and has never said another word about it.*

## Try being a COMMANDO PARENT 

**Express your feelings** Sometimes it seems as if you try everything and it isn't until you become apoplectic that your child gets moving. But have you ever taken the time to tell her directly and sincerely how you feel?

It's hard to believe sometimes, but most children genuinely want to please us. If you simply explain your feelings, she might surprise you by being obliging.

- *'I'm tired at night and I don't like having to remind you to turn off the TV.'*
- *'After I put you to bed, I've got work to do. We can't spend much time together so I would be much happier if we didn't waste it arguing.'*

**Give orders that don't sound like orders** She probably has a rough idea of the bedtime master plan; she's done it often enough. So try gently prompting to move her along. It's a much better way to get the job done than nagging. Here are some examples:

Ask what comes next:

- *'Now you've finished your bath. What comes next?'*

Describe what you see:

- *'I see you're ready for your pyjamas.'*

Give options:

- *'You can either finish this programme and go straight to bed, or come now so there's time for a story.'*

Say it in a word:

- *'Bed.'*

***'How can I get her to brush her teeth? She simply refuses.'***
Have you seen the *Pingu* cartoon where his mother sends him off to the bathroom to clean his teeth? She hears noises and thinks he is doing them, but we can see that he is actually brushing the side of the bathtub. You can't help but wonder if your children really are doing theirs when they say they are.

## Try being a TUNED-IN PARENT

*Imagine it could happen* Taking her reluctance to the fantastic extreme is a good way to sympathize and get her moving.

> *I said to my daughter, 'You really don't want to brush your teeth. I bet you wish you had an automatic little tooth-cleaning Hoover. You could just open your mouth and it would drive all around in there and – presto! – your teeth would be sparkling!' She laughed and so did I, and then she brushed her teeth.*

## Try being a SORTED PARENT

*Train them up* You could also talk her through anything she finds difficult. Some children don't actually feel confident about brushing their teeth properly, and so avoid doing it. It can help to spend time going through it together: first the flat parts, then all the way around the backs and all the way around the fronts, focusing on each tooth where it meets the gum.

## Try being a COMMANDO PARENT

*Give information* Waiting until she needs fillings isn't the ideal way of getting her to brush. It's better if you can teach her a bit about oral hygiene. Try showing her pictures of decaying teeth (your dentist will have some or try the internet). Disclosing tablets might also help. This may be enough to make her pick up her toothbrush, but don't be surprised if you also have to be tough and threaten consequences.

*Give consequences* Try coming up with consequences that mean something to her.

- *'For every five minutes I have to spend nagging you, I'm going to take five minutes off your story time.'*

Consequences work particularly well if they are directly related to what has to be done. If you want teeth brushed, don't threaten to cancel a trip to the park or swimming pool – say you'll cut down on your child's sugar rations.

> *My kids would always argue about cleaning their teeth – you'd think I was sending them to outer Siberia instead of the bathroom for five minutes.*
>
> *I said, 'Every night is the same. There are things that have to be done, and brushing your teeth is one of them. Sweets and puddings are full of sugar – which is bad for your teeth. So unless you get on with it, I won't be buying any more.*

### *'It's like she's trying to wind me up on purpose. It's infuriating.'*

Quite often children refuse to get ready for bed because it's a way of getting lots of attention. This can be maddening, but here are some things you can do.

## *Try being a CHEERLEADER PARENT*

***Notice the good, ignore the bad*** Swap things round so the attention you give her is the good kind. Do what you can to completely ignore her defiance, and praise her as soon as she makes even the tiniest move towards getting ready for bed.

## *Try being a PHYSICAL PARENT*

***Just be there*** There's often another type of attention-seeking at work – some children go through phases of needing or wanting a bit more of your time, even though they are seemingly too old for it.

> *For years my daughter got ready for bed on her own. But when she was eight she started fussing about it. It was infuriating.*
>
> *One day I asked her what the problem was, and she said she wanted me to help her. I felt so guilty! Why shouldn't I help her get her pyjamas on? She's only eight.*

*I spent lots of extra time with her, but then after a couple of weeks she wanted to do it on her own again.*'

## *Try being a COMMANDO PARENT*

***Give rewards*** If what she really wants is your attention, try using it as an incentive.

'*My son never wanted to get ready for bed, and I became a nagging mother – the type I never wanted to be. He must be getting something out of it, I thought, or he wouldn't carry on. I figured the only thing he could want was my attention, so I tried to think of something that we could do together.*

*I got out the backgammon and told him I'd love to play with him if we had time after he was ready for bed. I've never seen anyone get changed and brush their teeth so fast.*

*Now, instead of wasting hours every night, we spend twenty minutes playing a game together.*'

### *'She doesn't mean to drive me crazy. She's just in a world of her own.'*

Some children are pretty clued up about the whole countdown to bedtime. Then there are the dreamy types who look at you dumbfounded when you ask them to get into the bath, as though they've never heard of such a thing.

## *Try being a SORTED PARENT*

These children may need a little more hand-holding before they can make the big leap to doing things on their own. They might even need the whole process explained, but not at bedtime, when everyone is already tired and frazzled.

***Train them up*** Talk to your child and explain what needs to be done, making the steps short and simple.

*My son would dilly-dally about all evening. One day I sat down with him, and we made a list of what he had to do to get ready for bed. It was pretty clear:*

*Tidy up.*
*Have a bath and fold up the towel.*
*Brush teeth.*
*Put on pyjamas.*
*Get into bed.*

*He carried this list around with him for the next couple of nights. I could see he was mentally ticking off each item as he went. Since then he has got ready for bed in record time.*

If your child is very visual, or can't yet read properly, a picture of each step pinned to the wall can help enormously.

## Getting Your Child to Go to Sleep

### *'Now my children are ready for bed, how can I get them to stay there?'*

So you've made it through the busy part of the evening. Somehow you've managed to tick everything off that list: homework done, supper eaten, kitchen cleaned, house tidied, baths finished, teeth brushed, pyjamas on. You're nearly there.

On a good day, this is the best bit, when the house is quiet and the children are getting sleepy. At moments like these, when you have plenty of time to read them a story and everyone is calm, it is easy to remember why you like being a parent. There's time at last to listen to whatever your child wants to talk about and hold her tight, and to make everything right after a frenetic day. When it is good, it is really, really good.

But when it is bad it is horrid. Children keep springing out of their beds and siblings won't stop winding each other up, undoing all the good effects of your soothing bedtime story. Someone is arguing their case for a late-night snack, again. Who keeps turning the light on? Everyone is exhausted, bad-tempered and on the edge of tears.

You know you should keep calm – if you start shouting now you'll rev them up even more. But that Supermum mask started slipping ages ago; it's late, you're starving, there are seven messages on the answering machine, and you are desperate for a bit of down time before you check your emails, load the washing machine, put out the rubbish and collapse into bed.

So what's the trick? How do parents make that last lap to bedtime? How are you supposed to persuade your children to stay in their beds and stop bugging each other – and you?

## *Try being a PHYSICAL PARENT* 

**Physical Parents** know there can be simple reasons why their children won't stay in bed.

*Feed them well* Has your child eaten or drunk anything that might keep her awake? The most obvious offenders include fizzy drinks with caffeine, chocolate (caffeine again), and food that contains lots of sugar and additives. Some people are much more sensitive to these things than others.

> *Even one piece of chocolate after dinner is enough to delay my children's bedtime by two hours. If I have caffeine at night I can't sleep either, so I can understand why.*

> *Our son was having some behavioural problems. Our doctor said some children are sensitive to additives in food and we should try taking him off them. We did. Not only has his behaviour improved, but he is sleeping much better, too.*

*Get them to bed* Is your child over-tired? If she is getting irrational in the evening, ignore as much of the bad behaviour as you possibly can and try to get her to bed earlier.

> *At night my son completely loses it. The slightest thing hurts his feelings or tips him into a tantrum. He used to make bedtime hell for everyone.*
> *Finally, I got it. Trying to get him to behave when he is over-tired*

*is a complete waste of time. It's far better if I ignore his outbursts and get him to bed a.s.a.p.* ❞

For some children, it's the opposite problem: they simply aren't tired. If you are putting your child to bed too early (or letting her sleep in too late), she may keep bursting out of her room.

If you have a very young child who naps in the day and stays up very late, it might be time to change things around. Skipping the nap may be hard, but take her to the park, dance in the kitchen, sing songs, do whatever it takes to break her of the habit, so you can both get a good night's sleep.

*Get them moving* Is your child getting enough exercise? It's unbelievable how much exercise children can happily get without collapsing from exhaustion. We have a friend whose three-year-old can easily walk a mile and a half. We know a four-year-old who cycles for hours with stabilizers. Our friend's eight-year-old can walk to school, go swimming, have a judo lesson, and still have plenty of energy to play in the garden all evening. Yes, these children are tired afterwards, but that's the point. If your child goes to school in the car, watches TV most of the afternoon and isn't tired at bedtime, have a rethink.

## Make Your Child Feel More Secure

### *Try being a PHYSICAL PARENT*

Why do some children make such a fuss about going to sleep? One reason might be that it's just a blip in the history of man since we've had secure homes, and an even shorter blip since we've had our own beds and bedrooms. On a rational level, of course they know they're safe in their beds. But their instincts are still to stay close to us at night for protection.

*Just be there and be affectionate* **Physical Parents** instinctively know that to go to sleep, children need to feel safe and relaxed. There is nothing more comforting for a child than cosying up next to you for a story, or having a cuddle while she dozes off to sleep.

We've found that the parents who are least stressed at bedtime are **Physical Parents**, who automatically include time for these things in their child's bedtime routine. They don't pay the slightest attention to well-meaning experts who say children need to learn to go to sleep on their own. Far from worrying about doing it all wrong, they give their children lots of attention and affection at night and enjoy every minute of it.

*I'm sure you won't want to use me in your book because I just do everything my own way. After reading to my six-year-old I lie in bed with him until he falls asleep, then I hop in with my eight-year-old and chat with her about her day. They like it and so do I.*

*I put my kids to sleep in my bed because it's the only bed big enough for us all to fit in. I lie with them until they fall asleep, one under one arm, one under the other. My husband moves them into their own beds later.*

*I was amazed to hear that my friend holds her children until they fall asleep. But I have to admit, it takes her far less time to get her children to bed than it takes me.*

Because they are there with them, **Physical Parents** don't have to deal with children who keep getting out of bed for attention, or who are afraid of the dark. Their children relax and go to sleep happily because bedtime is so calm and cosy.

*It's a natural human instinct to relax when you are safe. So if my children want me to stay with them, I do. They also come into our bed if and when they want. But most of the time they go to sleep easily in their own beds. I think just knowing we'll be there if they want us makes them feel secure.*

Having some sort of bedtime ritual, doing the same thing every night, can also be soothing and reassuring for lots of children. If you get it right, it acts like a psychological trigger; telling your child that it's safe to relax and go to sleep. These little rituals can become very important.

*I remember when I was little my mother would always say, 'Goodnight, I'll see you in the morning.' But one night she forgot, and only said, 'Goodnight.'*

*I panicked. Wasn't she going to see me in the morning? Was something going to happen to her or me in the middle of the night? I couldn't let it go. I had to get out of bed and ask her if she was going to see me in the morning or not.*

### 'I'd love to stay with my children, but how will they ever learn to fall asleep on their own?'

Some parents worry that their children will become too dependent, but it doesn't seem to happen that way. The fact is, children naturally become more self-sufficient in their own time. How many adults do you know whose mothers still put them to bed? When they're babies, they love going to sleep in your arms. Toddlers and younger children like to go to sleep next to you or near you, and older children like it if you hang around and chat. Following that, you are likely to get the boot.

*I always cuddled my daughter until she fell asleep. But eventually she asked if I would kiss her goodnight and let her go to sleep on her own. And that was that.*

### 'Cuddling her is fine. The problem is the thousands of other things that I should be doing.'

Though it might be lovely to lie with your child for hours, work, chores, the telephone, other children and other adults all compete for your attention. So what do you do if getting her to sleep is taking far too long? Or if she has become used to lots of affection, but you can't always be there?

## Try being a COMMANDO PARENT 

**Give information** Try being honest and explaining the situation to your child. She may be surprisingly compliant if you do.

> *My children love me to stay with them, but when I'm busy, I tell them I can't stay long and why. Last night, for example, I explained that I had to get back to my desk and tackle a huge pile of admin. As long as they know what to expect, they're fine.*

## Try being a LAID-BACK PARENT 

**Ask for solutions** Children generally know what they need and what they can cope with, so they will often come up with unexpectedly good solutions for themselves.

> *Every night I would lie on my daughter's bed until she fell asleep. But this was taking longer and longer, sometimes up to an hour and a half, and I was getting quite resentful.*
>
> *She's exceptionally sensitive and I didn't want to hurt her feelings. So I decided to ask her advice. I told her I had a lot of things I needed to do at night, but not enough time to do them. She thought about it and then she suggested I leave her to go to sleep on her own. She said she would be fine without me, and she was.*

It's amazing how well this laid-back approach works. If this mother had given her daughter an ultimatum, there might have been tears and plenty of guilt about it. But as her daughter came up with the solution herself, they were both happy.

### *'My child just won't let me go. I don't want to be mean, but how do I extract myself?'*

What do you do if your child won't willingly let go of you?

> *At bedtime my daughter wraps herself around me like a limpet and whines, 'Don't go, Mummy. Just one more cuddle. I want you to stay here.'*
>
> *Of course I don't want to leave her, but I can't stay there all night. I have other children, and endless chores to do.*

*It sounds so mean, but sometimes I end up prying her fingers off me, one by one, dumping her back in bed, and standing outside holding on to the doorknob to keep her in her bedroom. I don't know what else to do.* ❜

## *Try being a SORTED PARENT*

***Sort your systems and give advance warning*** This may be one of those situations where your child picks up on your ambivalence. Children find all our weak spots. When you half want to go and clean up the kitchen and you half want to stay and cuddle her, you can send out mixed messages. It's no wonder she does anything she can to make you change your mind.

So start by working out what you really want or need to do. If you are going to stay, tell her you're staying and lie down and rest. Relax, put your feet up, don't threaten to leave (because you aren't going to), and don't be surprised if you wake up at three a.m. and wonder what on earth you are still doing there.

If you decide to go, tell her beforehand so she knows what to expect. Here's how one parent did it:

❛ *My daughter used to make a scene every night when I tried to leave. So I bought a kitchen timer. I told her I was going to stay for twenty minutes, and when the buzzer sounded it was time for me to go downstairs. That night when the buzzer rang, she didn't argue. For the first time ever, I kissed her goodnight and left.* ❜

### *'I love reading bedtime stories to my children, but they are insatiable.'*

One of the nicest ways for children to wind down is with a bedtime story. You might enjoy reading them too, but there comes a point when you've had enough or you've got to go. Instead of looking forward to 'just one more', you start looking forward to escaping.

## Try being a SORTED PARENT 

**Give advance warning** Be clear what you are going to read and for how long *before* you start reading and you can avoid all kinds of annoying wheedling.

> *I make it clear how many pages they're getting before I start and tell them I'm not going to change my mind. Secretly, of course, I'm tempted. But I've held my ground and they've finally stopped badgering me.*

### Sort your systems

> *Talking tapes from the library are a godsend. I read shorter books at bedtime, and he listens to longer ones, like Harry Potter, on his own.*

### *'My child uses any excuse she can think of to keep coming out of her bedroom. I'm beyond it.'*

When you've finally got your child to bed and you have a moment of peace and quiet, it's maddening if she reappears.

It isn't easy to know how to play this one. If you look fierce and order her back to bed, she might turn around, go back upstairs and stay there. But if you're so strict that she gets upset, you might have to spend ages calming her down again. Sometimes one last sliver of attention or sympathy is the quickest and most efficient option.

## Try being a TUNED-IN PARENT 

**Listen to their feelings** If you possibly can at this stage, try accepting how she feels.
So instead of:

- *'You are so naughty! Why can't you ever stay in your room?'*

Try, as an opener:

- *'You wish you didn't have to go to bed.'*

You aren't giving her the option of staying up, just showing that you understand. It sounds unlikely, but sometimes this will be enough to persuade her to go back to bed.

And if that doesn't work, here are some more ideas:

## *Try being a SORTED PARENT*

***Give advance warning and sort your systems*** Some children's desire for attention is so strong that they'll use all sorts of wily strategies to keep coming out of their bedroom.

> *My son will try anything to delay the inevitable. He comes out of his bedroom over and over again. He needs a drink, he wants the loo, he wants another story, he wants a toy from the kitchen, he wants to change his pyjamas. What can I do? It's driving me bananas. But what if he really does need the loo or a glass of water?*

In the end this mother got sorted. She sat down with her son earlier in the day and they worked out all the possible things he might need at bedtime. They decided they would check them off one by one each night, and then it would be time for bed.

> *Glass of water – tick.*
> *Trip to the loo – tick.*
> *Said goodnight to the dog – tick.*
> *Nightlight on – tick.*
> *Any special requests? – tick.*
> *That's it. Now I expect you to stay in your room. Goodnight.*

When things have got to change, tell your child in advance what the new system is going to be. That way when she comes down yet again, you won't have any qualms about sticking to the plan.

## *Try being a CHEERLEADER PARENT* 

***Notice the good, ignore the bad*** Instead of getting irritated, try praising any little thing she does right. If she is desperate for your attention, this can often work wonders.

- *'You stayed in your room for more than ten minutes after I put you to bed. Thank-you for that.'*
- *'Last night you only came down to get something twice. That's a big improvement from the night before when you got up five times. Well done.'*

One mother endured years of hideous bedtimes. She had to put her daughter back to bed dozens of times every night because she kept coming out of her room. However much she shouted, nothing changed. She finally decided that if she didn't have anything nice to say to her daughter, she wasn't going to say anything at all.

> *It could take me two hours to get my daughter to stay in bed, but I couldn't keep yelling at her any more. So instead, when she came down, I just pointed towards her bedroom. Every time she made a move towards it, I said something nice, like, 'Well done. It's time for bed now.'*
>
> *The first night was the same as usual; she came down so many times I couldn't count. The second night wasn't quite so bad. The third night she wailed, 'You only say nice things to me when I'm going to bed.' I told her she was right, and that was the end of it. She stopped coming down.*

Her daughter had finally got the message that she wasn't going to get any attention by coming downstairs.

When your child does go back to bed and stays there, it's nice to follow it up the next day with praise and positive attention.

- *'Thank-you for going back to bed last night. I really appreciated it.'*

## *Try being a COMMANDO PARENT* 

***Express your feelings*** Try telling your child how you feel.

- *'It's time for bed and I'm exhausted. I get really grumpy when it's this late and you are still up.'*

### *'My daughter stays awake for hours after I put her to bed. Is this a problem?'*

The simple truth is that you can't actually force anyone to go to sleep. If your child is a night owl, you may have to accept it. As long as she doesn't disturb anyone, it needn't be a problem.

But if she has trouble going to sleep and then struggles to wake up in the morning there are a couple of things you can do that might help. Do check to make sure she's relaxed and nothing is keeping her up (see **Physical Parents**, pp. 275–8).

## *Try being a PAUSE PARENT* 

***Calm down fast*** If your child won't, or can't, go to sleep there is no point in getting tense about it. If she knows you're stressed, it will only make it more difficult for her to get to sleep.

> *Sometimes our oldest can't fall asleep. Instead of putting her back to bed right away, we've always figured she just needs a bit more of our company. We see it as a rather lovely time to talk, read, or chat. Then we put her back to bed and she is happy to go. It's never been an issue for any of us.*

## *Try being a TUNED-IN PARENT* 

***Listen to their feelings*** It's worth checking to see if there is some underlying reason why she isn't able to fall asleep. Even older children can have separation anxiety or get freaked out by things they've seen on TV. Any problems with friends or teachers may also seem worse at night.

It's easy to forget how imaginative and sensitive children can be when it's late and they're tired. One girl we know found it hard to get to sleep for weeks after reading the beginning of *The Secret Garden*, where little Mary is left all alone. We've heard other stories about children studying Ancient Egypt at school and having nightmares about mummies. Your child's fears might seem very real, but by listening you can help to reassure her.

## *Try being a COMMANDO PARENT*

***Give information*** When your child can't sleep, the power of suggestion can be very helpful.

*'When my daughter had friends round for a sleepover one of the girls came into my room and said she couldn't sleep. So I got up, took her back to bed, and told her very reassuringly that everybody falls asleep, every night, so even if she tried as hard as she could to stay awake, she wouldn't be able to. She was asleep within moments, almost by the time I finished speaking.'*

## *Try being a LAID-BACK PARENT*

### *Ask for solutions*

*'My son could easily stay up until midnight every night. But when seven a.m. rolls around, it's like trying to wake a bear out of hibernation. But he came up with a good solution. He goes to bed early in term time and gets up every morning, no hassle. But during the holidays I let him go to sleep and wake up when he wants.'*

## *Try being a PHYSICAL PARENT*

Lots of children are chronically tired because they have a television in their bedroom and they stay up late watching it. Even if your child isn't upset by whatever she watches, she may not be able to wind down.

Try keeping the television in a family room where you can supervise it. If you've been thinking about this, but dread the confrontation, see Chapters Three and Eight on getting cooperation and difficult behaviour so you can work out your strategy and carry it through.

***'I find it impossible to get my children to sleep because I'm outnumbered. How do other people manage?'***

When siblings keep vying for your attention, the main factor is often jealousy.

> *'My children annoy each other, and me, and make bedtime take five times as long as it should. While I'm putting my son to bed, my daughter comes in begging for a drink or wanting to talk to me. Then she'll start making noises, bouncing a ball or doing anything she can think of to stop him from getting my attention.'*

Situations like this are enough to turn anyone into Evil Tyrant Parent, however patient you try to be. You are simply trying to devote yourself to one child, and once he is ready to sleep you will turn your attention to the other. But that's not how it feels to the one who's next door.

## *Try being a TUNED-IN PARENT* 

***Accept difficult feelings*** The child who is waiting is probably thinking:

- *'I'm bored. I want to be in there with you.'*
- *'It's not fair. You always spend longer with him than you do with me.'*

Even if you know it's not true, try showing her that you understand her feelings:

- *'It really bothers you when I'm putting him to bed and you have to wait'*

or:

- *'You want me to spend more time with you.'*

  If you tune in, she might stop being so annoying.

## *Try being a SORTED PARENT*

**Sort your systems** If your child keeps interrupting, try to find something she wants to do during that time. We hate to admit it, but this is one of those moments when the television or a DVD can be quite useful.

> *I was going nuts. There was no way I could get all my children to bed at night without some sort of system. So we talked about it and decided that I would put them to bed in age order, youngest first, and while I was putting one to bed those who were waiting would watch TV until it was their turn.*

Or you might try putting all your children into bed at the same time, and allow the older ones to read quietly while they wait for you.

## *Try being a COMMANDO PARENT*

**Express your feelings** Instead of pleading or shouting, have you remembered to try the obvious and tell your child why you're irritated?

- *'It really annoys me when you keep coming into your sister's room after I've read you a story and kissed you goodnight. I'd be much happier if you could do everything you need to do before I tuck you in.'*

**Give consequences** What do you do if none of this works? If you have already tried the soft stuff, there is absolutely nothing wrong with going for commando consequences.

> *When I put my children to bed I always spend some special time alone with each one. The others used to find every excuse to come in and interrupt, but I finally laid down the law. Anyone who interrupts loses*

*five minutes when it's their turn, and I'll take it off the next night if necessary. Persistent offenders lose a night of special time altogether.*

*I was amazed how well it worked, and also quite touched. It turned out that even the threat of losing five minutes alone with me was enough to make them behave.* ’

## How to Deal with Interruptions

You don't stand a chance of getting your children to go to sleep if there are constant interruptions at bedtime.

- Put on the answering machine

‘ *The phone used to ring all evening while I was putting my children to bed and I'd rush off to answer it. Finally I only answered my mobile if it was my husband or teenage daughter. Everyone else could leave a message on the house phone and I'd get back to them later.* ’

***'My problem is my husband. He keeps coming home right after my children have gone to bed. Then they're wide awake again and get all wound up. It makes me so angry.'***

Here's how different parents would handle this:

- A **Sorted Parent** would stick to the schedule and ask her husband to come home earlier, or later.
- A **Tuned-In Parent** would know how happy it makes her children and her husband to see each other and would try to accommodate them.
- A **Physical Parent** would think getting to sleep was important, so she'd ask her husband to give each child a cuddle to help settle them down.
- A **Laid-Back Parent** would ask him to take responsibility: if he wants to play, he can settle them afterwards.

### *Try being a LAID-BACK PARENT* 

**Get help** No matter how competent you are, if you are outnumbered you might simply need another pair of hands at bedtime.

> *'After the baby was born there was no way I could get the other children to bed on my own. At six o'clock she'd start grizzling, just when I was trying to get the two older ones settled down for the night. So I hired a lovely girl for two hours every evening to help me. What a godsend. It was worth every penny.'*

Some mothers get so tired with a new baby in the house that they forget to ask for help, or feel that it is their job to do everything. But there is no point in getting exhausted. If you need help, ask for it.

# Getting Your Child to Sleep Through the Night

### *'My children have night terrors, insomnia, wet their beds. How am I supposed to get any sleep?'*

Sleep deprivation is the bane of most parents' lives. If you don't get a good night's sleep the next day is a write-off: you can't string a sentence together because you lose your train of thought halfway through, and you constantly feel as though you are running ten miles an hour but moving backwards.

You think it's going to end once your children are no longer babies, but it doesn't – even when they reach school age. The broken nights can go on for years: your children still come into your bed, they still wet their own, they still get nightmares and tummy aches. Then, at some horrible hour of the morning, just when you've finally got back to sleep, they're up, raring to go and wanting breakfast.

When they're a bit bigger, you might have a respite for a few years when they sleep through the night and get up at roughly the same time as you do. If your children are at this stage, enjoy it while you can, because when they are teenagers their sleep pattern changes again. Then you're either up at two a.m. because of the thumping music or because you are worrying sick about when they'll get home.

But for now, what can you do if you can't get any sleep?

## *Try being a SORTED PARENT*

**Sort your systems** Bedtime rules and routines can be great, but if no one is getting any sleep, we suggest you chuck out all the parenting books and find a solution that works for you. In the end, your entire family is going to be better off if every member of it is getting enough sleep. Just do whatever works.

> *My son spent months screaming his head off for me in the night. I tried going to him and I tried letting him cry himself back to sleep. But nothing worked. My husband's work was suffering because he wasn't sleeping, and we were so tired we fought constantly. Finally, I pulled a mattress on to the floor of my son's room and slept there with him for a couple of months.*

This mother was given all sorts of warnings and 'friendly advice':

- *'How will he ever learn to sleep on his own?'*
- *'How does your partner feel left on his own?'*
- *'Surely it isn't right to give your child that much power?'*

But because none of them had been getting any sleep, she ignored it. So what if she slept on a mattress on her son's floor for a while? The whole family could function again. Problem solved.

### *'I'm sure I'm doing it all wrong, but when my children wake in the night they hop into our bed.'*

Join the club! A huge number of parents have told us that they let their children either sleep in their room or get into their bed if they wake up in the night, and the more children they had, the more relaxed they were about it. Yet most of them prefaced their confession with 'I'm sure I'm doing it all wrong, but . . .' as though they were divulging some personal secret that might disqualify them from being a good parent. There were lots of variations on this theme.

*'I don't mind them coming to my bedroom if they've got a problem. I don't want to get up and go to their room to settle them. In fact, I'd rather not wake up at all. If they want to bring in their duvet and sleep on my bedroom floor, they're happy and so am I.'*

*'We never used to let our older children sleep with us. But now we've got two younger children I can't understand why we were so rigid. It is so much easier, and the whole family gets more sleep.'*

*'When my husband goes away I let my children sleep in our bed as a special treat. They really love it and I sleep better, too.'*

*'With three children, I never quite know who I'm going to find in which bed in the morning. My wife might cuddle one of them back to sleep and fall asleep in their bed. Meanwhile someone else might come in and get in bed next to me. I sleep through the whole thing.'*

### 'I don't mind letting my child climb into bed with me, but once my husband gets woken up by a kick or a nudge, he can't get back to sleep. Then his next day is hell.'

Most parents who let their children sleep in their bed say they wouldn't do it differently, but it simply doesn't work for everybody. If your partner can't sleep, or if it bothers you, then it's not the right answer for your family.

*'Our youngest is a real wriggler. There's no chance we could sleep with her in the bed. She kicks, sleeps horizontally and hogs all the space. But she can sleep on the sofa in our room if she wants to.'*

*'My husband doesn't like having the kids in bed with us, so if one of them comes in I put them on my side and put a chair beside the bed so they don't roll out. He doesn't know the difference.'*

*'I can't sleep if my children are with me. So I keep a futon made up under my bed. If one of them can't sleep, they come into my room, pull it out and sleep on it.'*

If your child is used to sleeping in your bed, even getting her to sleep on a mattress beside you might be an issue at first. But don't worry if she makes a fuss.

Persuading her to stay in her own room can be difficult too. Here are some ideas that will help you to get her either out of your bed, or out of your room.

### *'How can we get her to sleep in her own room? We want our privacy back.'*

Children usually want to sleep in their parents' room less and less as they get older. Eventually your child won't want to come in at all. But what do you do now if your bedroom is being invaded? Threatening her with punishment doesn't work.

> *'We were desperate to get our daughter to sleep in her own bed, so my husband told her that if she didn't, he would start taking her cuddly toys away. The next day I saw her taking them down the garden in her wheelbarrow, and I asked what she was doing. She said she was getting rid of them because she would rather be with us.'*

Parents who have been clear from the beginning that their children should stay in their own rooms get off lightly here. But changing things doesn't have to be a problem, and there doesn't have to be an all-or-nothing system. Perhaps you don't mind her coming in if she is ill, or at the weekend when you don't have to get up so early, but not every night.

## *Try being a SORTED PARENT*

***Give advance warning*** The kindest way to make changes is to tell your child in advance what to expect and why. You can avoid histrionics at bedtime by talking to her during the day about a week beforehand, and giving her a chance to get used to the idea.

> *'I told my daughter it was time for her to move out of our bedroom because we didn't sleep well when she was there. She was upset at first, but after a few days she was fine about it.'*

## *Try being a TUNED-IN PARENT* 

**Listen to their feelings** If she is upset about the changes, listen to and accept her feelings. It's also worth finding out if there's something she's worrying about. There may be all sorts of reasons why she wants to stay, but if the problem is night fears, see pp. 294–6.

## *Try being a CHEERLEADER PARENT* 

**Notice the good, ignore the bad** When she does spend the night – or even part of it – in her own bed, be positive and praise her for it the next morning.

- *'Well done. You stayed in your own room for half the night last night.'*

## *Try being a COMMANDO PARENT* 

**Express your feelings** If you are all talked and listened out and she is still not staying in her own room, try telling her how you feel.

> *We always had an open-door policy towards our children in the night, but our youngest pushed us to the limit. He had a series of bad dreams after watching* The BFG. *Of course I was sympathetic, but over time he got into the habit of coming down every night and wanting more and more attention. He started jumping on the bed and dancing around the room to make us wake up and talk to him.*
>
> *Finally I sat down with him and told him I was shattered, and that if he wanted me to be kind to him instead of angry all day, he had to let me sleep.*
>
> *I couldn't believe it – he understood what I meant. The next night I slept for ten hours. Bliss! In the morning I told him how much I appreciated it.*

### *'My child suffers from nightmares and is petrified of the dark. How can I help her?'*

## *Try being a PHYSICAL PARENT* 

***Just be there and be affectionate*** Children who are allowed into their parents' room usually have fewer problems with night fears because they feel safe.

> *I remember thinking that shadows from the curtains were giants by the windows when I was a kid. So I would go in and sleep on the floor in my parents' room. There were giants in their room too, but I knew my dad wouldn't let them get me.*

If you decide to put your child back in her own bed, you could reassure her that you are nearby, leave her bedroom door open or cuddle her until she falls back to sleep.

## *Try being a TUNED-IN PARENT* 

***Listen to their feelings*** Monsters under the bed, ghosts in the cupboard, terrible nightmares or even just the dark can keep children awake for nights on end. If you do need to settle your child, it's no good starting off by telling her that her fears aren't real. To her they are, so start by tuning in.

This can stir up a bit of a moral dilemma for you – you might worry that taking her fears seriously will make the experience more real for her. But by tuning in to her you aren't agreeing that the monsters are there. You are only accepting that she is afraid of them.

- *'You think there is a monster under your bed. That's scary. No wonder you're upset. I'd be scared if I thought there was a monster under my bed.'*

Her fears might be caused by something specific. So many things can tip the balance: a frightening film, an idea from a book, moving house, a strict teacher or a test at school.

> *My daughter's nightmares started when we got divorced. I just tried to be very sympathetic and reassure her that I wasn't going to leave her. After a few months she stopped getting them.*

## Try being a COMMANDO PARENT 

**Give information** Once you've spent a moment tuning in and listening to how she feels, you can tell her the truth and try to reassure her.

> *Sweetheart, I know how scared you are, but there isn't anything or anyone under your bed. It's just your imagination.*

But be ready to prove it by checking the evidence yourself. It's no use telling her there's nothing there while you are still lying in bed. How do you know?

> *My son came running into our room in the middle of the night shouting that there was an alien in his cupboard. I told him there couldn't possibly be one, and sent him back to bed. I felt like the meanest mother in the world next day when we found a bird trapped in there.*

## Try being a PHYSICAL PARENT 

> *My son gets woken up by terrible nightmares. I told him he would feel less scared and more in control if he did some deep breathing. We practised breathing out very, very slowly before taking in another slow breath.*

> *In the end we banned television after six o'clock because our son couldn't sleep. He is very sensitive and he was working himself into a state about burglars and terrorists in his room every time he watched the news.*

## Try being a LAID-BACK PARENT 

### Ask your child for solutions

> *I asked my daughter what would make her less scared. She said that she'd be fine if her room wasn't so dark, and asked if I could get her a night light. Now there is one in her bedroom and one in the bathroom, and she's fine.*

## Overcoming Night Fears

Here are other suggestions from parents who have found ways to help their children with night fears. They may or may not feel right for you.

- Some 'got rid' of the problem

*'My husband pulled that invisible crocodile out from under the bed and took it downstairs to the dustbin. Then the rubbish men took it away for ever.'*

*'Our daughter was afraid of the bogeyman, so her older brother dressed up in his fencing gear, went into her room and closed the door behind him. He made a big commotion, and when he came out he said the bogeyman was gone. He'd finished him off.'*

- Some tried to help their child feel safe

*'I told my daughter to think of a little warm glow in her heart when she gets scared. The more attention she pays to it, the stronger she will feel.'*

*'I helped my daughter get over her fear of monsters by talking about her guardian angel who is there to protect her all the time. She closed her eyes and said she could see it. It was bright pink – like her Barbie.'*

If these approaches don't work for you, stick to tuning in and giving information. Your child will feel more secure if you are sympathetic and reassuring.

### *'Our child simply needs less sleep than we do. She's up at the crack of dawn and wakes the whole house up. It's awful.'*

This is a tricky one, particularly if she is quite young. An older child can read, do puzzles, or watch a video. But you never know what a small child might get up to.

*When my son was little he would wake up and roam around the house in the middle of the night. He'd meddle with everything, leaving the bathroom taps running and fiddling with the knobs on the gas cooker. I thought of locking him in his room at night, but I was afraid of what would happen to him if there was a fire. On the other hand, if I let him wander around the house on his own, he might start one.*

Even if they sleep all night, little children are often up and charging around at unearthly hours of the morning, and they have to be supervised. We'll get the most painful, obvious solution over with first. If you have a small child who is up and wandering around the house, you are going to have to wake up too, however tired you are.

If she will stay in her room, you might try putting out lots of toys to keep her busy, or get her an alarm clock.

*I bought my daughter the kind with bunny ears that pop up when it goes off, because she is too young to tell the time. I told her I need to sleep until seven o'clock, when the bunny ears pop up, and asked her to stay in her room until then. Thank heavens she does.*

## *Try being a LAID-BACK PARENT*

***Ask for solutions*** It's great if you can find an answer together.

*My son used to come and wake me up at five in the morning, which drove me mad. Finally I told him I couldn't take it any more and asked him what we could do about it. He suggested he could watch a video, but he didn't know how to turn it on.*

*What a great idea. We taught him the basics and now we leave one loaded for him at night in case he wakes up early.*

## *Try being a COMMANDO PARENT*

***Give orders that don't sound like orders*** Try giving options:

- *'If you wake up in the middle of the night you can read a book or watch TV quietly, but you can't do anything that wakes other people up like playing music or the piano.'*

*Give consequences* If your child is a repeat offender, go ahead and lay down the law by giving consequences.

- *'You know the rule about watching TV loudly in the middle of the night. If you wake us up one more time, there will be no television for a week.'*

### *'My daughter still wets the bed. Her best friend hasn't worn a nappy since she was two. Why can't we be normal?'*

Some parents worry if their child is no longer a toddler but still wets her bed. The extra laundry is boring and inconvenient, but try not to tell her off. She probably can't help it. Though bed-wetting can be a symptom of other issues, like anxiety, in most cases it is just one of those things, and in time she will grow out of it.

If it wasn't so embarrassing to talk about, you'd probably find she has a fellow classmate or two who also wets the bed.

> *'My daughter, who is seven, still wears a nappy at night. If she spends the night at a friend's house, she sneaks into the bathroom to put it on. Among her friends, two others admitted they still wore nappies at night as well. That makes three children in her class that we know of.'*

Older bed-wetters shouldn't be made to feel ashamed, so don't fuss about it. To give you some idea how common a problem it is, you can buy night pants for up to twelve-year-olds in the supermarket. This isn't a specialist medical issue where you need to order them from the chemist.

## *Try being a PHYSICAL PARENT* 

If your child is a bed-wetter, the obvious practical things you can do about it are physical. Limit the amount she drinks after dinner, take her to the bathroom before she goes to sleep, and then again before you go to sleep. But don't expect to solve the problem entirely. Some children are very deep sleepers, or have small bladders, and you just have to wait for them to grow out of it.

## Try being a SORTED PARENT

*Sort your systems and train them up* If your child frequently wets the bed, she can wear night pants. But if the problem is intermittent and she is reluctant to wear them, teach her how to deal with her sheets in the middle of the night.

> *My daughter occasionally wets the bed, but refuses to wear night pants. She used to wake me up in the middle of the night to change the sheets until I showed her what to do.*
>
> *Over her bottom sheet we put a plastic-backed sheet, then another sheet on top. When she wets the bed she takes off the top layers, turns over her duvet, changes her pyjamas and gets back into a dry bed. She can have a shower in the morning.*

Some parents have found visualization techniques to be helpful. There are bedtime stories available that can help you with this. Try the internet for suggestions.

## Try being a COMMANDO PARENT

*Give consequences* If she is a persistent bed-wetter, but refuses to wear night pants, she can be in charge of stripping her sheets and putting them in the washing machine. But remember, this is a consequence, not a punishment, so be kind about it.

### *'I can't stand being woken up in the middle of the night. Can I forbid my children from doing it?'*

Some sleepless nights are inevitable. Apart from waiting for your children to grow up, there is no miracle cure. At some point you are going to have some broken sleep because there can't be a child on this planet who cheerfully goes to bed every night, falls asleep and stays that way.

Whether we like it or not, our children are dependent on us morning, noon *and* night. They are going to have fevers and get tummy bugs. Some have nightmares, some want more attention, some are light sleepers, and some need less sleep than we do.

Almost all of them go through phases of being unsettled. There will be times when you are just going to have to rise to the occasion and deal with it as best you can.

Even though they're tired for years and years, many parents don't look forward to the time when their children won't need them at night.

> *I adore holding my daughter's hand or letting her rest under my arm until she drops off to sleep. In the middle of the night, I know that I can comfort her when she's ill or frightened just by being near her. It means a lot to me. It's bittersweet knowing it will all end one day.*

# 8

# Dealing with Difficult Behaviour

## From Minor Grumbles to Major Tantrums – It's Not Easy, but You *Can* Do It

Does your child ever get moody and withdrawn, answer back or have tantrums? Does he ever swear, throw things or kick you? Or refuse to do what he is told?

Well, join the club. We'd like to tell you that none of our children have ever done these things, but it simply wouldn't be true. Over the last fifteen years, we've survived toddler tantrums, teenage mood swings and everything in between.

Being a parent is so simple when your child is in a good mood and behaving well. You talk nicely to him. He talks nicely to you. It's easy. But catch even a cooperative child on a grumpy day, and it's another story.

> *I asked him twice to turn off the TV. Nothing. Then, after the third time, he went ballistic. 'No! Why should I? Stop telling me what to do. You're so mean. I'm NOT turning it off.'*

Being a parent when your child is being foul can be demoralizing. With so much stress and anger swirling around, it's enough to push even the most easygoing, civilized parent over the edge. You might try to console yourself by being cynical about other people's perfect children – they're sure to rebel big-time in their teens, aren't they? But you have to admit, it would be so much more pleasant if everything would just run smoothly.

When your child is rude and surly, all the good parenting stuff can fly right out of the window. You can go from Super Parent to the Great

Dictator in nought to ten seconds, yelling things you'll regret later.

*I've had enough of you and your mouth. Turn that blasted TV off right now! You drive me demented. Get up this minute and go to bed. And don't even think of answering me back or there'll be no TV – ever. I'm going to pick it up and fling it out of the window.*

What are you saying? Who knows! You are furious and out of control. Your voice rises, your blood pressure soars and it is hard to think straight. Your child behaves worse and worse – and so do you. After a hideous scene, you can feel overwhelmed, exhausted and guilty.

*One day, my son refused to get dressed after his swimming lesson. But we had to go – the children for the next session had arrived and we weren't allowed to hang around. I was struggling to put on his clothes, and he kept stripping them right off again. He started having a huge tantrum so I picked him up, half dressed, and carried him to the car.*

*He screamed his head off the whole way, biting and kicking me. Three different people in the street, including a builder, called out 'You're not fit to be a mother' and 'People like you shouldn't have children.' Then, when we got to the car, a bunch of policemen screeched up in two squad cars to see what the problem was. A member of the public had actually called the station to report me!*

*My older son set the policemen straight. 'Don't worry. It's just my younger brother having one of his tantrums.' I was so humiliated. I sat at the wheel and cried for ten minutes before I could gather the strength to drive home.*

This mother was still so upset a year after it happened, she had to fight back tears when she told us this story.

If your child tends to be tricky, you might feel paranoid and isolated, and assume that everyone else's children are always impeccably behaved. Don't kid yourself. Toddlers and teenagers get the worst press, but all children have their grumpy days. It might give you some comfort to know you aren't alone, but if your child is particularly temperamental, sensitive, reactive or headstrong, you're probably in for a bumpier ride than the average parent.

*'I keep thinking, 'Why me? Why does my son keep putting me through this?' All I wanted was a normal life. My husband and I are quiet people, so these tantrums are a real shock.'*

*'I'm actually quite scared of standing up to her. I feel like I am holding my breath all the time to avoid saying the wrong thing. It's like having a snarling dog in the house. One false move and she snaps.'*

Lots of parents find their problems don't come in isolation; it's generally more of a package deal, with a couple of added bonus problems on top. A child who is rude and uncooperative with you may also torment his siblings, refuse to do his homework, be aggressive at school or hyper-sensitive to loud noises.

### *'What's the right thing to do when my child is being difficult? I honestly haven't got a clue.'*

Ideally, unhappy, angry feelings could be sorted out immediately and they'd never escalate. But some days, whatever you say or do seems to be wrong. The good news is that whether your child is difficult occasionally or most of the time, the situation isn't hopeless and every one of the parenting skills can help. Once you are communicating better your child will be more inclined to listen, and his behaviour will improve. You'll find it's much easier to tackle problems when there is a good atmosphere and you feel you are both on the same side.

We're not saying you can change your child's temperament entirely, or that you should even want to. His stubbornness, his impulsiveness, his sensitivity – whatever it is that drives you crazy – is what makes him unique. What you *can* change is the way you respond to him, so he feels loved, accepted and understood.

# Reasons Why Your Child May Be Difficult

Though every child is different, when we talked to parents, the same broad themes kept coming up time and time again. It might be helpful to see if your child's behaviour fits into any of these patterns. The idea isn't to label him for ever, but to target more precisely what's going on.

## He may be sensitive

It's surprising, but lots of children who seem difficult and temperamental are extremely sensitive. Many of them were fussy babies who were hard to feed or had trouble getting to sleep, or tricky toddlers who threw tantrums if things weren't exactly the way they wanted them. Some are physically sensitive children who can't tolerate loud noises, too much sugar, food additives, or ordinary washing powder. Or they might be emotionally sensitive and burst into tears at the mildest teasing or unintentional criticism.

Because they find things hard to bear, sensitive children can seem difficult or even aggressive.

*'My daughter is very sensitive to noise – always has been. She can't stand loud music in shops or children's parties. At home, if someone is being too loud she'll yell, 'SHUT UP! I CAN'T STAND IT! SHUT UP!' She has even done it at school.*

*The irony is that when she's screaming she makes far more noise than whatever was bugging her in the first place.'*

*'My son takes things to heart and can't handle criticism. If he feels he's been wronged – like if I say he has to do his homework when he has already finished – it's all too much for him and tears start rolling down his cheeks.'*

Some sensitive children are also extremely tuned in to the emotion around them. They pick up on all the family frustrations and on all of your frustrations, too. They may not know what's wrong, but they can feel something isn't quite right. If this makes them feel insecure or irritable, they can start acting up.

This is the child who will ask you why your voice was so fake on the telephone during a difficult conversation, who will have a fit at Christmas dinner when you are straining to impress your in-laws, or who will start whinging in the car when the traffic is solid and you are rigid with tension.

Some therapists call it 'expressing the shadow in the family'. Unless you are very alert to what is going on, you can feel permanently irritated with this child because he always seems to be at the epicentre of whatever is going wrong. You may not have noticed the simmering tension, but he has. He starts misbehaving, and then he gets it in the neck for apparently being the trigger.

Sensitive children aren't usually trying to wind you up on purpose. More often they are just reacting strongly to something. They are not rejecting the broccoli you've cooked to spite you. To them that broccoli tastes bitter. The label on their vest does feel unbearably itchy. A casual, tactless remark really does hurt their feelings.

## He may be reactive

Some children have a very short fuse. They blow up over the slightest things, and when they erupt they rampage round the entire house. But they don't lose their cool on purpose to get attention. They just can't seem to help themselves.

> *If anyone accidentally bumps into my son, his adrenalin shoots right up and he'll punch them or kick them back.*

This type of child becomes consumed with feelings and emotions, but then doesn't know what to do with them. After making a scene, he might be ashamed of losing control. One father told us:

> *My son is known for his terrible outbursts. Once, I was using my video camera and filmed him just as he lost a board game. He flew into a temper, yelling, 'It's not fair! It's not fair! You cheated!' Later we*

*played the video and he saw the whole thing. He was so embarrassed I actually wished I hadn't shown it to him.* ’

## He may have a strong character

Some children know their own minds and can drive you mad, either by being incredibly demanding or by refusing to do what you say.

‘ *My son has lots of energy and no fear. He stands up to me all the time, and when he wants something, he won't take no for an answer. I admire him, but it drives me up the wall because he never does anything I ask.* ’

This kind of child has a strong internal drive and knows exactly what he wants. When he's hungry, he wants food immediately. When he doesn't want dinner, you can't get him to the table. Although he may be a pain now, you can't help but think he'll do very well in life if he can manage to channel his incredible drive in a positive way.

## He may be over-protected

Some children are over-protected by their well-meaning parents. The whole family has to tiptoe around so they don't burst into tears or have a tantrum.

Sometimes parents become over-protective if their child has been seriously ill. Maybe he was very premature or a sickly baby. Maybe as a toddler he had a life-threatening illness, an operation, or developed a severe food allergy.

Other parents are like this because they feel guilty. Perhaps they didn't bond properly when he was a baby or feel they don't spend enough time with him.

Of course, it's natural and admirable to want to do all you can for your child, but the reason you were cautious and protective in the first place may no longer apply.

*My son had meningitis and he was very frail afterwards. But that was when he was four. Now he is thirteen he is a real pain. I realize that it is partly my fault. I have never told him off or set limits. I've always thought, 'Poor Rob, it's not his fault. He needs looking after.' Now I regret it.*

## He may not pick up on social cues

Some children have great difficulty picking up on social nuances. They just don't realize that they irritate other children or adults. They might behave too exuberantly, say things in an annoying way, tug too hard at your arm to get attention, get too close to your face when they are talking, or expect cuddles at inappropriate times.

*My daughter doesn't know when to stop. She doesn't notice the change in my voice and she carries on until she gets into serious trouble. With the others, just a look or a gesture is usually enough.*

These children don't quite understand the social cues the rest of us take for granted. Apart from not properly decoding what other people mean, they may act oddly because they don't realize what normal behaviour is. If your child is like this, you may have to spend a lot of time with him teaching him how to get along with people – how to look enthusiastic, say 'please' or 'hello' – to get the response from people he wants or needs (see Chapter Four).

Confusingly, some children who on the one hand seem oblivious to social cues can also be hyper-sensitive to them. They feel criticized, even when you have no intention of criticizing them at all, and pick up on your subtle changes of voice and body language, assuming the worst.

*If I tell off my children for being noisy, my oldest child will scowl, 'Why do you always pick on me?' She takes everything personally and assumes every criticism is meant expressly for her.*

## He may be a slow processor

Some children get stuck in a mood. From your perspective, there is so much else going on and so little time, you just want to sort his problems out and move on. But if he's not the type to work through emotions quickly, it might take a while.

> *My daughter comes to me and starts droning on about her problems at school. Although I'm pleased she can talk to me, I start to feel trapped. She wants my advice, but whatever I suggest she says, 'Yes, but . . .' and carries on complaining.*

This type of child might get in your face when he's got problems, growling at everyone and putting you down, because he doesn't know what else to do with his unhappy feelings.

Other slow processors need to be alone to calm down. They may not want you near them because they feel overwhelmed, or even ashamed of being in the grip of such strong feelings.

## He might be different from the rest of the family

Your child may seem like quite hard work to you, but in another family his behaviour might not be unusual at all.

> *My son is always bouncing around, irritating his sisters and generally driving us all mad. He is more active and noisier than the rest of us put together, and his sisters are always complaining about him. I always secretly wondered whether we had some behavioural issues.*
>
> *Then we went to stay with some friends, a family with three boys, and our son fitted right in. Now I feel guilty, like we gave him a bad rap he didn't deserve.*

It isn't uncommon for one child to seem difficult simply in contrast to his siblings. In *The Simpsons*, Bart is clearly cast as the difficult child next to brainy Lisa and cute baby Maggie. But put him in a family with some of the playground thugs from the series and he'd seem pretty harmless. It is all relative. It's so easy to label the one who doesn't fit in as the difficult one. As one father told us:

*I had four brothers. The others loved sports, like wrestling and playing rugby, while I just wanted peace and quiet. My mother used to tell me how difficult I was, but I just wasn't like them.*

Not everyone is the same. Take a look at your child's friends and other families – maybe he isn't so unusual after all.

## He may have difficulty reconciling expectations and reality

Some children are very easily disappointed. Like perfectionists, they have a strong sense of how they want things to turn out, and get upset when life doesn't go the way they've imagined. The problem is that their disappointment can make them sound unreasonable and spoilt.

*We'd been told about a fantastic public swimming pool. But when we got there the curly slides and wave machine weren't open. My girls wanted to swim anyway, but my son freaked out. 'Why did we come to this horrible pool?' he snarled. 'You're so stupid. Why did you bring us here?'*

Often these children haven't told anyone about their expectations; they assume you know about them through telepathy. Sometimes even they don't know themselves how much they mind about something until it goes wrong.

## He may have difficulty making transitions

Lots of children are happy doing whatever they are doing, but find it hard to adjust to doing something different. Many parents have realized that transitions can be the most difficult times of the day.

*It's hard to get my daughter out of the door in the morning, but once we're actually walking to school, she's fine. She won't get undressed, but once she's in the bath she loves it. Getting her out of the bath and into bed is tough, but she's OK once she's tucked under the covers.*

Sometimes difficulty with transitions follows patterns. You might find that your child comes home with attitude after playing at a friend's house or staying away for the night. He might have trouble getting used to a new set of teachers each September. And lots of parents dread the beginning of the school holidays.

*'My children behave appallingly and fight like crazy for the first few days. But once they've got used to hanging around, without the structure and routine of school, they get into it and enjoy themselves.'*

## He may have learning difficulties

If you were to describe a child with learning difficulties and a classic 'difficult' child, you would probably tick most of the same boxes. Dyslexia, dyspraxia, Asperger's Syndrome, autism and Attention Deficit Disorder are called learning and behavioural disorders because their symptoms often overlap. In many cases, the brain processes both information and emotions in a different way to most. These children can display a whole range of difficult behaviour, from sensitivities to tantrums.

Academic problems might be diagnosed at school. What can be harder to spot is when children struggle to cope with situations their friends take in their stride. Petty frustrations can be hard for them to handle, and they might react inappropriately. A timetable can seem incomprehensible, and just finding their way around school can be overwhelming. Statistically they are more likely to be bullied than other children.

It can be hard for parents to crack down on bad behaviour if they feel sorry for their child, don't know how to handle him or find it hard to admit that he has a problem.

## He may be going through difficult circumstances

A child with a difficult temperament, coping with difficult circumstances, is a hell of a combination. If you are also having a tough time, it can be very hard to be sympathetic.

*My son was upset when we moved house, so I worked flat out all day unpacking his bedroom before he got back from school. When he walked in he said rudely, 'I'm not sleeping here. It hasn't even got a curtain.'*

*I could have killed him. I'd had a million other things to do, and he wasn't even grateful.*

*My husband and I are splitting up, and my children are pushing me beyond the limit. Can't they see how hard this is for me? I'm struggling, doing the best I can, and all they do is give me grief.*

If your family is going through difficulties and you can barely keep your own head above water, it's hard to find the extra strength to support your children. But if your child is behaving badly, try and be compassionate, because it's probably a signal that he isn't coping very well.

*When I started a new job with longer hours, my daughter started picking on her brother, hitting him and being really nasty. It took a lot of untangling before she admitted she was upset because I wasn't spending much time with her.*

Some children are actually very good at dealing with difficult situations, but their circumstances are so bad that they are still considered to be 'problem' children. As one teacher told us:

*There was one little girl in my class who was very hard to deal with. I found out that her mother had been in and out of rehab, and in two years she'd had twenty different nannies. Once I knew that, I was amazed how well she'd coped.*

## He may be going through a difficult phase

Some stages of emotional development (not to mention hormonal ups and downs) can be hard to deal with. If your child is going through a bad patch, even minor events like an argument with a friend can seem overwhelming. But instead of letting you in so you can comfort him, he might push you away.

Sometimes the only thread you can hold on to is that things will change – eventually. You can also console yourself with the thought that by going through these difficulties now, your child is learning how to handle problems while he's safe and secure under your roof.

## Strategies for Dealing with Difficult Behaviour

### Stand Back and Stay Calm

***'I want to turn my child's behaviour around, but where on earth do I begin?'***

#### *Try being a PAUSE PARENT* 

The first thing to do is to take yourself out of the fight. Every time the emotional temperature starts to rise, make a mental decision to pause. Call a personal ceasefire. Stop focusing on the arguing, rudeness, screaming or violence. It is a waste of time. Do yourself and your child a big favour and keep calm. You can work on changing his behaviour afterwards, but while he is behaving badly you are wasting your breath.

> *My son was out of control and had the most incredible temper tantrums. I took him to loads of places looking for help: Harley Street doctors, child psychologists, the lot. The doctor who finally helped me told me what I should do* before *and* after *my son was difficult, and said I should stop focusing endlessly on the tantrums themselves.*

At first this advice seems to go against basic common sense. When your child is being horrendous, whinging, screaming, arguing, answering back – all that unacceptable behaviour that sends you gibbering up the wall – you want him to stop immediately.

But if he isn't behaving rationally, he isn't feeling rational. So you aren't going to get anywhere by reasoning. In fact you will probably end up even more furious and frustrated with him, and him with you. The temperature needs to come down before you can solve the problem.

When he is in the grip of such overwhelming feelings, he simply can't hear you. At that moment you can't argue him out of his foul mood or tantrum. As we have heard, you can't persuade an irrational child to get dressed after swimming, or to do anything else. Reasoning just doesn't work. It's like shouting into a storm; the words fly right back in your face.

Because you are physically bigger and louder than your child, you might be able to force him to cooperate. But this can backfire badly because he'll then feel even more angry and resentful.

***Zip your lip*** Though it might be hard to admit, if the two of you keep clashing, whatever you're doing isn't working. So it's time to try something different. The next time you sense trouble brewing, pause. Take a deep breath, keep quiet, and remind yourself that this unbearable situation is only temporary and you can't fix it now. You can stay in the room without speaking, or walk out. It may take you five minutes, it may take twenty, but let yourself calm down and get some perspective. If you give your child time to calm down too, you can both start again.

This can also help if your child doesn't fly out of control but simply refuses to do what you say. If he is sitting, arms folded, face set, entire body tensed in silent resistance, it may drive you mad, but do your best to pause. Give yourself some time out to collect yourself before you try something else.

If your child is behaving appallingly, you might think that pausing flies in the face of reason. After all, you are the parent. You are supposed to be in charge and he shouldn't be allowed to behave that way. You may be worried that if you give in now, there'll only be more trouble next time. But we aren't saying you are going to let him get away with anything.

***Wait until later*** Instead, come back to the problem in five minutes or five hours, when you can address it rationally and your child isn't resistant. You'll be amazed. By that time you might even be able to get him to do what you want without a battle at all.

*My son would never brush his teeth unless I nagged him. Sometimes I'd force the toothbrush into his hand and make him brush. Or prise open his mouth so I could do it. It was awful for both of us.*

*One day I decided to change tack. I said, 'OK, teeth time.' He immediately started into the big resistance routine. I could feel myself getting angry. How many hundred times had we been through this?*

*So I went straight upstairs, splashed my face with cold water and put on some hand cream, deep breathing the whole way. I went back down again, feeling more calm. Then I said, as if nothing had happened, 'Now, what were we talking about? Oh yes, teeth.' To my surprise he started getting up. 'All right, all right. Will you read to me tonight?' We didn't argue. He did his teeth, and that was it.*

One of the most difficult times to pause is when your child acts up in a public place. If he is defying you in front of your friends, or causing a scene in the street and everyone is turning round to look at you, the humiliation can be unbearable. The pressure is on you to do *something*.

But by taking a deep breath and refusing to lose your cool you *are* doing something. You are giving yourself the space to think through your next move.

There are all sorts of other things you can do to rescue the situation, and we will lay out a lot of ideas in this chapter. But almost always, pausing is the first step. There are so many ways to help your child in the calm between the storms. Don't waste your time and energy on the storms, yours or his. It's not worth it.

### *'I take your point. But once I lose my temper, I have a hard time steadying myself again.'*

***Calm down fast*** You may have good intentions of staying calm, but when your child is being difficult, all sorts of stress hormones start whizzing round your body, whether you want them to or not.

You probably know some quick ways to reduce stress, and if you are anything like us, you've been meaning to get round to actually doing some of them when your child starts winding you up.

## Physical Ways to Calm Down

- Take in a couple of deep breaths and slowly let them out
- Count to ten
- Circle your shoulders
- Shake out your arms and legs
- Wash your hands
- Punch a pillow
- Run up and down the stairs
- Go out for a run
- Vigorously sweep the garden or scrub the floor (yeah right, but it does work)

## Mental Ways to Calm Down

- Lock yourself in the bathroom for five minutes' peace
- Put on some music and sing
- Read a quick chapter in a book or an article in a magazine
- Close your eyes and imagine that you are somewhere calm, like a meadow or by a waterfall
- Imagine you're a tree, with deep solid roots going down into the ground

These things are pretty simple if you can remember to do any of them. But when your child is driving you crazy, it's hard to remember anything. So don't worry if you can't manage it. We'll give you loads of ideas in this chapter how to deal with your child, and we guarantee some of them will work for you. It's an upward spiral, and once he starts to behave better and you see a glimmer of light, you will find it easier.

# Notice the Good, Ignore All the Rest

## *Try being a CHEERLEADER PARENT*

This chapter is about turning round your child's behaviour, but if he's a tough nut, he is going to resist everything you try. You may be wondering if you'll ever be able to get through to him.

Surprisingly, one of the best things you can do is also the simplest. It takes almost no effort, just a small mental shift on your part. All you have to do is make a silent decision to start noticing anything good he does. Stop criticizing, comment nicely when he does something right, and you will start seeing some results. By consciously ignoring it, the bad stuff is more likely to fade away from lack of attention, while the good stuff expands to fill its place. Your child's behaviour will improve and you will feel much more positive.

*Notice the good* If you are normally painfully aware of your child's bad behaviour, noticing his good behaviour will seem strange at first. It's as though you are ducking your responsibilities and letting him walk all over you.

But what you are doing is subtle and powerful. You are not letting him get away with being difficult. You are setting out to change his behaviour in a totally new way. Most children love the positive attention, so their behaviour starts to improve immediately.

*'When I first started telling my son all the things he was doing right, it was so unnatural for me. But he listened every time I said anything nice to him. It made me realize what an old battle-axe I must have been.'*

*'As far as I was concerned, there was absolutely nothing my daughter ever did right. She picked fights with the other children and argued constantly with me. She was the root of every problem.*

*But once I started looking, I began to spot little things. She taught her younger brother how to work the DVD player, and she is kind to the dog. It was like taking blinkers off my eyes.*

*I'm not saying all our problems ended overnight. But now I realize the situation isn't so hopeless.'*

Once you stop obsessing about his annoying habits, you might even realize your child isn't really so difficult at all.

'*I always thought my son was extremely difficult. He is always late for everything – he holds the whole family up.*

*He used to drive me absolutely insane. But then I looked at the big picture. He actually does pretty well at school, he has lots of friends, and all round he's doing fine. So he irritates me because he's not a great timekeeper. But we can work on that. I realize he's not so bad in the big scheme of things.*'

By deciding to be a **Cheerleader** you aren't being an ostrich, sticking your head in the sand and opting out of your responsibilities. Nor are you being a Pollyanna, insisting that everything is going well with your child when it quite clearly isn't. It's about refocusing the beam of your gaze on to the things that genuinely are going well, instead of getting overwhelmed by the chaos and trouble.

'*I struggled with my son for years. The turning point definitely came when I started pointing out what I liked about him.*'

Children often use bad behaviour to get attention. Although they may enjoy provoking a reaction and putting themselves in the limelight, they don't actually like being criticized. You can change things around by putting them in the spotlight for what they do right.

***Be specific*** If your child manages to do anything good, no matter how small or seemingly insignificant, make an effort to point out *exactly* what it is, and why you like it. The mother who made the rounds of the Harley Street doctors and child psychologists described in detail the advice that helped her.

'*This incredible doctor said I should talk to my son at bedtime, and tell him three to five things he had done well during the day. On tough days, when I couldn't think of anything, I should mention any times when he could have had a tantrum but didn't.*

*At first it was hard to think of anything good to say, so my daily list included all sorts of odd things like 'You didn't hit your brother, even when he bumped your leg with his scooter' and 'Although you were still angry at bathtime, you didn't bite me again. I really appreciate that.'*

*The doctor also said I should write down all the good things my son did and put them in a folder – even though he couldn't read at the time! He called it a Feel-Good File. That way my son would have proof of all the good things he had done and I could help him change his sense of himself.*

*My son's behaviour started to improve and I was so busy looking for good things to tell him that I felt a lot happier.* ’

You could also try writing down all the good things your child does and pinning the list up on a wall so he can see it.

Some parents find their child's behaviour gets worse when they first start praising him. If he is feeling quite paranoid and persecuted, it might take a while before he can open up and let you in, so be prepared.

‘ *For a while, when I tried to appreciate my daughter, she behaved worse. She was rude and sarcastic, and I was tempted many times to snap back at her. It took me a while to realize she was feeling bruised and suspicious.*

*At first she didn't believe the nice things I told her, or that I was sincere. But I didn't give up and it's got easier and easier over time to give her genuine compliments.* ’

If your child is uncomfortable being praised, it helps a lot to be specific. If he isn't feeling 'marvellous' or 'wonderful' or doesn't think he's a 'good boy', these kinds of compliments won't mean anything. But by being specific you can say things that are true and are no big deal:

- *'You hung up your towel.'*
- *'Thanks for feeding the fish.'*

Keep your voice neutral and don't gush, because gushing can make a prickly child embarrassed or make you sound insincere. Lots of children, especially when they are older, feel uncomfortable when you praise them. So you might have to be more subtle about it. Try giving a quiet thumbs-up, a kind look or a quick nod and smile when he does something right.

Though it is nice to compliment your child on the spot, if he is incredulous or thinks you're trying to manipulate him, leave it until bedtime. You'll have his full attention, and it will be obvious that you don't want anything from him.

### *'I'm trying so hard to be positive, but he's still getting to me. It's almost impossible to ignore his bad behaviour.'*

*Ignore the bad* It's very hard not to take the bait when your child tries to drag you into an argument. It's like pausing in the face of continuous and extreme provocation. But you have to make it clear to your child that you are not going to give him any attention until he starts behaving.

Many children are used to getting exactly what they want, when they want it, by being difficult. They behave badly because it works.

> *'I dread taking my son to the supermarket. He badgers me for biscuits and sweets. I usually give in just for an easy life. The couple of times I've said 'no' he's had a tantrum, a complete screaming fit in the middle of the supermarket with everyone staring at us.*
>
> *Now he has moved on to demanding toys and videos as well. I really don't know what to do.'*

Lots of parents give in because they want to be kind and don't like confrontation. Working mothers and divorced parents can easily fall into this trap. You don't want to waste precious time with your child arguing, and you would do anything to make him happy. So it's easy to get into the habit of giving in to requests. But before you know it, you've created an ungrateful, insatiable monster. As *Daily Mail* journalist Fiona McIntosh put it:

> *'After a long day at the office, many of us are too tired, too busy and too guilty to hand out the prescribed dose of textbook discipline*

*required to keep our children in check. If you only have an hour with your children before bedtime, you're far more likely to give in to their demands than spend the next precious forty minutes locked in a screaming match.* ’

Whether we work or not, we are all in danger of the same thing. Most of us will do anything for a quiet life. But if your child knows your weak spots, he can start controlling the show.

Ignoring bad behaviour is tough, because some children can take control of every conversation, weeping and whining, shouting and complaining, begging for something they don't need or shouldn't have, and taking up your whole field of vision. When you ignore their bad behaviour for the first time – and we mean literally carrying on with your business as though the temper tantrum on the floor isn't taking place, the door isn't being viciously kicked, or no one is wrapped around your ankles screaming at you until they are blue in the face – it is going to be a battle of wills that your child isn't used to losing.

Don't feel foolish if you just can't stomach the emotional fallout. Most parents whose children act this way keep giving in because they can't bear it. Try this only when you are feeling strong enough to carry it through. If you can, block out an entire afternoon when you know you are going to be at home. It will be much easier to get through the ordeal without friends, neighbours or random people in the street looking at you as if you are a psycho mother with a psycho child.

If you don't get sucked in and react as usual, your child might throw a huge out-of-control fit while he tries everything under the sun to rope you in. So be prepared for the worst. It could carry on for hours, until he has completely exhausted himself. But your advance preparation – telling him how things are going to change and mentally gearing yourself up for it – might make it that bit easier and help him realize you mean business.

## How to Overthrow a Mini-Tyrant

The BBC Programme *Flesh and Blood* highlighted the case of Kate McElroy and her four-year-old daughter, Alice. As a single working mother, Kate felt guilty about not spending enough time with her. She tried to make up for this in the evenings by being super-nice and doing everything her daughter wanted.

Alice had turned into a mini-tyrant who screamed and demanded and fussed about everything, everywhere they went. The more Kate did for her, the worse she behaved. On the programme, family therapist Noel Janis Norton, of the New Learning Centre, told Kate to ignore her daughter when she was behaving badly, and give her lots of attention and praise the second she stopped.

The first time her mother didn't do what she wanted, Alice had a forty-five-minute tantrum on the floor and her mother looked absolutely stricken. You suspected she'd have cracked if Noel hadn't been there to back her up.

Kate found it so difficult and out of character not to give in immediately to her daughter's demands that she carried around little Post-it notes to remind herself what to say when Alice started acting up:

- *'It sounds to me like you are giving me an order. In this house Mummy is in charge.'*
- *'I can see you aren't feeling very friendly and I can see you don't want to do what I asked. When you are ready to be friendly, you can come and talk to me.'*

After a few weeks, Alice was a changed child – smiling, happy, laughing. She could be taken anywhere, and Kate was finally the head of the household. Instead of dreading her daughter's behaviour, she loved spending time with her.

What shone through was that manipulating her mother with bad behaviour didn't actually make Alice happy. Being in charge is far too great a burden for children, and can leave them feeling out of control.

# Look for Physical Causes

If you keep your cool and ignore as much bad behaviour as you possibly can, there will already be much less drama in your house. Now is the time to start working on longer-term strategies to turn your child's behaviour around.

He might be behaving like a rabid dog, but is he really disturbed or just ultra-sensitive to Coca Cola or worn out after going to bed too late too often? It may not be easy to change his diet or bedtime, but if you manage to find the culprit and take action, you'll start to see results within days, or even hours. The main physical triggers of mood swings and bad behaviour are: high or low blood-sugar levels, food additives, food sensitivities and intolerances, dehydration, lack of exercise, lack of sleep, or simply needing more time with you.

## *Try being a PHYSICAL PARENT* 

## Avoid sugar highs and sugar blues

When it comes to bad behaviour, the most familiar suspect is sugar in its many forms. When it zooms into the bloodstream it can lead to bursts of unfocused energy, and then leave you feeling downright depressed. If you suspect your child can't cope with sugar highs or the sugar blues which often follow, try cutting right down on biscuits, cakes, sweets, fizzy drinks and chocolate, which also contains caffeine – another stimulant.

*When she came home from a birthday party, my daughter would be in a vile mood, showing off and shouting one minute, and weeping the next. You wouldn't believe how temperamental she was.*

*And then it hit me. It was so simple. It was all to do with too much sugar and chocolate. She can't cope with it. I realized there was no point in shouting at her. Instead, I put her on my lap and she cried herself to sleep.*

## Look out for low blood sugar

When children behave appallingly for no apparent reason, it can simply be because they can't go for too long without food and they need a little extra energy.

> *We took our children out for lunch. They whinged and complained. They didn't like the café, there was nothing on the menu they wanted to eat, on and on. At first I was so irritated that I threatened to take them home, but then I realized and whispered to my husband, 'Low blood sugar.' Sure enough, within five minutes of the food arriving they were back to normal.*

> *My son gets really grumpy if he doesn't eat. He can be horrible to me when I collect him from school, but within a few minutes of giving him a snack, he's fine.*

If you think your child's foul moods are caused by low blood sugar, resist doling out sweets to solve them. The trick is to lower his glycaemic load by focusing on foods that release sugar more slowly – nuts, muesli bars, oatcakes with cheese, that kind of thing, as they'll probably help keep him together for longer.

## Avoid food additives

The next culprit to consider is food additives. You might be able to transform your child's behaviour by cutting various things from his diet.

> *My daughter used to get hyperactive, and would practically bounce off the walls. I read a book which suggested she might be sensitive to additives. Over time we found she can't tolerate the red dye found in cola drinks and hot dogs.*

> *We had five years of hell. My son could turn into a monster in a heartbeat. We went to endless doctors and even a child psychiatrist. The breakthrough came when we cut out processed food from his diet.*

Unfortunately there are hundreds of different colourings, flavourings and additives out there, so how on earth do you narrow them down to find out which one is causing the problem? It sounds extreme, but some parents find the simplest way forward is to try and cut out all the processed food in their child's diet. Otherwise it's a matter of excluding different foods until you find the culprit.

Making these changes and persuading your children to go along with them may sound like a huge pain. But if you are already living with difficult behaviour, your life isn't easy now. If changing your child's diet can solve the problems, it's actually a quick fix because you'll see improvements straight away. Look for foods without artificial colourings, flavourings or preservatives. Even if it turns out that he isn't sensitive to any of these things, you won't have lost anything because your whole family will be eating better food. (See Chapter Five.)

## Look out for food sensitivities and intolerances

Some parents find that hyperactivity and mood swings can be exacerbated by food intolerances. Many children with ADHD are said to improve on the Feingold programme, which removes major food groups like wheat and milk (as well as processed food and salicylates) from their diet. And some dyslexics improve when they cut wheat from their diet. If you suspect that your child might be intolerant to a food group, you might try eliminating it from his diet for a few weeks and see what happens. While the symptoms of food allergies are usually quite easy to spot, those of food intolerances are more subtle and can vary. Talk to your doctor or check out the internet and books on the subject for more advice.

## Look out for dehydration and poor nutrition

Sometimes you might need to add things to your child's diet rather than take them away. The very first thing to check is that he is getting enough plain old water. If he tends to be grumpy or lethargic, he might be slightly dehydrated.

Try to make sure he's getting enough vitamins and minerals by improving what he's eating or your doctor might recommend a supplement. Research also shows that some children with learning and behavioural difficulties can improve with the right balance of Omega fatty acids in their diet.

**Get them moving** When your child is being a complete pain, sometimes the best answer is to get him outside into the fresh air. Even if he complains bitterly and drags his heels, the battle will be worth it. You'll feel better without all the noise and aggravation bouncing off the walls. He'll feel better too, especially if he can move around and get his endorphins going.

Don't wait until you can't take any more and it's a matter of either getting him out of the house or strangling him. All children (and all adults) need to get out and exercise. The increase in feelings of happiness and well-being are well documented.

Most children make trouble if they sit around with nothing to do.

*I like letting my children relax and chill out over the school holidays, but they get bored and argumentative. After the Christmas break, with everyone fighting endlessly and pulling each other's hair out, I knew I couldn't go through it again. So in the Easter holidays I booked them swimming and rock-climbing sessions at the local sports centre, and took them to the park. They were a thousand times more pleasant.*

The hardest part is getting sedentary children going. If your children never do anything more strenuous than lift their forks to their mouths, see **Physical Parents**, pp. 43–4 for advice on how to get them moving.

**Get them to bed** Even the most placid children and adults can be positively evil if they haven't had enough sleep.

*Bedtime is such a battle with my daughter that sometimes I let her stay up just to avoid a showdown. But she is so rude and tearful the next day that it's never worth it. The fact is, she needs her sleep and I've got to get her to bed earlier or it isn't fair on either of us.*

Changing the sleeping habits of any child can be tough (see Chapter Seven for more help and advice).

***Just be there*** Sometimes children act up because they want more of your time and attention. They need you to be around more, to be nearby. This may be hard to believe if your child says he hates you and acts up every time you walk through the door. But he might be trying to tell you in his own peculiar way how much he needs you.

In his book *Raising Boys*, Steve Biddulph writes about a truck driver whose eight-year-old had been diagnosed with ADD (Attention Deficit Disorder):

*Don read the diagnosis and, for want of better information, decided it meant his son Troy wasn't getting enough attention. Don set himself the goal of getting more involved with Troy. He had always taken the view that raising children was best left to the 'missus' while he worked to pay the bills. Now all of that changed. In the holidays, and after school when possible, Troy rode in the truck with his dad. On weekends, whereas Don had often spent the time away with mates who collected and rode classic motorcycles, Troy now came along too . . .*

*The good news: Troy calmed down so much in a couple of months that he came off his Ritalin medication – he wasn't 'ADD' any longer. But father and son continued to hang out together because they enjoy it.*

Steve Biddulph concludes:

*We are not saying that all instances of Attention Deficit Disorder are really dad-deficit disorder – but quite a lot are.*

Sometimes it can be mum-deficit disorder too. One mother, a full-time barrister, told us:

*I was working very long hours on a complicated case. When I did manage to get home my children raised hell as soon as I walked in. They were so belligerent and uncooperative I wished I'd stayed at my chambers.*

*Our nanny kept saying, 'I can't think what the matter is. They've been so good all day with me.' This really upset me and made me feel it was my fault. But when the court case finished I took a month off and my children calmed down completely. I think their bad behaviour must have been their way of letting me know they missed me and wanted me around more.* ❜

She told us that even though she cannot take off as much time as she would like, she now makes much more of an effort to spend time with her children when she comes home.

❛ *Even if I have to stay up until one in the morning to get through my papers, I set aside an hour to get them ready for bed, spend a little time with them, and kiss and hug them goodnight. If I am really tired, we just sit together on the sofa. Now if they are demanding, I take it as a compliment. It's their way of letting me know they need me.* ❜

***Be affectionate*** If your child is upset or angry, he may desperately need affection. A hug can comfort him more effectively than words and show him that you love him, difficult behaviour or not. But this is often the time when he is most likely to push you away.

It is very bleak when your child won't let you get close to him, and though he might pretend otherwise, he probably feels it worse than you do. You might desperately want to turn back the clock so you can hold him in your arms and cuddle him again. Even if he won't admit it, deep down, he probably longs for that connection too.

If you want to get closer to him, start by just hanging out with him in the same room. If he tells you to bog off, don't take it personally. Put it down to the weather and try another time.

You could try making a nice comment or getting involved in what he is doing. To get through to an autistic child who rocks all the time, a therapist may spend the first twenty minutes rocking in time with him. The idea is to build a bridge into his world before expecting him to cross over into yours. With some children it is hard to build that bridge, but it's worth trying.

Even if you think you have nothing in common any more, make

the first move. Listen to your child's favourite music with him; walk down to his favourite shop and discover why he likes it; watch *Match of the Day* highlights on television with him, even if football bores you rigid; sit for two hours on the touchline watching him play rugby and be prepared to discuss the game on the way home. You might even have to get interested in computer games.

*My son decided he was too old for bedtime stories. So reading to him at night was out. At mealtimes he wouldn't sit next to me. He only seemed to be interested in computer games. Horrible things. I thought they were violent and pointless, but I was desperate to do something with him, so reluctantly I sat and watched him.*

*I could see he was very fast and skilful, and I told him so. It was the first nice thing I said to him that seemed to get through. It opened the door a chink. He actually let me kiss him goodnight.*

Another parent said her child wouldn't do any of the 'soppy stuff' like hugs and kisses, but she kept the contact going by sitting next to him on the sofa watching television, and giving him the occasional back rub or foot or head massage. Now, two years down the line, he will hug her again.

If you can make the breakthrough, affection can help a lot if your child isn't good at expressing his feelings. If you try and discuss his bad behaviour with him, he may not want to talk. He may even be as baffled as you are about what has gone wrong. So instead of dredging through what happened, try sitting next to him and comforting him without saying anything at all.

If your child starts to feel more connected to you, his behaviour should improve a notch. This will be a big help, because the next step is to tackle his difficult feelings more directly.

## Listen to Feelings

How your child behaves is directly linked to how he feels, so if he is behaving rudely, there is probably something going on under the surface that he isn't expressing in an appropriate way. Try tuning in to his feelings. Listen with your full attention and accept whatever he has to say.

## *Try being a TUNED-IN PARENT* 

When your child isn't being difficult, you might already be tuning in to his feelings at the first sign of bad behaviour; it's a very good way to head off trouble and stop it escalating.

But if he's being very difficult, you may not want to. Huge outbursts of emotion can be overwhelming, and make lots of parents feel uncomfortable. If he's shouting or whinging, you probably want to make him stop as quickly as possible, any way you can. These are the kind of things you might already say:

- *'Please don't do this, darling.'*
- *'Oh no, don't start up again. I can't bear it.'*
- *'Stop fussing. You are making a big deal out of nothing.'*
- *'See. It's not so bad.'*
- *'OK sweetheart. You can have another chocolate biscuit.'*
- *'Oh, look at that cute little bird outside the window.'*

Does any of this work? Usually not. If your child feels strongly about something, you can't fob him off by pleading, shushing, trying to cheer him up or distracting him. It's more likely that he'll complain harder or shout louder to get his point across.

It's actually far more effective to allow his feelings to bubble up, listen to them and accept them. Some children are like volcanoes; when they blow they lose it entirely and explode all over the place. What they need is a constant outlet for all the emotions that build up inside them.

So instead of telling him off for being obnoxious, try tuning in instead. It's a brilliant way to cool down difficult situations and help unhappy, angry children to move on. When he feels understood he will calm down. You might calm down too, because you'll see the situation from his point of view.

*We were organizing my daughter's birthday party. Suddenly, with no warning, she demanded to open her presents early. What? Within seconds we had got into such a blazing row that she was screaming at the top of her voice that she hated me.*

*I felt like telling her she was a spoilt brat, but with great difficulty I managed to say, 'You sound very upset. You are desperate to open your presents.'*

*Then it all poured out. She knew I'd got her some compilation CDs, and she wanted to check them out long before her friends arrived, so she could play songs at the party. She had this whole hidden layer of expectations that I simply didn't know about. What seemed spoilt and bratty before, suddenly made sense. I got an apology and she got to open the CDs early.*

### 'OK. I'm willing to have a go. So what do I actually do when he's making a scene?'

**Listen to their feelings** The easiest way to begin is to listen to whatever your child is shouting, crying or complaining about, and repeat back what you hear. This feels very strange at first. Most parents' first impulse is to contradict their child or try to cheer him up:

- *'I hate Theo.'*
  *'No you don't. He's your best friend.'*
  *'I said I HATE him. He's a stinky butt-head.'*
  *'Of course he isn't. Don't be silly. He came to your birthday party.'*
  *'I HATED that party and I HATE HIM!'*

This kind of argument can go on for ages as your child becomes more and more determined to prove he's right. But if you tune in, he is more likely to let go of his feelings and move on:

- *'I hate Theo.'*
  *'You must be* really *angry with him. What happened?'*
  *'I want to smash his face in. He knocked my elbow in art, I got in trouble for spilling the water, and it ruined my picture.'*

*'How annoying.'*
*'And when I looked at him he was smiling, and it wasn't funny. He didn't even say he was sorry.'*
*'No wonder you're furious with him.'*

With an angry child on your hands, agreeing that he really is angry seems risky. With some children it can seem positively suicidal. Won't he just get worse? What if he starts hitting people or smashing things up? Many parents are afraid that if they allow their child to express his unpleasant feelings, it will be like pouring petrol on a bonfire.

The bizarre thing is that this works the other way round. When your child is angry, his brain has no room for rational thought. Trying to argue the feeling away doesn't work. In fact it will probably make him feel even angrier.

Acknowledging his anger has the opposite effect. After venting his feelings, all that rage will die down and he will finally have enough space in his head to listen to you properly. Better still, he may even have enough room to work out the answer to his problem on his own.

- *'No wonder you are furious with him.'*
  *'I am. But it doesn't matter. I'll do another picture tomorrow.'*

It is more than likely that if you'd suggested that in the first place he would have thrown it back in your face. But it's a different story if he reaches that conclusion himself.

With older children you may have to be more subtle. They can find it irritating or patronizing when you repeat back how they feel. Instead, quietly acknowledge you understand what they're saying. Listening and nodding might be all you need to do.

### *'I'm trying so hard to listen, but I still can't get him to open up. What do I do now?'*

Lots of children have a hard time expressing themselves with words. So how on earth are you supposed to find out how they are feeling?

*My children are so different. My daughter will sit on my knee, pour out her problems and listen to my advice. But my son just sits there simmering. If you ask him what the matter is he'll yell, 'Go away. Stop bugging me. Just shut up.' If I try to hug him he shrugs me off. If I give him advice he blocks his ears and walks away. I try to be sympathetic, but I usually end up shouting at him and sending him to his room.*

Often children don't know exactly how they feel, apart from fed up with the world in general and with you in particular. Some children don't talk about their feelings at all. They just lurk around the house in a bad mood.

It can be infuriating if you've made the conscious decision to listen to your child, but you can't get a word out of him. He senses you are up to something, so he clams up. Or perhaps he wants to communicate with you as well, but he doesn't know how to go about it. Don't give up on him. Instead make a guess about how he might be feeling:

- *'You're upset.'*
- *'Looks like you've had a bad day.'*
- *'Something happened today at school.'*
- *'You seem pretty annoyed about something.'*

The trick is to make a non-threatening, unemotional statement rather than ask directly what's wrong. A statement can seem less intrusive than a question and can encourage a non-communicative child to tell you more. Don't worry if you guess wrong; he will correct you, so you'll still end up with the answer you were looking for.

- *'No, it wasn't school. Jerry was picking on me on the bus home.'*

If he can't, or won't, elaborate further or even respond to you, don't feel rejected. It is incredibly common for children to need time on their own to calm down and process their feelings before they can discuss them. If he isn't ready to talk, he may snarl at you rudely. Again, don't feel rejected.

- *'Looks like you are upset.'*
  *'Well what do you think, stupid?'*

When your child is this rude, it's like a smack in the face. If you know you are about to lose your temper, take a deep breath and walk away. But if you are feeling particularly relaxed and on top of things, you can try some more tuning in. Sometimes it works, sometimes it doesn't.

- *'Looks like you are feeling upset.'*
  *'Well what do you think, stupid?'*
  *'That bad, huh? Maybe you'd be happier to be left alone.'*
  *'Stop using that stupid voice, Mum.'*
  *'I'll be next door if you need me.'*
  *'Blah, blah, blah. Stupid woman.'*

This may be more than you can stand, but don't get hooked into an argument. You might be desperate to have the last word, but you won't get it if he is in this kind of mood. If your child can't or won't communicate, pause to give him some space and time. It'll be easier to talk about his feelings after he has calmed down.

### *'What do I do when he says he hates everything?'*

If you keep tuning in, you can help your child to understand exactly what's bothering him and to become more emotionally literate. It won't happen overnight. He may say he hates you and hates the world, but if you start helping him untangle exactly what he means, he will be better equipped in the future to start decoding his feelings for himself. A good way to do this is to start giving him names to describe his intense feelings:

- *'It must have been devastating when that happened.'*
- *'It's so frustrating that last piece won't fit.'*
- *'No wonder you felt defensive when he yelled at you like that.'*

It doesn't matter if you use long words. He will understand what you mean. You'll know it's working when you hear him use them in another situation.

*My son has a very short fuse when he can't do something or things don't go his way. I finally felt we were getting somewhere when I heard him tell the baby, 'It's so frustrating when you can't reach your toy. I'll get it for you.*

If he isn't very verbal, keep encouraging him to name his feelings, and try to come up with other ways for him to express himself. Take a tip from **Physical Parents** and get him to punch a pillow, or run up and down the stairs or round the park. For a younger child, you could ask him to draw how he feels.

### *'It's not that my son won't talk, he talks too much. When he wants something, he simply won't take no for an answer.'*

***Imagine it could happen*** When your child is being demanding, it's hard not to get drawn into an argument. Instead, try acknowledging his feelings by imagining what it would be like if his wishes were fulfilled. He won't end up getting what he wants, but if he feels understood he may stop being so unreasonable.

*We went to Toys R Us to buy my nephew's birthday present. My son started whinging, 'I want this, I want that.' At one point he was lying on the floor in the aisle refusing to move unless I bought him a seventy-pound remote-control car.*

*Then I had a stroke of genius. I said, 'Wouldn't it be amazing if this car only cost ten pence? Then you could buy one every single weekend with your pocket money. You could have twenty in your bedroom and we could get the whole class round for a big race. If you got another hundred cars for your birthday we could invite the whole school.'*

*He was so taken with this idea he actually put the car down and we carried happily on round the store.*

Don't worry. He knows he isn't going to get a hundred cars, or even one. But instead of saying 'no', you are acknowledging how much he wants a car, and this may be enough to satisfy him. It sounds unlikely but it works, particularly with young children.

*Accept difficult feelings* If your child is worked up, some of his feelings might be overwhelming to hear and hard to stomach. But your aim is to help him express himself with words, rather than by behaving badly. So if you do get a volcano erupting, be grateful, even if what comes out seems shocking.

One mother brought this problem to her parenting class:

*'Last week was horrific. My daughter has been pinching the baby and being awful to him. I started out trying to be kind and listening to her feelings. But almost immediately she burst out with, 'I hate the baby. I hate him.'*

*I couldn't bear it and I panicked. Suppose she hurt him? I said, 'That's a horrible thing to say. Stop being so nasty to him. He is just a little baby.' She had a complete tantrum, and started screaming that I love him more than I love her. I yelled at her and then I cried my eyes out.'*

She asked the other parents in the group what else she might have done.

*'One mother said, 'I think she sounds perfectly normal. I hated my little brother too. He used to knock over my games, and my mother always took his side. Why don't you admit she has a point? Maybe you could say something like, "Yes, baby brothers can be annoying."'*

*When I went home I tried to show Ellie that I understood how she felt. I said, 'Sometimes you wish he hadn't been born. You wish it was still just you and me.' I told her that feeling angry was OK, that she could come and talk to me about it and I would listen. Or she could ask me any time for a cuddle or a story.*

*It felt very odd to talk like that, but it helped a lot. She's been much nicer to the baby and thank heavens, she has stopped pinching him.'*

It can be especially hard to accept your child's feelings when he turns against you and hurts yours.

*'When I have an argument with my daughter she sits on the stairs and chants, 'I hate you. You're a fa-a-t p-i-i-g.' Wherever I go in the house I can hear her, and it gets me every time.'*

Sometimes the hardest feelings to accept aren't the angry ones, but the sad ones. We want our children to be happy and when they aren't we can't bear it. Lots of perfectly wonderful parents blow it here. They can't stand hearing their child's troubles, so they feel compelled to bandage everything up or argue the feelings away in a desperate attempt to make him feel better.

- *'No one likes me.'*
  *'You've got plenty of friends. Ed came round to play only last week.'*

- *'I'm stupid.'*
  *'No you aren't. Don't say that.'*

- *'I'm rubbish at sport.'*
  *'Not to me. You're my little Superman.'*

Saying these kind things might help, but your child may not be able to take them in until he feels you understand him. So first, tackle the sad feeling directly.

- *'No one likes me.'*
  *'You feel like you don't have any friends.'*
  *'Not one single person likes me.'*
  *'What happened?'*
  *'Ed's supposed to be my partner this week, but he wouldn't sit next to me in science and ran away from me during break.'*
  *'I bet that wasn't much fun.'*
  *'If he does it again I'm going to ask my teacher for a new partner.'*

Your child may or may not have friends, be coping at school, or be good at sport. But he will deal with his problems better if he feels understood.

The more tender-hearted you are as a parent, the harder it can be to accept your child's feelings without getting worked up about them or inadvertently making him feel worse. You may not even realize you're doing it. Here is one mother's incredible story:

*For three years my son was so angry and unhappy that I worried about him all the time. The breakthrough came when we took him to an educational psychologist. She set up a family of five cardboard boxes, like post boxes. Each one had a name – mum, dad, brother, sister and baby. She gave him an envelope and said it was a sad letter, and asked him to post it in one of the boxes. Then she gave him an angry letter, and so on through a whole range of feelings.*

*The bizarre thing was that no one got any letters except the baby. When asked why, he said he whispered all his secrets to the baby (aged three months) because she was the only one who would listen to him.*

*He especially didn't want to tell me anything, because he hated it when I got sad or made a fuss. He couldn't handle my distress as well as his own. It was tragic. I always thought of myself as kind and sympathetic. But it was true. It would really upset me if he was unhappy.*

*It was hard, but I had to learn to say 'You sound upset,' or 'No wonder you're angry.' As soon as I stopped trying to rescue him and let him be unhappy, he started being able to sort himself out.*

It can be so difficult to stay calm when our children are upset or rude. But they need to know we won't be knocked off balance by their feelings. They will only come to us when they have problems if they feel we can cope with them.

*When I came home from work, my daughter used to be so unpleasant that sometimes I'd have to send her to her room.*

*After a while, one of our neighbours asked if I knew what our childminder was up to. She'd seen her in the garden pulling my daughter by the hair and twisting her arm. I was beside myself.*

*When I talked to my daughter about it, she said she hadn't told me because she thought I would be too worried about her, or I might get angry with her for being naughty. How awful – she felt she couldn't cope with my reaction on top of everything else.*

It's not easy to discuss painful feelings without getting emotional. But if you simply acknowledge them, your child will feel a lot better. It will give him a deep sense of security to know that whatever happens and whatever he does, you will listen.

***'My son overheard me complaining about him to a friend. Although he claims he doesn't care, he says he's never going to speak to me again.'***

*Respect their feelings* Your child might swagger around pretending he doesn't care what you say, but underneath he definitely does. Though he may seem like your tormentor or nemesis, he is just a child who doesn't yet know how to express himself in a civilized way. So no matter how badly he behaves, try your hardest not to hurt his feelings or complain about him in front of other people.

When you are at your wits' end, you may be tempted to say all sorts of things, just to relieve your own feelings:

> *That one is my nightmare. He is always so badly behaved. I'm sick to death of him. He never listens to a word I say. Do you know what he did today? . . .*

Even if you are desperately worried about him and want advice, keep your thoughts to yourself until he is out of the room, asleep or, best of all, out of the house altogether.

*Reconnecting* However hard you try, there are going to be times when your child's behaviour gets under your skin, you say and do things you regret, and you end up feeling dreadful. When it happens it's definitely best to go back and put things right so neither of you has to suffer.

> *Every time my daughter behaves badly, I lose my temper and start shouting at her. Then I feel a complete failure and guilty. Even when she's calmed down and playing quite happily, I still feel terrible.*

A friend told us how upset she was feeling two hours after her children had gone off to school.

> *My children were fighting this morning, and I made everything worse. My daughter stomped off to school and wouldn't even say goodbye to me, and when I dropped my son off, he was still close to tears.*

*I can't help re-running the situation over and over in my mind. What should I have said? What could I have done differently? I feel awful about it. I'd like to rewind the tape and start all over again.* ❞

So what can you do? If you lost your temper and yelled at your child, go back after you've calmed down and tell him you're sorry.

As well as soothing your guilt, this is a chance to show him how to deal with uncomfortable feelings. If you can be big enough to apologize, you are also teaching him what to do when he makes mistakes. Arguments happen, but they don't have to be a disaster because you can always start again.

Some parents feel they'll lose authority by apologizing. But this is about reconnecting, not grovelling to your child. By owning up to your part in it, you are giving him the opportunity to say sorry to you in return.

## Sort Out Problems Before They Arise

Once you've identified your child's problem areas you can start to work out what to do about them. Don't wait until he is being difficult. Your goal is to try to change his behaviour and deal with trouble spots long before they come up again.

### *Try being a SORTED PARENT*

*Give advance warning and set up rules* **Sorted Parents** tell their children in advance that things are going to change. It's the best way to make rules, because it gives children time to get used to them.

Sorting things out beforehand isn't just for your benefit; many children act up because they don't have the emotional maturity to cope with surprises. They hate being rushed, they hate being unprepared, and they hate plans going wrong at the last minute. We aren't saying you have to anticipate everything, but taking time to chat through plans with your child can ease a lot of stress.

*My in-laws are so organized. When we stay with them for Christmas, they tell us the night before what time we have to be up and ready for church. They tell us what time we're going to eat and how they expect us to dress. It sounds stressful, but actually it's great. We all know what we are doing – very different from our house.*

Some children feel much happier and in control when they are given a simple set of rules so they know what's going to happen and how you expect them to behave. If they have to judge things for themselves, they can keep getting things wrong.

*My son and his best friend at school kept wrestling and calling each other names, and every day one or the other ended up in tears.*

*I'd say, 'Please remember you can wrestle – but not too hard,' or 'You can call each other funny names – but not hurt feelings.' But they kept upsetting each other.*

*The teacher said they needed a firm set of rules because they couldn't judge where playing crossed over into fighting, and she was very direct with them about what was acceptable.*

*I always thought it was natural for little boys to scuffle. But they are both happier now they don't have to figure out the limits.*

***Train them up*** Some children are a pain because getting organized doesn't come easily to them. They simply need more help.

*My daughter always puts away her school stuff. It's automatic. I don't even need to remind her. But my son doesn't get it. We're often late for school because he can't find some vital part of his homework or sports kit.*

Giving children like this a clear path can be much less stressful for them than leaving things to chance. Take time to explain and show your child, in detail, what you expect of him.

- *'The only way to keep track of your homework diary is to keep it in your back pack at all times. After you use it, put it back. Otherwise it will get lost.'*

Remind him what he needs to do, and then when he does it right, tell him how pleased you are.

You may not feel you can spare the time to talk him through the routine and train him up. But you'll be saving time in the long run and, more importantly, you are changing the atmosphere in the house. With luck, he will cooperate and welcome the fact that he is no longer being nagged or yelled at for leaving his stuff lying around.

## How to Make Changes

- ***Give him advance warning*** of what is going to happen and when. Use as neutral a voice as you can manage. Then remind him a couple of times over the next few evenings what you said.
- ***Let him moan*** In fact, expect it. Tune in to his feelings, but don't change your mind unless there is a very good reason.
- ***Enforce the plan*** This part shouldn't be as hard as you might think. By the time the rule starts, it should be a done deal.

If it helps, pin the new rules up, Supernanny-style, on the kitchen wall where your child can see them. If he has enough time to get the complaining out of his system beforehand, he may be surprisingly compliant when the moment comes and do what you say.

*Bite the bullet* We know that having this kind of conversation is much easier said than done, and many parents would rather not go there. Even if you start off being friendly, if your child is feeling prickly and defensive, he will do everything he can not to listen to you.

He may twist and turn, refusing to talk to you or to look you in the eye. He might try to provoke you by coming up with silly comments. He might stick his fingers in his ears and hum. He might even walk off in the middle of the conversation. It can be hard to hold on to your courage or your temper.

Many parents back down just to keep communication going – any communication. They keep trying to be nice and hope their child will finally get the message. Other parents simply don't know what to do or say. But it is possible to stand your ground and have a productive conversation, and we'll give you lots of good advice on how to make it happen.

The thought of tackling your child's deep-rooted habits may seem daunting, but if you want him to change, you are going to have to talk to him about it. If your relationship is complicated, you might be putting this off.

> *Things have been so bad at home. The times when we get on are so precious to me that I don't want to spoil them by rehashing old arguments. You must be joking!*

Why ruin a nice moment by bringing up a sore topic? Because if you ignore it, it won't go away. It will still be there, waiting to jump out at you like the bogeyman in the cupboard. Suddenly, out of the blue, you're facing the same argument, the same histrionics, all over again.

You will save yourself a lot of time and trouble in the long run if you gather up your courage and deal with the problem head on. Even if you have to give up some precious quiet time with your child, think of it as an investment. You are making the sacrifice to get a system in place; a system that will lead to happier times in the future.

## How to Have a Difficult Conversation With Your Child

### Choose a time when you are both calm and not distracted

Don't talk if you are racing against the clock to get Sunday lunch on the table, manoeuvring your way through traffic or in any other situation that makes you tense. It may seem as if there is no opportunity, except when he is glued to the television or the

PlayStation. But don't bring the subject up then either; you will be competing with the box, and it will win. Instead:

- *Try at bedtime.*

He is likely to be far more receptive when he is tucked up under the duvet. But if the problem has been a huge issue that very day, you may want to wait another twenty-four hours before tackling it.

- *Try taking him to a café.*

He might like to be taken out on his own, and he'll probably behave well on neutral ground in a public place. You could also try sharing a picnic on a park bench.

- *If he is old enough, try starting the conversation via text or email.*

> *'Hi, we both went over the top this morning. Let's go to the café after school and sort things out for next time. Love Mum.'*

- *If you can't wait until bedtime or manage a trip to the café, try to pick a time when the house is as quiet as it's going to get, when you won't be disrupted by siblings or the telephone.*

## Approach the conversation with a friendly attitude

This is not the time to tell him off or punish him. It's a chance to look at a trouble spot and say:

- *'This isn't working very well for you and it isn't working very well for me. What can we do about it?'*

Show your friendly intent by telling him something you genuinely appreciate about him. As you might remember from the Cheerleader section, it helps to be sincere and specific. If you gush he'll be embarrassed or think you are trying to manipulate him.

- *'I noticed you held your sister's hand crossing the road this morning. Thank you for that.'*

Extra bonus points for you if the compliment can be relevant to what you want to talk about.

- *'I really like it when you two are getting on. How can we make it happen more often?'*

If you can't make it relevant, just move on to whatever you need to say.

- *'I want to find a way to get everyone to bed without a fight. Let's work out a plan.'*

## Express your feelings

If you start off on the attack:

- *'What the hell are you doing, disturbing the whole house every day? Turn it down or I'll have to confiscate your speakers'*

it might work and he might cooperate. But if he feels resentful and refuses, you'll have a fight on your hands.

It's less risky to express how you feel:

- *'I'm getting a headache from your constant music. Could you please turn it down?'*

## Don't rise to the bait

Even if you pick a calm time, start with a friendly attitude and express your feelings, you may still have problems. Your hope is that laying this groundwork will help you to get through to him. But if he goes into the sarky-comments-and-fingers-in-the-ears routine, this is the time to grit your teeth and pause, however intimidated or angry you feel.

You could try going back to tuning in:

- *'It looks like you don't want to talk about this right now.'*

This might be enough to get the conversation back on track.

If not, add some praise.

- *'I can see you don't want to listen to me, but thank you for staying in the room and not shouting.'*

If you are still getting nowhere, let it go and postpone the discussion. Don't panic, there will be another opportunity. He can't play a power game if you aren't getting annoyed. So pause, tell him you will discuss it another time, and if necessary walk away.

### *'But what do I do if he walks off in the middle of our conversation?'*

Don't follow him, however angry you feel. It's a tremendous temptation to run after him shouting:

- *'Now you come back here right now and listen to me, young man! You will* not *walk off when I'm talking to you.'*

But if he is being very difficult, there is no point. If you shout you might temporarily relieve your feelings, but you can't force him to be receptive, and if you try he'll probably hate you more.

Luckily our children usually need things from us more often than we need things from them. If you don't chase him, he will come back to you. There is always going to be something he needs, whether it's a snack, clean socks, a cuddle, some money, a ride somewhere or help with homework. The time to carry on the conversation is when he comes back to you.

- *'Oh yes, what were we talking about? Loud music. Now what do you reckon we can do about it?'*

You may not believe this will ever work, but at some point everything will click into place and he'll listen to you. When he does, you won't believe how easy the conversation can be.

It may all seem like a lot to remember, but you won't have to tiptoe around like this for ever. You are changing habits that have built up over years, and the first conversations are often the hardest. Once he is used to discussing things in a non-confrontational, matter-of-fact way with you, you can shorten the whole process. You will be more confident that you are getting through to him, and you'll find you won't have to wait until the conditions are perfect to bring up tricky subjects.

## Preparing Your Child in Advance for Difficult Situations

You can't anticipate all the things that are going to throw your child into a frenzy, but you can help him prepare specifically for some of them. If he tends to overreact playing board games, for example, you can sit down at a quiet time long before the next game comes out, and talk it through. First he needs to understand what bothers him. Then you can help him work out what he should say when he starts getting irritated.

- *'It really annoys me when people keep rolling the dice and it isn't their turn. Could you please stop?'*
- *'I don't like it when you shout. It hurts my ears.'*
- *'I hate it when people are winning and they gloat about it. Please don't.'*

To help him remember what to say, give him the list to keep in his pocket or pin it up on the wall. Then help him to explain his feelings to the rest of the family:

- *'Before we start, let's make a deal not to cheat, and not to move other people's counters along.'*

### Teach him how to calm down before he tips over the edge

Explain to him that getting angry is usually a gradual process. One tiny thing can make you lose your temper if you are already feeling on edge about something else. Long before he reaches the tipping point, he can start to notice how he feels. Talk to him about pausing before he explodes; for example, taking three deep breaths, getting a glass of water, or walking away to calm down.

One mother taught her son how to work off his anger physically:

*I told him he could go to a room and beat up a pillow if he was angry. He thought that was stupid, but said he would like a punch bag. So we hung one in the corner of his room. It's better than thumping his sister.*

## Tell him what to say so he doesn't irritate people

If he feels strongly about something, he has to find acceptable ways of expressing himself. You can show him how to get the result he wants next time without annoying everyone else.

- *'No one wants to listen when you shout. Even though you might have a good point, it hurts our ears. Next time, come and tell me or Dad what you want.'*

### *'All this forward-planning seems unnatural to me.'*

If you want to make serious changes to your child's behaviour, we can't over-emphasize how useful and effective the sorted tools are. In fact, we think you can't do without them. We've heard stories time and again from parents who have tried wonderful methods of child control from books or parenting courses, and failed. Not because there was anything wrong with the advice, but because these parents tried to implement them out of the blue, without warning, right in the middle of a flare-up.

*My parenting book suggested putting my child in a quiet corner of the room, to stand and think until he was ready to calm down. I tried it with my son, who was messing around at Sunday lunch.*

*'If you don't stay sitting on your chair,' I said, 'you will have to stand in the corner until you calm down.'*

*'I won't,' he said and jumped off his chair.*

*'OK, into the corner,' I said firmly, 'until you are ready to sit nicely.'*

*'No,' he said more defiantly, 'I won't.'*

*I marched him to the corner. He escaped and ran around the table, laughing.*

*'OK,' I said. 'You can go to your room.' My husband and I carried him, kicking and wriggling, upstairs. I held his door shut from the outside.*

*'MU-U-UM, I need to go to the loo.' I opened the door. He ran out shouting, 'Ha, ha. Tricked you.'*

*We caught him with some difficulty and put him back in his room. I told the others they could have their ice-cream. A little voice called out, 'I don't care. I don't want ice-cream anyway.'*

*After ten minutes he said he'd be good, but when I opened the door, he burst out and then ran laughing round and round the kitchen, the centre of attention again. He didn't get his ice-cream, but the whole meal was a complete failure.*

*Later that evening I sat him on my lap and explained why I wanted him to behave. As Sunday was the only day when we could all eat together, I wanted a good atmosphere at lunch so we could talk to each other.*

*'Oh,' he said. 'Why didn't you tell me that before?'* ❜

She said the next Sunday lunch worked a thousand times better. Her son even asked her to remind him what to do, in case he forgot.

## Teach Your Child to Take Responsibility

### *Try being a LAID-BACK PARENT*

Encouraging your child to take responsibility for his behaviour is a fundamental step in turning it around. **Laid-Back Parents** are extremely good at making this happen.

***Ask for solutions*** You can start simply by asking him:

- *'What do you think you should do?'*

As well as working in practical terms, encouraging responsibility can help your child feel better about himself. Instead of seeing

## Taking Emotional Responsibility

The television programme *Brat Camp* focused on a group of troubled teenagers. Drinking, drug-taking, stealing – you name it, these children did it. In desperation, their parents send them off to a ranch in Utah to turn their lives around. Watching the programme it's noticeable that the unhappiest children are those who keep blaming their circumstances, their parents and everyone around them for their problems. The teenagers only graduate from camp and go home when they take responsibility and start to think their way out of them.

himself as the rebel who always messes up, he will begin to see that he's the kind of person who has good ideas, makes good decisions and can be trusted to carry things through.

One mother discovered how useful this can be:

*My son kept tramping mud into the house. I nagged him a million times to take off his trainers, but most days he'd forget or get stroppy with me about it.*

*One evening I said to him, 'I don't know what to do any more about those shoes. You're going to have to come up with something – because I can't.'*

*It was a cry of despair, really. I was giving up.*

*I couldn't have been more surprised when he came down the next morning with a sign he'd made.*

*It said 'SHOES OFF', and he pinned it up with Blu Tack by the front door. The problem stopped that day.*

If your child isn't the type to come up with good ideas spontaneously, you can help him to problem-solve. This can be as easy as sitting down for a chat with him, one-to-one. But if you are still having difficulties communicating, here are some tips to help the conversation go smoothly. The process is very like getting sorted, so set it up the same way.

- *Pick a time when you aren't distracted.*
- *Approach the conversation with a friendly attitude.*
- *Express the problem, along with your own feelings.*
- *Then tune in to what he has to say.*

It is helpful to have a large piece of paper and a pencil with you to write down his ideas, then agree to try the ones you both like. If you've done your groundwork, this should be quite simple. But what do you do if he is still resistant?

## What to Do When Problem-Solving Isn't Working

**If he starts moaning or refuses to come up with any ideas:**

- *'This is stupid. Why do we have to do this? What's the point?'*

**Try something like:**

- *'Go on. There's no right answer. Think up any old thing. I'd like to hear what you have to say.'*

**If he throws out stupid ideas to annoy you:**

Even if he starts spouting gibberish, just write it down. You are brainstorming together and all sorts of good ideas might come out of the silly stuff – eventually. Stay friendly, even if some of his ideas are horrible,

- *'Cut off the baby's head if he annoys me.'*

He knows you aren't going to take this one seriously, so don't overreact.

**If he still won't cooperate:**

Explain exactly what you are doing and why:

- *'I would like to hear what you think. You don't like it when I tell you what to do. This is your chance to give me your ideas. Then we can decide what to do together.'*

Once he realizes you are genuinely interested, he might be more forthcoming.

**If he doesn't agree with the solution you want:**
You may have to be open-minded here. By inviting him to brainstorm with you, you can't trick him by pretending his ideas are important, and then impose your own. If you come to an impasse, try tuning in to his feelings:

- *'So you don't like this idea, because . . .'*

or expressing your own:

- *'I'm not so sure about that one because . . .'*

**If he won't agree to try out the plan:**
Suggest you try it out for a day or a week. He may agree if he knows that he isn't promising to do it for ever.

*Ask the family for ideas* If your child is behaving badly it can affect the whole family, either because he's driving everyone else mad, or because they're driving him crazy. In most families it's a combination of the two. So you may want to encourage everyone to help solve the problem.

You can either formally call a family meeting, or just have a chat around the kitchen table. Tell everyone the rules – no interrupting, no ganging up and no squashing down other people's ideas – then ask them for suggestions so they all feel included.

*'We gave our son a drum set for his birthday, but he played it late at night and early in the morning, and it drove his sisters to distraction. After lots of discussion he eventually agreed to stick to more reasonable hours.'*

# Take Charge!

Some children behave badly because they hate being nagged and bossed about. You might remember how resentful you felt as a child. But families don't work when children are in charge. So how do you get the balance right? How can you be authoritative without getting your child's back up?

Parenting experts say over and over again that we need to set boundaries, discipline our children, be firm, be consistent. None of this is a problem when your child is behaving. When you say, 'Please do this' or 'No, you can't,' he'll say, 'OK,' and mightn't even moan about it. Even if you have a difference of opinion, you can generally talk it through quite amicably.

But when he's being a pain, it's a different story. There's no chance you can just assume he's going to do what you say. It's too risky. It's far more likely he'll refuse and see what reaction he gets. Even ordinary daily tasks can become frustrating and exhausting, and take up a huge amount of time.

> *It takes a lot of courage for me to ask my son to do anything. Every time I'm mentally bracing myself because I don't know how he's going to react. He might do what I ask, or I might have an enormous fight on my hands. Sometimes it just isn't worth the effort.*

Many parents find there's nothing left they can threaten or do to get their child to obey them. A despairing father told us:

> *We've had so many clashes, so many stupid pointless arguments, that my son is quite fearless. There is no threat or punishment that will make him back down and do what I say. If I tell him he has to go to his room or I'll cancel his pocket money, he just looks at me like, 'Whatever. Do your worst. I don't care.'*
>
> *I think he really does care, and I know I do. But I don't know how to handle him.*

There is no point backing your child further into a corner or, like a trapped rat, he'll probably bare his teeth and fight harder. But you can't let everything slide. If your child has taken over, you'll both be much happier if you get back in charge. Though at one level he might enjoy the power, he will feel more contained and secure if he knows you are the boss.

> *I couldn't get my two boys to do anything and I was a wreck. I asked my doctor for advice. 'Let me give you a tip,' she said. 'The secret to raising children is boundaries. What you need to do is set up a few more boundaries for your boys.*
>
> *It made me want to scream. Boundaries is such a wind-up word. It's all very well to talk about setting up boundaries, but how do I do it?*

So the sixty-four-million-dollar question is – how do you actually make it happen?

The short answer is right here in this section on how to take charge. But the long answer is that it's a holistic process. This entire chapter – this whole book, in fact – is about changing your relationship so your child no longer sees you as the enemy or a doormat. It is about changing his view of himself so he knows he is someone who can do the right thing. It is also about changing yourself, building yourself up so you have some natural authority without turning into a dictator.

If the two of you have a volatile and hostile relationship, this may still seem a long way off. But if you lay the groundwork, you'll get there. It's no accident that we've taken you through so many other parenting tools in this chapter *before* getting on to discipline. Pausing, praising, tuning in, getting sorted, encouraging responsibility and checking out any possible physical causes for your child's behaviour are the stepping stones. They will help you to create a better atmosphere at home.

When it's time to get tough, add some more **Sorted** strategies to strengthen your authority, then some **Commando** techniques to get back in charge.

## *Try being a SORTED PARENT*

**Set up rules** The best way to boost your authority is by establishing rules in advance. If you bark orders without any preparation, you are setting yourself up for defeat. Your child will probably ignore you or defy you, and make your life such a misery you'll wish you had never raised the subject. Instead, set up rules beforehand to maximize your chances of success. If the word 'rules' puts you or your child off, call them something else: plans, systems, strategies, ideas, policies or whatever.

**Sort your systems** If you give yourself time to think through new rules, you'll have a much better chance of enforcing them. When you look and sound confident, your child is more likely to do what you ask.

However badly behaved he is, if the situation is dangerous and you tell him to *'Get off the road – NOW!'* he'll do what you say. You have no doubts. You know you are right. You automatically have that extra edge, and he can hear it in your voice.

But you don't have that advantage when it comes to everyday requests. If there is any doubt in your mind about following through, children sniff it out and exploit it. Getting your rules sorted in advance is the best way to get that extra oomph into your tone, so you don't have to plead or yell.

**Give advance warning** We can't emphasize this too strongly: if you are serious about turning your child's behaviour around, don't wait until he is driving you mad. It works much better to talk him through the rules beforehand.

Try to sound friendly, but firm. Here is how the conversation might go:

- *'Starting next week, there is going to be no PlayStation after six o'clock, because that's the time for homework. I'm going to give you a ten-minute warning so you can save your game and then I expect it to be off at six – not one second later. If you argue, I will confiscate the PlayStation for the next day and you will miss out on it. If you carry on fussing, Dad and I will take it away for longer if we have to.'*

Sounds impressive, doesn't it? Obviously you can adapt this dialogue for whatever circumstances you are tackling. You should be fine if you stick to the main ingredients:

- *Decide in advance what you are going to say.*
- *State the new rule, the consequences, and the start date.*

If you feel you can set these rules up democratically, by all means ask your child for good ideas, or have a family meeting.

If your child has more problem areas than most, you may need to have more rules than other families. The more ambiguity you can get rid of, the less opportunity there will be for him to argue about the holes in the system. It's a matter of pinpointing the things that don't work and doing something about them.

But it's important to pick your battles. Some family therapists recommend tackling all your child's trouble spots in one go. But as mothers against masochism, we think it's much more realistic to start with either the problems that don't seem too intimidating, or the ones that are driving you insane. Once you've successfully changed a few things, you'll have more confidence to start working on others.

## *Try being a COMMANDO PARENT*

**Give orders that don't sound like orders** Organizing rules in advance can take care of a lot of problems. But what do you do when you need your child to do something right *now*? Try giving orders that don't sound like orders.

Instead of ordering him to do something 'Because I say so,' this is a way to get him to *want* to do the right thing. In simple terms, you do this by presenting him with information so he can come up with the answer himself.

You say matter-of-factly:

- *'The cats are hungry'*

or:

- *'The coat is on the floor.'*

Then, with a bit of luck, he realizes:

- *'Oh yes, it is my job to feed them today'*

or:

- *'Oh yes, I'll stick it on the peg.'*

The beauty is that you aren't ordering him directly, so he's not tensing up to disobey you and there's no power struggle. He thinks of the answer so the impetus comes from him. Here is a quick recap of orders that don't sound like orders. You might find that you've started using some of them already.

## Orders That Don't Sound Like Orders

- ***Give options*** *'Teeth first or pyjamas?'* This lets him keep his dignity by choosing.
- ***Say it in a word*** *'Coat.'* One word can work better than a long, boring explanation.
- ***Describe what you see*** *'The water spilt. We need a cloth.'* Say it in a neutral voice, and let your child figure out the next step.
- ***Ask your child what comes next*** *'I'm opening the door. What's the first thing you need to do?'*
- ***Give a quick reminder*** *'There's something else you need to remember'* is better than *'How many times do I have to remind you to put your plate in the dishwasher?'*
- ***Whisper*** *'Spoon.'*
- ***Give thanks in advance*** *'Thanks for taking your wet towel off the bed.'*
- ***Write a note*** *'Please flush.'* If it is written down, he might take the request seriously.
- ***Refer to the rules*** *'It's six o'clock. What's the rule about the PlayStation?'*

These work best if you've already set up your family rules. But even if you haven't, the chances are your child already knows the score. How many times have you told him over the years to get into his pyjamas and brush his teeth? Even if you try using one of these soft orders and it doesn't work, you haven't lost anything, because you can add another layer on top.

### *Give information*

If you've already said:

- *'The water's spilt. You'll need a cloth'*

and nothing happens, you can always add something like:

- *'The cloth is in the sink'*

or:

- *'If you knocked it over, you are the person who needs to mop it up.'*

The point is that you are stating facts. There is no toxic edge to your voice, which makes your child want to defy you.

## Some Useful Phrases

If your child won't cooperate, give him information and he may stop being defiant.

- *'You're carrying on because you think I'll change my mind. But I mean what I say, and I won't.'*
- *'When you don't help me, it makes me not want to help you.'*
- *'When you annoy the others it annoys me. So now I'm irritated with you.'*
- *'You are going to find that if you talk to me like that, we are going to have a big problem.'*
- *'I'm sure you don't realize how you sound.'*

Be sure to leave it here and let your child think for himself. Don't be tempted to carry on with a lecture.

Whatever you choose to say, stick to statements presented reasonably in a non-threatening, matter-of-fact way. You're giving him information he needs to know.

***Express your feelings*** Blast! You did your best to hold back, but you ended up yelling at your child again. As long as you didn't turn into a totally-lost-it maniac, it's quite all right. In fact, it's often helpful.

If you're angry because you've found yet another apple core buried in the sofa, you have every right to tell your child how you feel. You aren't getting personal and calling him an idiot. You aren't ordering him to pick it up (or not yet, anyway). You are stating a fact. If you aren't happy about something, go right ahead and say so.

- *'I'm furious. I've just found another apple core that should be in the bin.'*

Some people have natural authority and can do this easily. But many parents find it hard to express themselves strongly without feeling guilty, and many more don't know how to hit the firm spot halfway between friendliness and raging fury.

It's much easier for teachers or grandparents to be appropriately tough. They sound firm enough to have authority, but not so strict that the child becomes defiant. It's much harder for parents to be straightforward and assertive because we are so closely connected to our children. When they wind us up, it is hard not to back down or overreact.

According to Steve Biddulph, the parents who end up over-reacting and hitting their children often aren't, surprisingly, the firm, consistent ones. They're the nice, kind, soggy parents who try and try to get through, and then lose it.

- *'Maybe you could quieten down now, please darling?'*

Then:

- *'Be a bit quieter, darling.'*

Then:

- *'Please, darling. A little quieter.'*

Then suddenly they flip out of sheer frustration:

- *'I SAID SHUT UP!'* Thwack.

It's not always easy to express your feelings appropriately, so here are some ideas.

## Some Good Ways to Express Your Feelings

Start by saying what you feel. Instead of 'You always . . .', try:

- *'I don't like it when you use those words. Please use different ones to tell me.'*
- *'I don't like the shouting. You need to find a different tone of voice.'*
- *'It's hard for me to be nice to you right now because you've been yelling at me. You'll have to wait for a few minutes until I calm down.'*
- *'It embarrasses me when you are rude to me in front of others.'*
- *'I expect you to listen to me. Please turn off the television.'*
- *'I mind a lot about rubbish lying around. I want it in the bin.'*

***Stand your ground*** With some children you have to be even more assertive because they only half listen to you. They might be distracted or deliberately defiant, but either way, if your child is ignoring you, you are going to have to make eye contact and stay in his space. For a refresher on how to do it, see p. 60. It takes a bit of time, but it works if you can stay centred and patient.

When you stand your ground you are calling his bluff. You need to show him you are going to stay there, not getting upset, until he gets moving. It takes a bit of nerve.

Sometimes it's your only option when you need to enforce rules. If he won't turn off the Nintendo Wii at bedtime, point out the rule. No luck? Then turn it off yourself and stand there. If necessary, unplug it. Even if he starts shouting and trying to push past you, don't lose your temper. Repeat, firmly, 'You know the rule,' and stay there. Standing your ground is usually the farthest you'll have to go. It's a rare child who will literally wrestle you to the ground to get the screen turned back on.

If your child is used to getting his way because you usually back down, he will struggle and plead his hardest to make you change your mind. Keep reminding yourself you are not being mean by not giving in. He is pushing the boundaries to test whether they are really solid. In the long run he will feel more secure if they are.

Once you've taken the plunge and stood your ground for the first time, you'll find it's much easier to follow through in the future. You'll feel more confident because you know you can do it, and your child will realize you mean what you say. You'll probably be pleasantly surprised when he obeys you, so follow through by telling him how pleased you are that he is cooperating.

If you're still finding it hard to be assertive, or find that your tone keeps slipping into desperate pleading or sounds aggressively toxic, then pause and don't speak until you're more calm. Eventually he will get it that you are in charge and you mean business.

***Give rewards and consequences*** To reinforce what you say, you can also throw in some incentives. You can reward your child when he behaves well and set up a system of consequences for when he doesn't.

## Rewards

Rewards might entice your child to behave, but we aren't talking here about bribing him with sweets and toys. Believe it or not, what he really wants is your recognition and to spend time with you. So reward him by telling him when he's done something you like, and being specific about what it was. You'll find more on how to set up rewards on pp. 61–2.

## Consequences

When you set up new rules, you might want to agree on the consequences of stepping out of line. Lots of parents would prefer not to get to this point. They'd far rather be soft and loving than be law-enforcement officers. Keeping tabs on everything can be a huge pain, and how on earth are you supposed to enforce the consequences in any case?

But you can't ignore all of your child's bad behaviour. Some of it is unacceptable, like hurting other people or smashing things on purpose. There are going to be some things you really mind about. If you don't impose consequences, you risk losing your temper and threatening random punishments you have no intention of carrying out, or punishing your child far more severely than you ever intended.

It's better to come up with logical consequences for bad behaviour in advance so it's a rational rather than an irrational process. You love your child, but you don't like the bad things he does, so you are making it ultra clear to him where those boundaries are.

Consequences even work if you can't pre-legislate against the crime.

- *A **punishment** for breaking a window is being grounded for the afternoon.*
- *A **consequence** is needing to apologize and offering to pay for the new glass.*

Even a difficult child can see there's a sense of fairness, a logical connection between the two.

Your child might push you to see if you really will follow through. But more likely than not he will surprise you and toe the line, and you'll have less trouble than you think.

*When my son was demanding and rude, I tried being kind. I explained that it bothered me, and told him how to ask nicely for things. But it didn't work. His behaviour got worse and worse. He called the babysitter a stinky bum and refused to go to bed. His best friend went home in tears, and his brother and sister were so fed up they wouldn't play with him. I decided I had to get tough.*

*I spent a week telling him that starting on Friday, if he was rude to us we wouldn't want to be with him, so he would have to go downstairs for five minutes.*

*Friday finally came. Within the first minute of sitting at the breakfast table he told his sister to 'Shut up!' Immediately I told him to go downstairs. I was surprised because he didn't argue the point at all. He accepted it and walked straight down.*

*When he came back up, I said I would be looking out for good behaviour. Five minutes passed and his behaviour was fine, so I gave him lots of praise. 'You've been really good for five minutes. Well done. . . . You've been upstairs now for fifteen minutes. You're doing really well.' The whole rest of the day he didn't have to go back downstairs.*

*He was so proud that when his father came home he told him, 'I got to stay upstairs all day today.'*

Following through with consequences is no big deal if you can easily enforce them, for example picking your child up and depositing him outside the room. It's much harder to deal with older children who persistently misbehave. Either they're fearless because they know you don't have the stomach to stand up to them, or they are defiant because they have been yelled at and punished so many times they feel there is nothing more you can do to them. But even if your child is six foot two and you can't force him out of the room, you still have two consequences you can keep up your sleeve.

If he won't leave the room, walk away from him yourself, partly to calm down, and partly to deprive him of your company. Even if he pretends he doesn't mind, this can be surprisingly effective.

It sounds like a high-risk strategy, especially if your relationship is fragile already. But present it as a logical consequence of his behaviour rather than spur-of-the-moment emotional blackmail.

- *'I don't want to be with you when you are rude to me or shout at me. If you won't leave the room, I will.'*

Don't be put off if he crows with delight when you walk away – deep down he cares. But even if he pretends not to, there is another consequence you can use. You can refuse to do something for him next time he asks you to, like lending him money or driving him into town. As one mother put it:

> *If I ask you for some help and you just sit around doing nothing, I can't make you do it. But next time you want a lift or something to eat, I might not feel like helping you either. It's your choice.*

This is an important life lesson you are teaching your child. If you are polite, respectful and have a helpful attitude, people are more likely to treat you the same way.

### *'I'd feel really bad about walking off, and I wouldn't like to say no to him. If he's asking me for something at least he's talking to me.'*

It may not feel good, but if you've told your child what to expect, it's important to step back and let him take the consequences. We know you don't want to dive head-first into another bad place. But you've got to carry through with what you've said. If he is nasty to you, do you really want to be with him? If he doesn't help you, do you really want to help him?

When it comes to the crunch, you might not want to go through with this. But if you back down his behaviour won't get any better. Even if you manage to stand your ground and he refuses to talk to you, don't despair. While he is getting used to the new regime he may be angry and resentful, but this isn't the end of your relationship. Go back to the beginning of this chapter and see if you can do anything else to connect and show you are on his side. If you have a child who has been quite difficult, working behind the scenes really is a long-term project.

### *'But what if there's a good reason for his bad behaviour. Do I still have to enforce consequences?'*

If you think your child has a point, you may want to adjust your consequences accordingly. Even schools have trouble enforcing rules and consequences if a child feels misunderstood.

*My son got into a fight, and jabbed his pencil into another boy's cheek. The consequences seemed fair. He got a blue slip and a detention and had to write down ten reasons why poking people with pencils is dangerous.*

*But when the headmaster told him this, he refused. 'I'm not doing it! He has been beating me up all year! I'm sick of him picking on me and I refuse to be punished!'*

*Once he knew the background, even the headmaster had to admit there were two sides to the story. He compromised a bit on the punishment and the other boy was punished as well.*

When you stand firm, the time you've spent tuning in isn't wasted. If you've listened to your child, he will be less angry and more likely to accept the consequences.

### *'This commando stuff does work most of the time. But what do I do when it doesn't?'*

If you've tried every trick of the **Commando Parents** and your child won't obey you, you may have to run through any other parenting skills you can think of until you come up with a winner. Time and again we've found tuning in can be the best one in a crisis. One mother reported back to a parenting class:

*I was in the bath and my son took my expensive new soap rack, put it on the floor and stood on it. He was rocking on it like a seesaw, and I was trying my best, from my bath, to get him off it.*

*I tried being firm: 'Get off!' Nothing.*

*I explained: 'That rack is made of metal, and when you stand on it, it bends out of shape.' Laughter from him.*

*I pleaded: 'I really like that soap rack, and I don't want it to break.' Still nothing.*

*I threatened: 'If it breaks, you're going to have to buy me a new one.' He carried on rocking and said, 'Make me!'*

*What could I do now? By this point I was so angry I felt like shouting at him. But by some miracle I remembered to try to see it from his point of view.*

*'You're bored,' I said, 'because I am in the bath and the others are busy. You want someone to play with. You want me to get out of the bath and spend time with you.'*

*Yes – jackpot! He got straight off the rack. I told him I would play with him in ten minutes if he went to find a game. So I finally got some peace and quiet, and we played when I got out.* ’

Being difficult isn't a life sentence. Off the top of our heads we can think of four well-adjusted friends who swear that they were difficult children. One screamed so loudly at her mother she popped a blood vessel behind her eyes and couldn't see properly for weeks; another got expelled from three schools; another smashed down a wall in the house with a sledgehammer; and another admits to being constantly mouthy, argumentative and furious.

You might argue that we must have some pretty strange friends, but if you met them you'd never guess how difficult they used to be. As well as being devoted mothers, they all have successful careers. So don't worry that your child is lost and gone for ever. Be open-minded and think of him as someone who is finding this particular stage of his life difficult.

Despite his behaviour, keep reminding yourself he has a lot going for him. Even though he can be a pain, you might admire the way he has his own agenda and tries to call the shots. He may end up accomplishing great things one day instead of following the herd. Hyperactive children have lots of energy; stubborn children are able to stand up for themselves; mouthy, angry children express themselves honestly; fussy children notice nuances the rest of us miss; sensitive children understand feelings. With luck you can help your child keep his individuality while smoothing enough rough edges to help him fit into normal life.

Keep trying and don't give up. If you have to deal with a lot of difficult behaviour, you will probably have to go deeper, read more widely and take less well-trodden paths through the parenting jungle. It can be a tough journey because your child needs more of your time and understanding than the average child. What works for your niece, or the boy next door, or the majority of children in his class, may not work for him. It can take time to understand what makes him tick, but with your help he can learn to make sense of the world and to respond to it differently.

# Resources

## Parenting Courses and Counselling

If you need more help to put these ideas into practice, try:

**Karen and Georgia.** www.KarenandGeorgia.com
We run some parent courses and workshops, based on all the Seven Secrets of Successful Parenting. See our website for availability.

**The Family Caring Trust.** www.familycaring.co.uk **028 3026 4174**
We can highly recommend their parenting course material, which is clear, simple and very effective. They are particularly strong on Tuning-In, Cheer-leading, Commando and being a Laid-Back Parent.

**The New Learning Centre.** www.tnlc.info **020 7794 0321**
These are great people to turn to if you have a serious problem. As well as teaching Tuning-In and Cheerleading, they are also very good on Sorted and Commando.

**The Parent Practice.** www.theparentpractice.com **020 8673 3444**
Excellent, positive parenting workshops, based in south-west London.

**Parentline Plus.** www.parentlineplus.org.uk **020 7284 5500**
They offer a twenty-four-hour, confidential, free telephone advice line 0808 800 2222, (though this can be busy). They also run parent groups and workshops all over the country.

**Julie Johnson.** **Julie.johnson@virgin.net** **020 8672 0311**
Counsellor who works to address bullying with individuals and schools, mostly in the London area.

# Books

These are some of the books which we've found particularly inspiring over the years:

*How to Talk So Kids Will Listen and Listen So Kids Will Talk* (Piccadilly Press, 2001)
*Liberated Parents, Liberated Children* (Piccadilly Press, 1985)
*Siblings Without Rivalry* (Piccadilly Press, 1999)
We love all these parenting books by Adele Faber and Elaine Mazlish, and can't recommend them more highly. Especially good on Tuned-In, Cheerleader and Commando parents.

*The Bully, the Bullied and the Bystander*, by Barbara Coloroso (HarperCollins, 2005)
Practical suggestions if your child is being bullied, or is bullying. Uses most of the parent types.

*The Continuum Concept*, by Jean Liedloff (Penguin, 1989)
Great on establishing a deep connection with your baby. Especially good on Physical, Tuned-In and Laid-Back techniques.

*The Highly Sensitive Child*, by Elaine N. Aron (Thorsons, 2003)
About Tuning-In to your child's needs.

*Raising Boys*, by Steve Biddulph (HarperCollins, 2003)
How to love and appreciate boys.

*Three in a Bed*, by Deborah Jackson (Bloomsbury, 2003)
About the importance of physical affection for babies, by a great author.

*What Our Children Teach Us*, by Piero Ferrucci (Simon & Schuster, 2002)
Loving and compassionate, good on Pausing and Tuning-In.

*When Your Kids Push Your Buttons*, by Bonnie Harris (Piatkus, 2005)
What to do when it's hard to Pause.

# Food

For good advice on healthy food, we like:

*The Food Our Children Eat*, by Joanna Blythman (Fourth Estate, 2000)

*Not on the Label*, by Felicity Lawrence (Penguin, 2004)

*Boost Your Child's Immune System*, by Lucy Burney (Piatkus, 2003)

# Learning and Behavioural Difficulties

There's loads of information out there, so start with the internet.

Good books for physical and emotional strategies include:

*The Gift of Dyslexia*, by Ronald D. Davis (Souvenir Press, 1997)

*Right-brained Children in a Left-brained World*, by Jeffrey Freed and Laurie Parsons (Prentice Hall, 1998)

**The Dore Institute.** www.Dore.co.uk **01926 514 033**
They have developed physical exercises said to have dramatic results. There are centres all over the country.

# Acknowledgements

We particularly want to thank everyone at Transworld, our publishers. The dream team was headed by our lovely editor Brenda Kimber, and included Katrina Whone, Kate Samano, Alison Barrow, Helen Edwards, Zeb Dare, designer Julia Lloyd and many others to whom we are eternally grateful. We are indebted to our magnificent agent, Caroline Michel, for being our champion, and to Araminta Whitley for early encouragement. Thank you to Ellen Hatvany, for generously lending your house and being our catalyst.

### *Karen's thanks*

Thank you, Pete, for your unwavering support and for making my life what it is, and thank you Natasha, Anya, Cian and Alexandra for helping me to be the best I can be. I am grateful to my father, James Weinberg, for always seeing the best in me, and to my mother, Patricia Weinberg, for not giving up.

Writing this I realize how many people I appreciate, and I so wish I could thank you all personally. I'm grateful to all of you who have stayed my friends despite my being so busy I couldn't even pick up the phone, especially during those early years with so many young children. Thank you to all my wonderful neighbours and the parents at my children's schools who have shared your stories and been so supportive. Special thanks to my close friends who have spent countless hours discussing the book with me: Judy Cummins, Heidi Larson, Caitlin Mavroleon, Tara Saglio, and my mentor, John Cummins. Thanks to my friends in California who've spent their summer holidays chewing over it, including Kathy Johnson, Georgene Mitsanis, Maria Farrow and Joanna Demetriou. Thank you, Molly Gervais, for inspiring me to be a better parent, Lisa Larson for still being there and Nick Woodward, my tutor at Oxford, for throwing me a lifeline.

Thanks to all of you who have helped to raise my children, including all the teachers and staff at their schools. Particular thanks to headmistresses Elizabeth Marsden and Jenny Aviss for understanding my children and believing in them. I'm grateful to the doctors, health visitors and staff at Holland Park Surgery, and my most sincere gratitude to paediatrician Dr Chantal Bricka at the Cromwell Hospital for helping us to avert a disaster.

Georgia, I am most grateful to you for making this book what it is, for being a joy to work with every day, and for all you have taught me about life.

### *Georgia's thanks*

Thank you to my amazing husband Nicholas for supporting me in every possible way, and to our four children Alexander, Freddie, Sophie and Tommy who have taught me so much. Thank you to my father George Metcalfe for always listening, my mother Elizabeth Ungley for letting me find my own path, my sister Becky for her creativity and Nick's family for being so welcoming.

So many kind people have given me their time and their ideas, and please forgive me if I don't mention you all individually, but I thank each one of you for your wonderful stories and generous encouragement. I am especially grateful to Elvira Langagan for her warmth and rock-solid support, and to Gillian Edwards from the New Learning Centre, whose inspiring parenting classes opened my eyes. Thank-you to Ingrid Ballard, Natalia O'Sullivan, Wendy Mandy and to my teachers at the CPS for your wisdom. Thank you to Jane Mays and Susie Dowdall at the *Daily Mail* for encouraging my writing. Thank you Katharine Barton, Brian Greenaway and many others at *Condé Nast* for so much practical help and advice. Thank you to Elvie Langagan for your unconditional warmth, Zdenek Schaffer and Michaela Vlasakova for your positive attitude and Andrew Fernandez for resurrecting my computer so many times. Thank you to my lovely bookclub and yoga friends for listening and encouraging me for so many years.

I owe a huge debt of gratitude to many other friends, including the staff and parents of all my children's schools; particularly Jane Cameron, Diana Maine and Shelley Gibson, Robin and Angela Badham-Thornhill, Mark Fielker and Carolyn Turner and Margaret Beamont.

Most of all I want to thank Karen. Working with you has been a huge pleasure and so inspiring, and I literally could not have done this book without you.

# Index